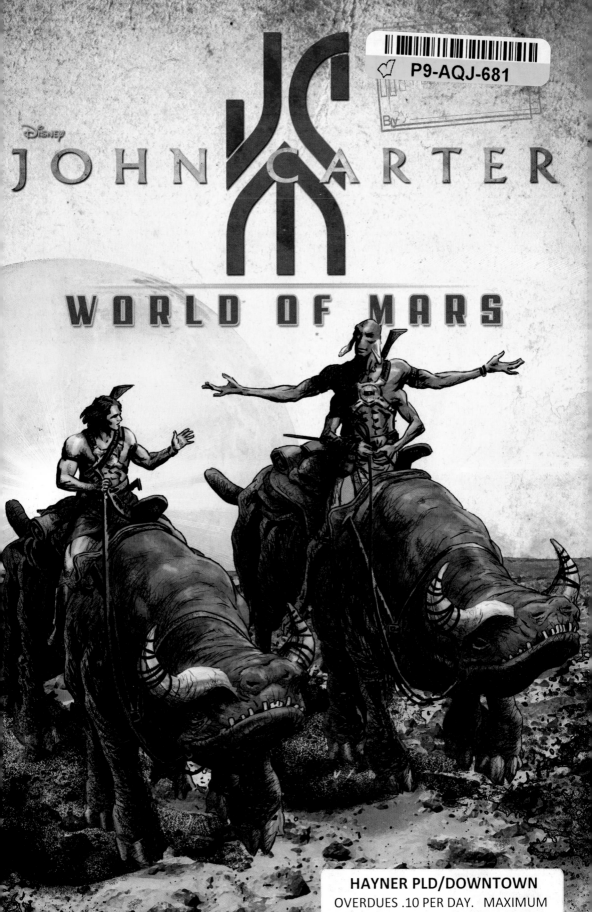

DISNEY

JOHN CARTER
WORLD OF MARS

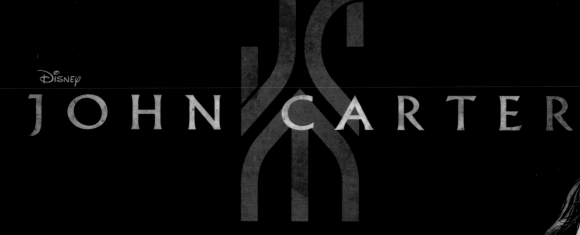

DISNEY

JOHN CARTER

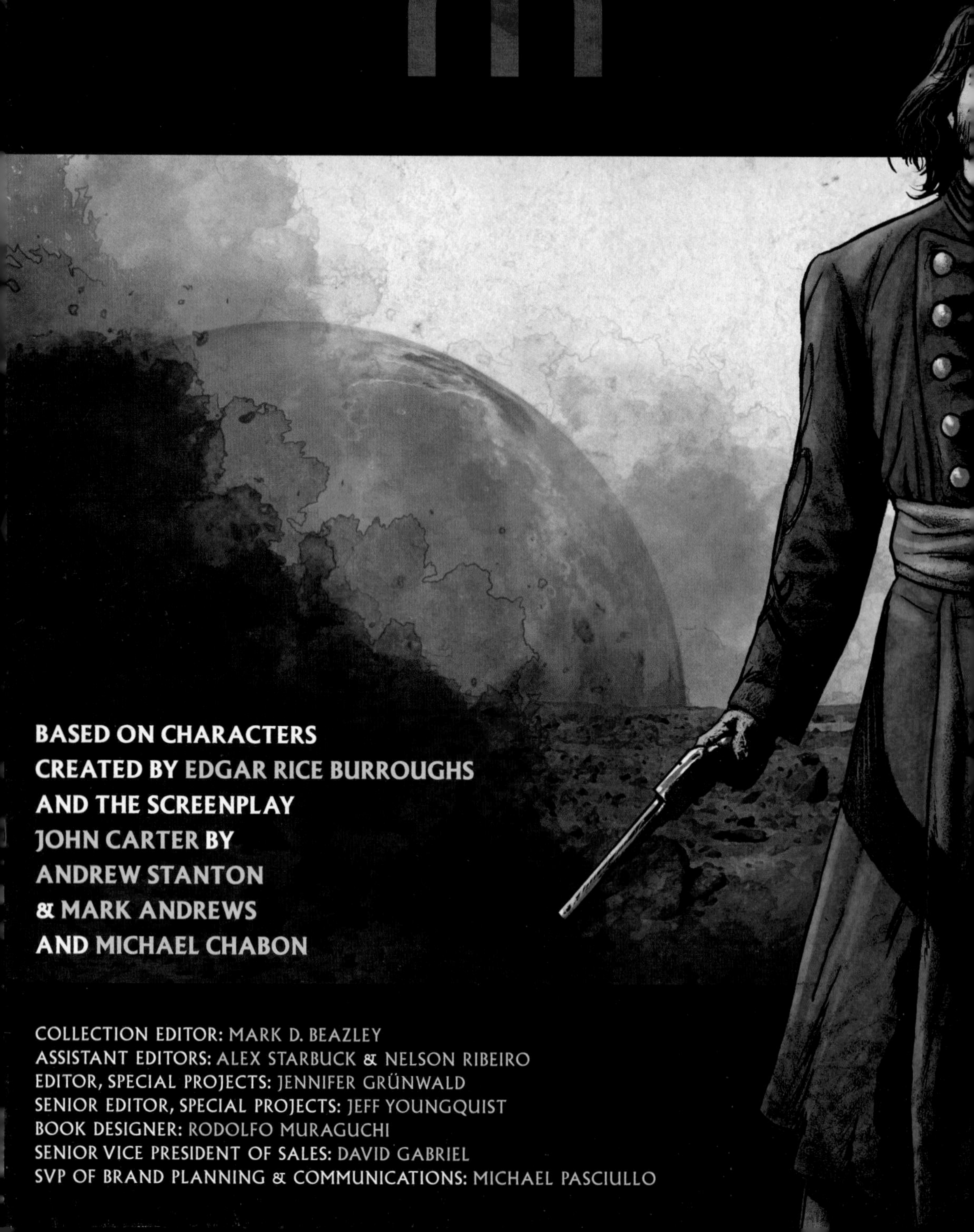

BASED ON CHARACTERS CREATED BY EDGAR RICE BURROUGHS AND THE SCREENPLAY JOHN CARTER BY ANDREW STANTON & MARK ANDREWS AND MICHAEL CHABON

COLLECTION EDITOR: MARK D. BEAZLEY
ASSISTANT EDITORS: ALEX STARBUCK & NELSON RIBEIRO
EDITOR, SPECIAL PROJECTS: JENNIFER GRÜNWALD
SENIOR EDITOR, SPECIAL PROJECTS: JEFF YOUNGQUIST
BOOK DESIGNER: RODOLFO MURAGUCHI
SENIOR VICE PRESIDENT OF SALES: DAVID GABRIEL
SVP OF BRAND PLANNING & COMMUNICATIONS: MICHAEL PASCIULLO

WORLD OF MARS

WRITER: PETER DAVID
ARTIST: LUKE ROSS
COLOR ARTIST: ULISES ARREOLA
LETTERER: VC'S CORY PETIT
ASSISTANT EDITORS: RACHEL PINNELAS
& JON MOISAN
EDITOR: SANA AMANAT

FRONT COVER ARTIST: ARIEL OLIVETTI
BACK COVER ARTISTS: MICO SUAYAN
& FRANK D'ARMATA

EDITOR IN CHIEF: AXEL ALONSO
CHIEF CREATIVE OFFICER: JOE QUESADA
PUBLISHER: DAN BUCKLEY

SPECIAL THANKS TO LAURA SANDOVAL, LESLIE STERN,
MATTHEW FRANK, KEVIN HURTZ, RALPH MACCHIO & IRENE LEE

WORLD OF MARS
GLOSSARY

Barsoom:	Mars, or Barsoom as it is referred to by its inhabitants, was once full of water but now it's a desert - ravaged by war and time. Barsoom is a world of sweeping landscapes, vast canyons and unique, technologically advanced cities that are home to many races. The ongoing battles between its native inhabitants, the Heliumites and the Zodangans, threaten to destroy all life and resources remaining on the planet.
Jeddak:	A Jeddak is the equivalent of a King in Barsoomian society. Jeddaks exist in societies among multiple Barsoomian races including the Zodangans, the Heliumites, and the Tharks. Jeddaks include Than Kosis, Sab Than's father, and Tardos Mors, Dejah Thoris' father.
Zodanga:	One of the major locations on Barsoom is the fearsome city of Zodanga which moves over the surface of the planet on hundreds of massive mechanical legs. Its massive hangar decks house the many airships that Zodangans use to attack their enemies, the Heliumites. The city itself has been through so many battles that it's been rebuilt and redeveloped over the various wars.
Zodangans:	The Zodangans are citizens of Zodanga and are Red Men of Barsoom. They are a hostile, manipulative, and aggressive people who wage war on the Heliumites, the Tharks, and any other enemies that cross their path.
Helium:	Helium is the other major city on the planet and is a civilization of sophistication, technology, and intellectual pursuits. For this reason, it's referred to as "the Jewel of Barsoom." Its wealth of resources and defendable position have helped it survive the various wars on the planet.
Heliumites:	The Heliumites are citizens of Helium and are also Red Men like the Zodangans. Unlike citizens of Zodanga, Heliumites are a regal and intellectual race. They are ruled by a sovereign, but have a representative government with a senate-like body. Their greatest enemy is the Zodangans.
Tharks:	The Tharks are a race of 9-foot-tall Green Men on Barsoom who live a nomadic life in the hinterlands. They have a rich history on the planet where they were once its dominant society. Since they were overtaken by the Zodangans, they have become more tribal and less sophisticated than the Red Men. While they pride themselves on being a tribe of strong and aggressive warriors, their populations has significantly decreased in size because of clashes with the Red Men, who view the Tharks as a threat.

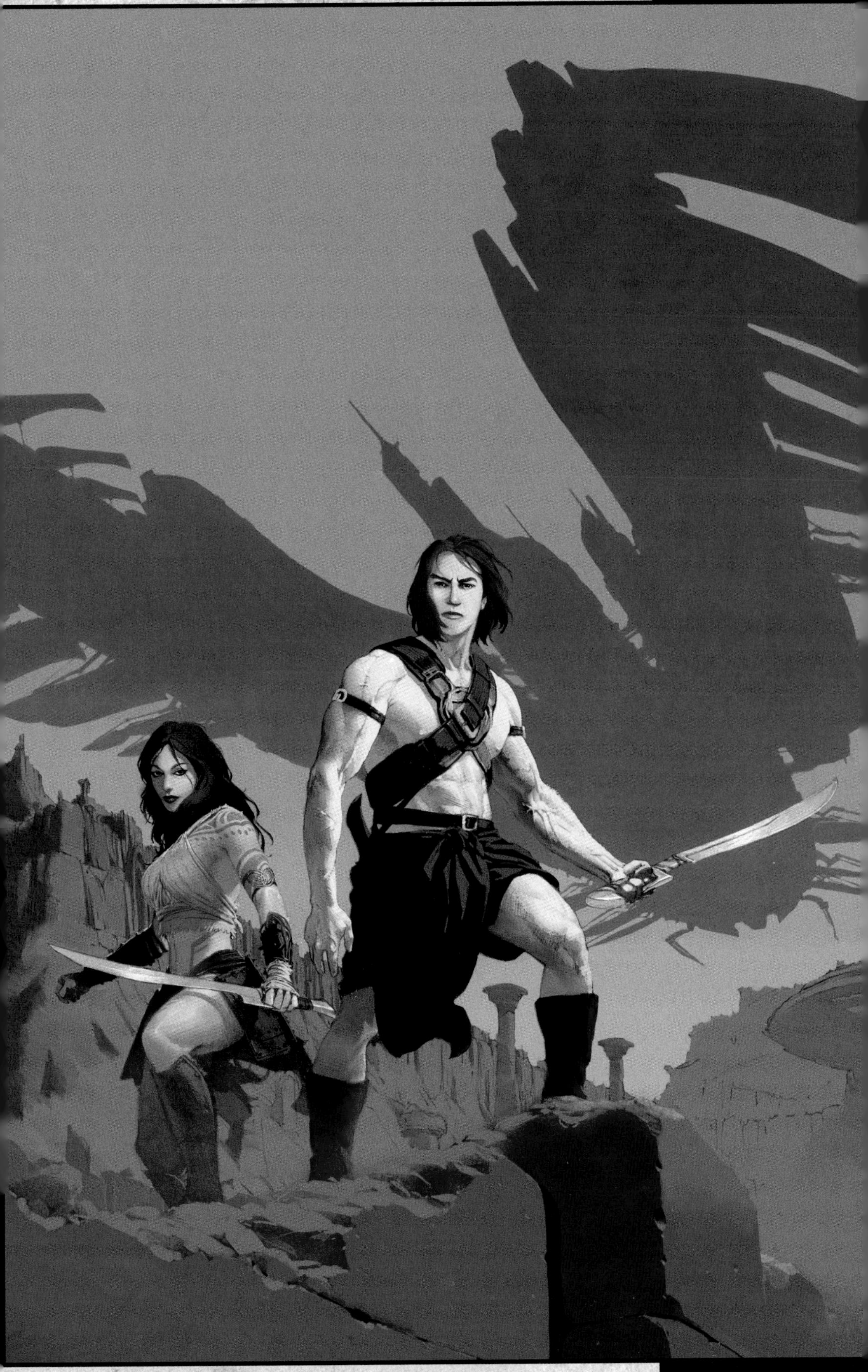

ONE

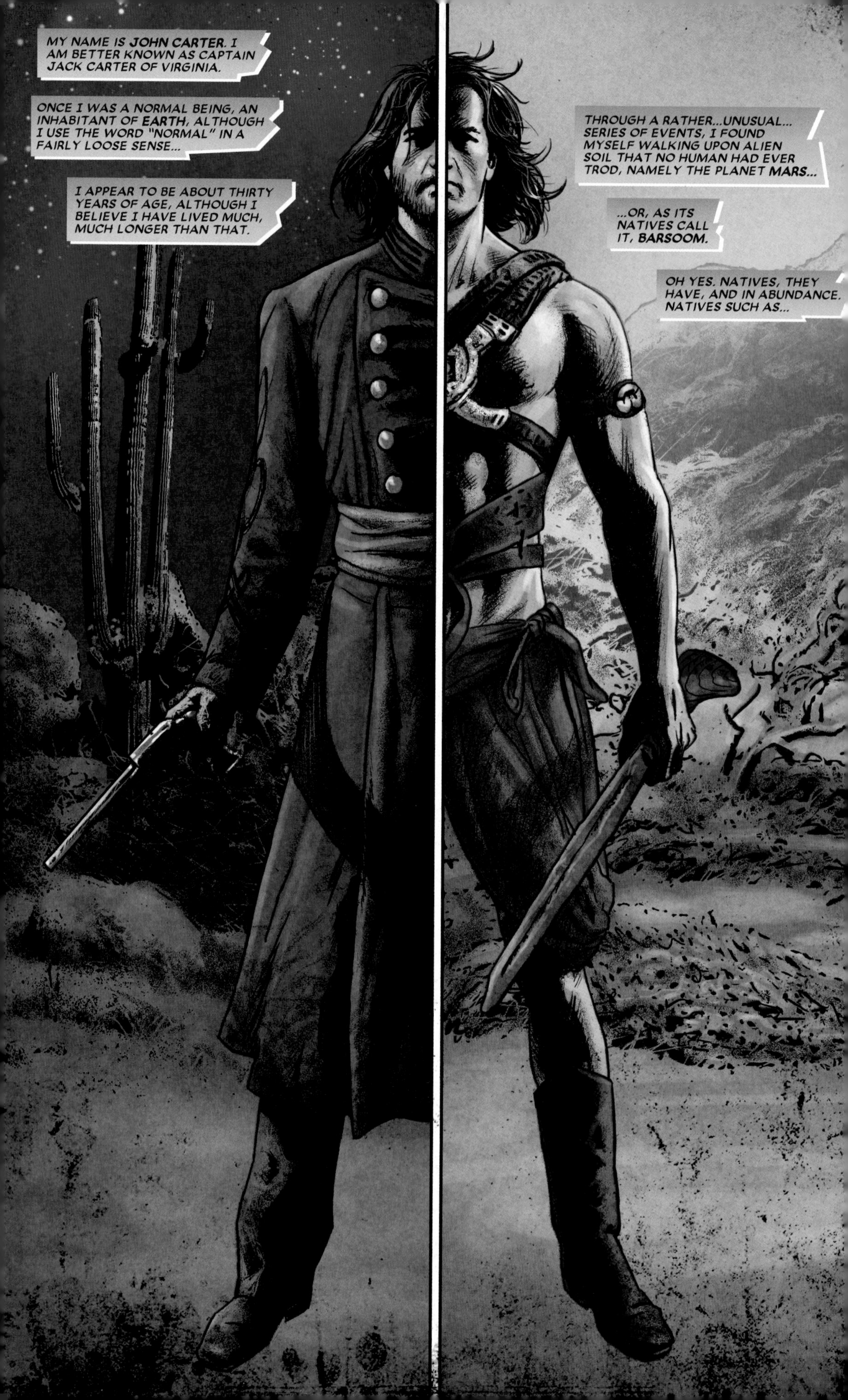
MY NAME IS JOHN CARTER. I AM BETTER KNOWN AS CAPTAIN JACK CARTER OF VIRGINIA.
ONCE I WAS A NORMAL BEING, AN INHABITANT OF EARTH, ALTHOUGH I USE THE WORD "NORMAL" IN A FAIRLY LOOSE SENSE...
I APPEAR TO BE ABOUT THIRTY YEARS OF AGE, ALTHOUGH I BELIEVE I HAVE LIVED MUCH, MUCH LONGER THAN THAT.
THROUGH A RATHER...UNUSUAL... SERIES OF EVENTS, I FOUND MYSELF WALKING UPON ALIEN SOIL THAT NO HUMAN HAD EVER TROD, NAMELY THE PLANET MARS...
...OR, AS ITS NATIVES CALL IT, BARSOOM.
OH YES. NATIVES, THEY HAVE, AND IN ABUNDANCE. NATIVES SUCH AS...

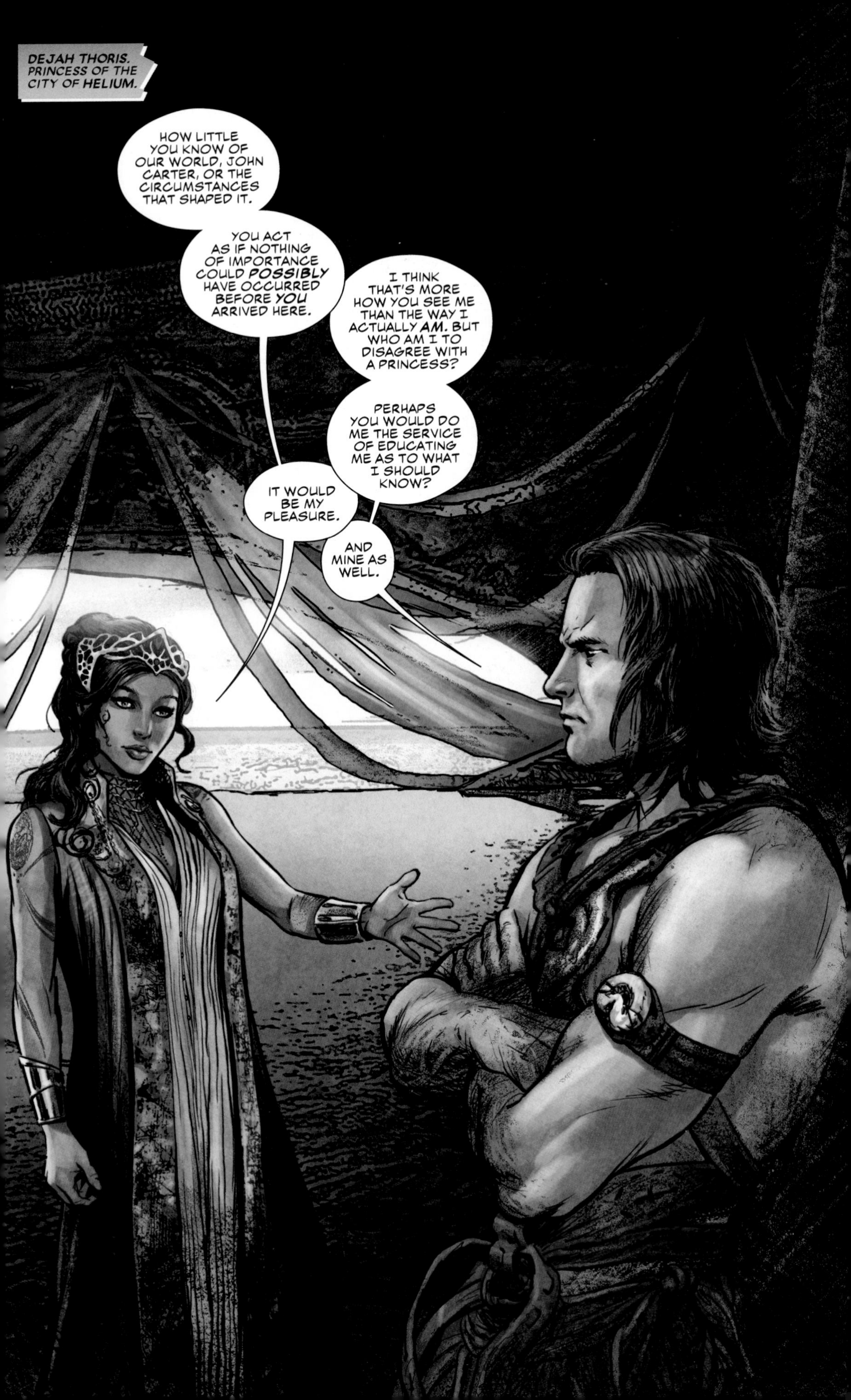
DEJAH THORIS. PRINCESS OF THE CITY OF HELIUM.
HOW LITTLE YOU KNOW OF OUR WORLD, JOHN CARTER, OR THE CIRCUMSTANCES THAT SHAPED IT.
YOU ACT AS IF NOTHING OF IMPORTANCE COULD POSSIBLY HAVE OCCURRED BEFORE YOU ARRIVED HERE.
I THINK THAT'S MORE HOW YOU SEE ME THAN THE WAY I ACTUALLY AM. BUT WHO AM I TO DISAGREE WITH A PRINCESS?
PERHAPS YOU WOULD DO ME THE SERVICE OF EDUCATING ME AS TO WHAT I SHOULD KNOW?
IT WOULD BE MY PLEASURE.
AND MINE AS WELL.

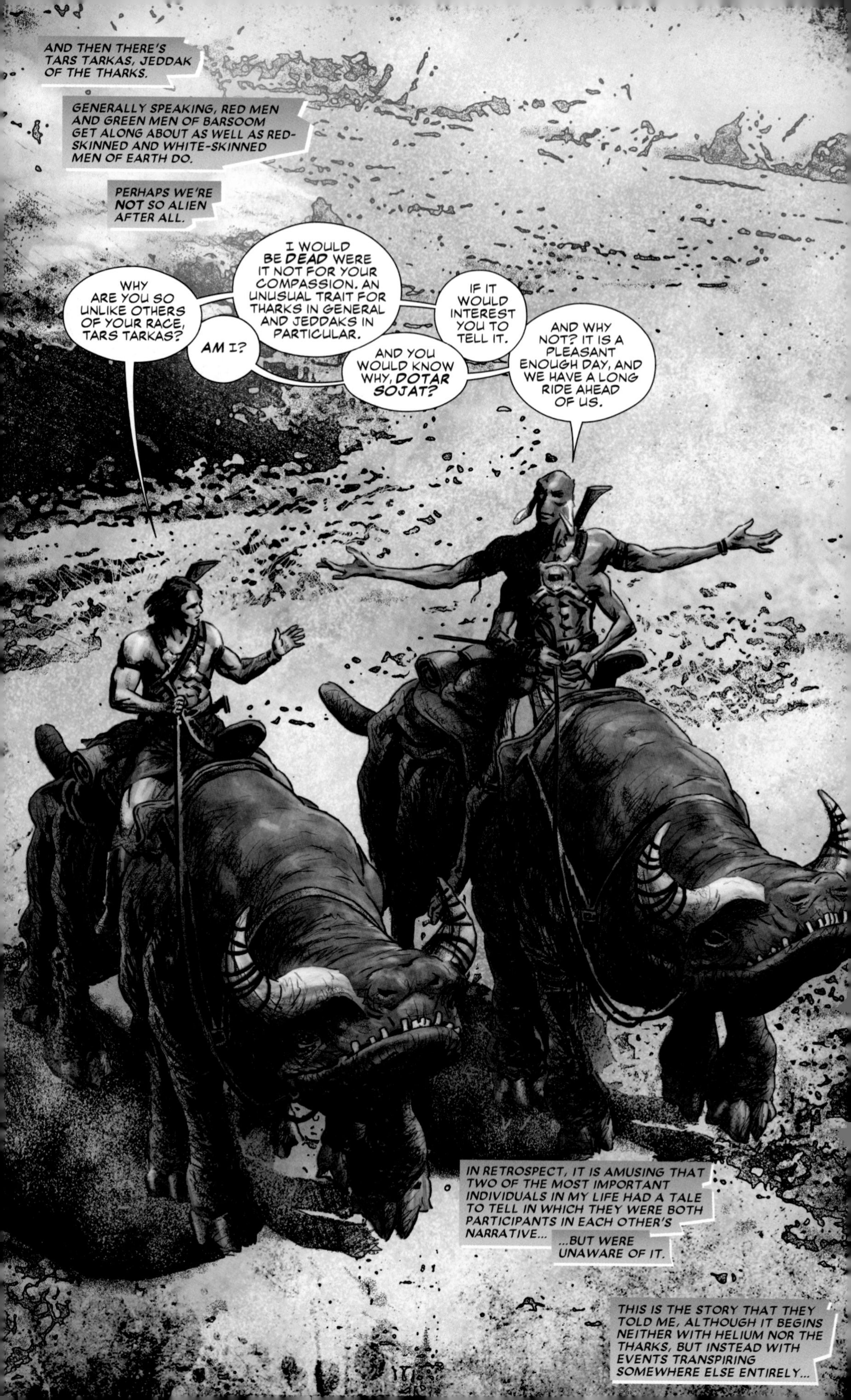
AND THEN THERE'S TARS TARKAS, JEDDAK OF THE THARKS.
GENERALLY SPEAKING, RED MEN AND GREEN MEN OF BARSOOM GET ALONG ABOUT AS WELL AS RED-SKINNED AND WHITE-SKINNED MEN OF EARTH DO.
PERHAPS WE'RE NOT SO ALIEN AFTER ALL.
WHY ARE YOU SO UNLIKE OTHERS OF YOUR RACE, TARS TARKAS?
AM I?
I WOULD BE DEAD WERE IT NOT FOR YOUR COMPASSION. AN UNUSUAL TRAIT FOR THARKS IN GENERAL AND JEDDAKS IN PARTICULAR.
AND YOU WOULD KNOW WHY, DOTAR SOJAT?
IF IT WOULD INTEREST YOU TO TELL IT.
AND WHY NOT? IT IS A PLEASANT ENOUGH DAY, AND WE HAVE A LONG RIDE AHEAD OF US.
IN RETROSPECT, IT IS AMUSING THAT TWO OF THE MOST IMPORTANT INDIVIDUALS IN MY LIFE HAD A TALE TO TELL IN WHICH THEY WERE BOTH PARTICIPANTS IN EACH OTHER'S NARRATIVE...
...BUT WERE UNAWARE OF IT.
THIS IS THE STORY THAT THEY TOLD ME, ALTHOUGH IT BEGINS NEITHER WITH HELIUM NOR THE THARKS, BUT INSTEAD WITH EVENTS TRANSPIRING SOMEWHERE ELSE ENTIRELY...

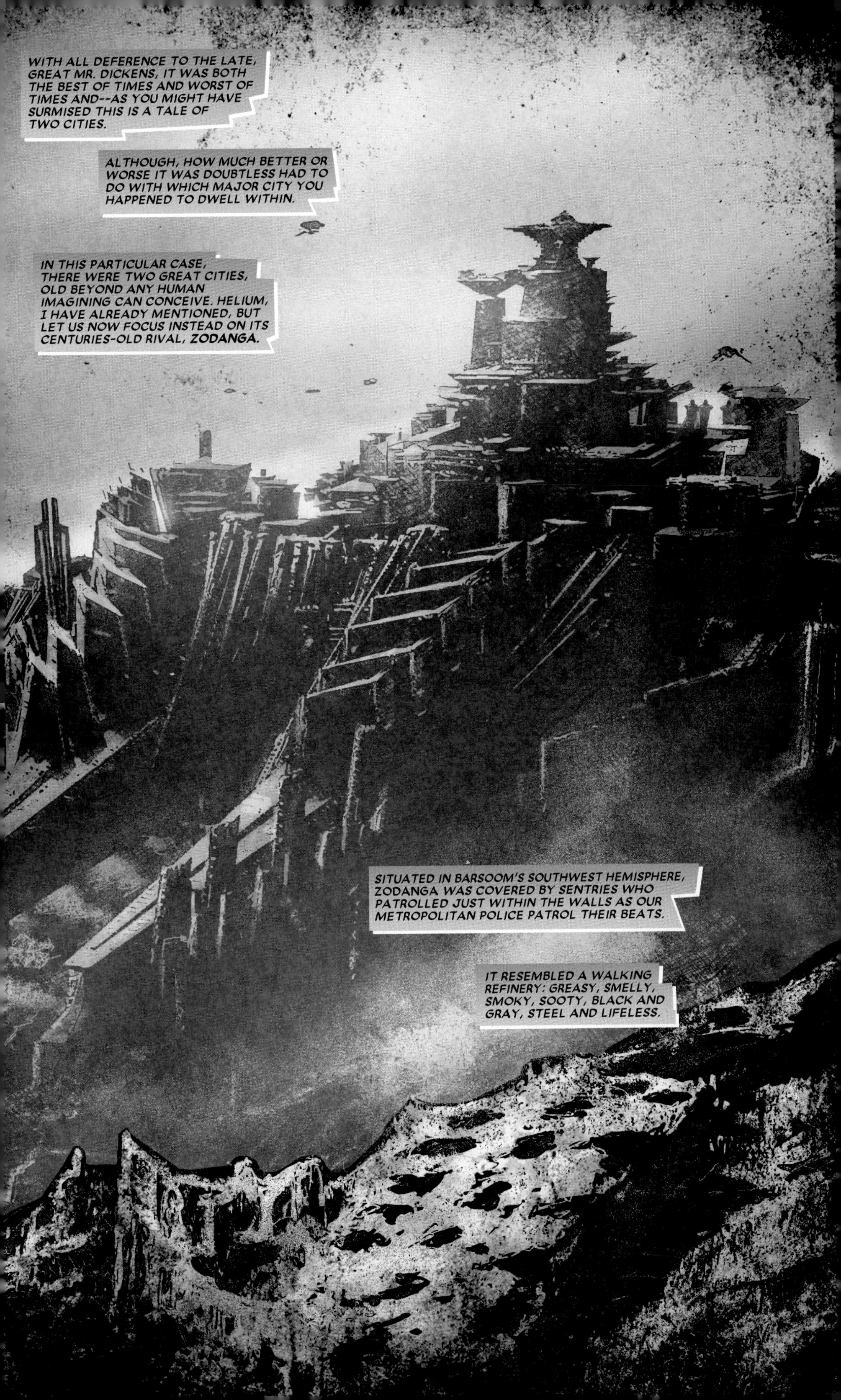
WITH ALL DEFERENCE TO THE LATE, GREAT MR. DICKENS, IT WAS BOTH THE BEST OF TIMES AND WORST OF TIMES AND--AS YOU MIGHT HAVE SURMISED THIS IS A TALE OF TWO CITIES.
ALTHOUGH, HOW MUCH BETTER OR WORSE IT WAS DOUBTLESS HAD TO DO WITH WHICH MAJOR CITY YOU HAPPENED TO DWELL WITHIN.
IN THIS PARTICULAR CASE, THERE WERE TWO GREAT CITIES, OLD BEYOND ANY HUMAN IMAGINING CAN CONCEIVE. HELIUM, I HAVE ALREADY MENTIONED, BUT LET US NOW FOCUS INSTEAD ON ITS CENTURIES-OLD RIVAL, ZODANGA.
SITUATED IN BARSOOM'S SOUTHWEST HEMISPHERE, ZODANGA WAS COVERED BY SENTRIES WHO PATROLLED JUST WITHIN THE WALLS AS OUR METROPOLITAN POLICE PATROL THEIR BEATS.
IT RESEMBLED A WALKING REFINERY: GREASY, SMELLY, SMOKY, SOOTY, BLACK AND GRAY, STEEL AND LIFELESS.

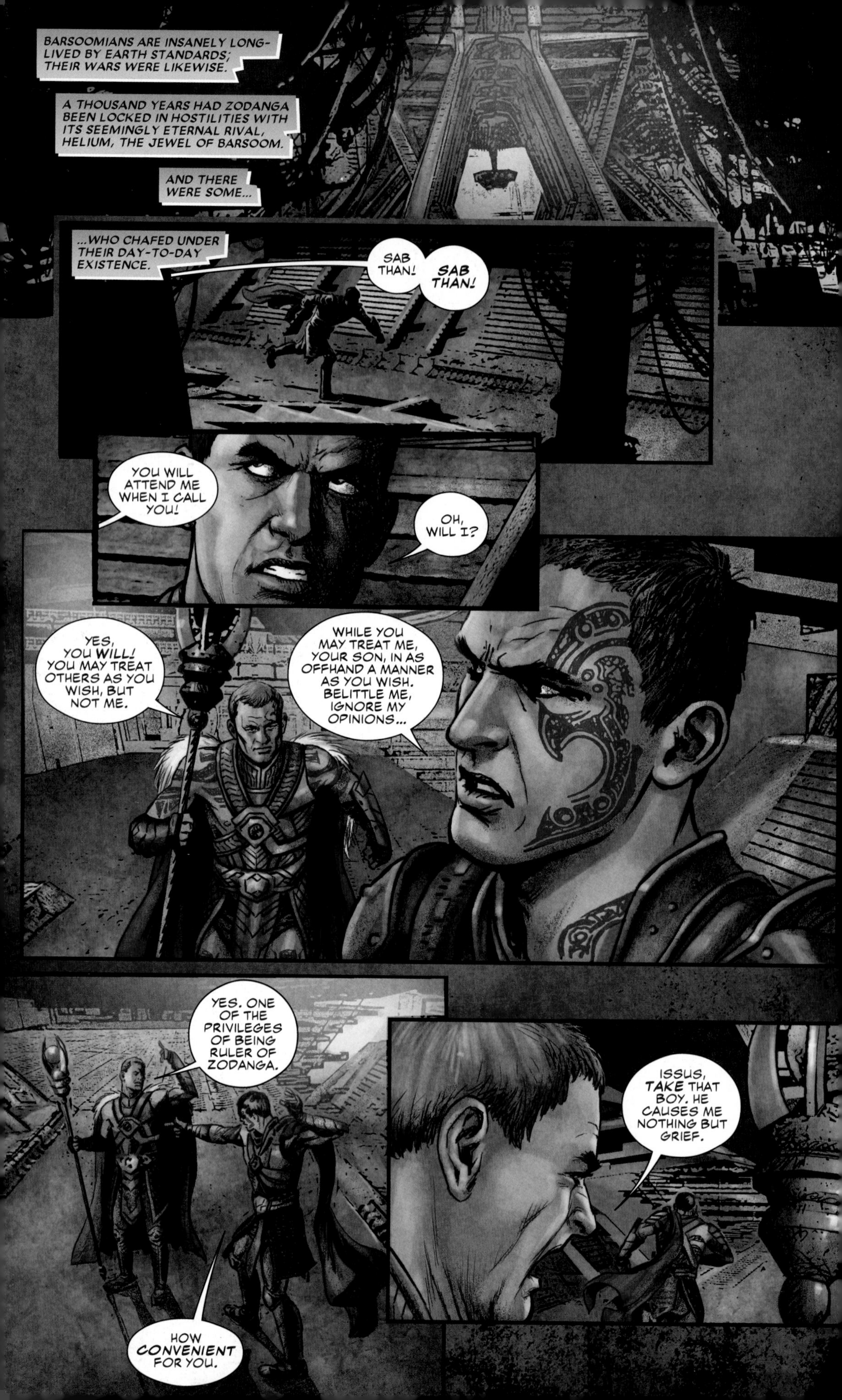
BARSOOMIANS ARE INSANELY LONG-LIVED BY EARTH STANDARDS; THEIR WARS WERE LIKEWISE.
A THOUSAND YEARS HAD ZODANGA BEEN LOCKED IN HOSTILITIES WITH ITS SEEMINGLY ETERNAL RIVAL, HELIUM, THE JEWEL OF BARSOOM.
AND THERE WERE SOME...
...WHO CHAFED UNDER THEIR DAY-TO-DAY EXISTENCE.
SAB THAN!
SAB THAN!
YOU WILL ATTEND ME WHEN I CALL YOU!
OH, WILL I?
YES, YOU WILL! YOU MAY TREAT OTHERS AS YOU WISH, BUT NOT ME.
WHILE YOU MAY TREAT ME, YOUR SON, IN AS OFFHAND A MANNER AS YOU WISH. BELITTLE ME, IGNORE MY OPINIONS...
YES. ONE OF THE PRIVILEGES OF BEING RULER OF ZODANGA.
HOW CONVENIENT FOR YOU.
ISSUS, TAKE THAT BOY. HE CAUSES ME NOTHING BUT GRIEF.

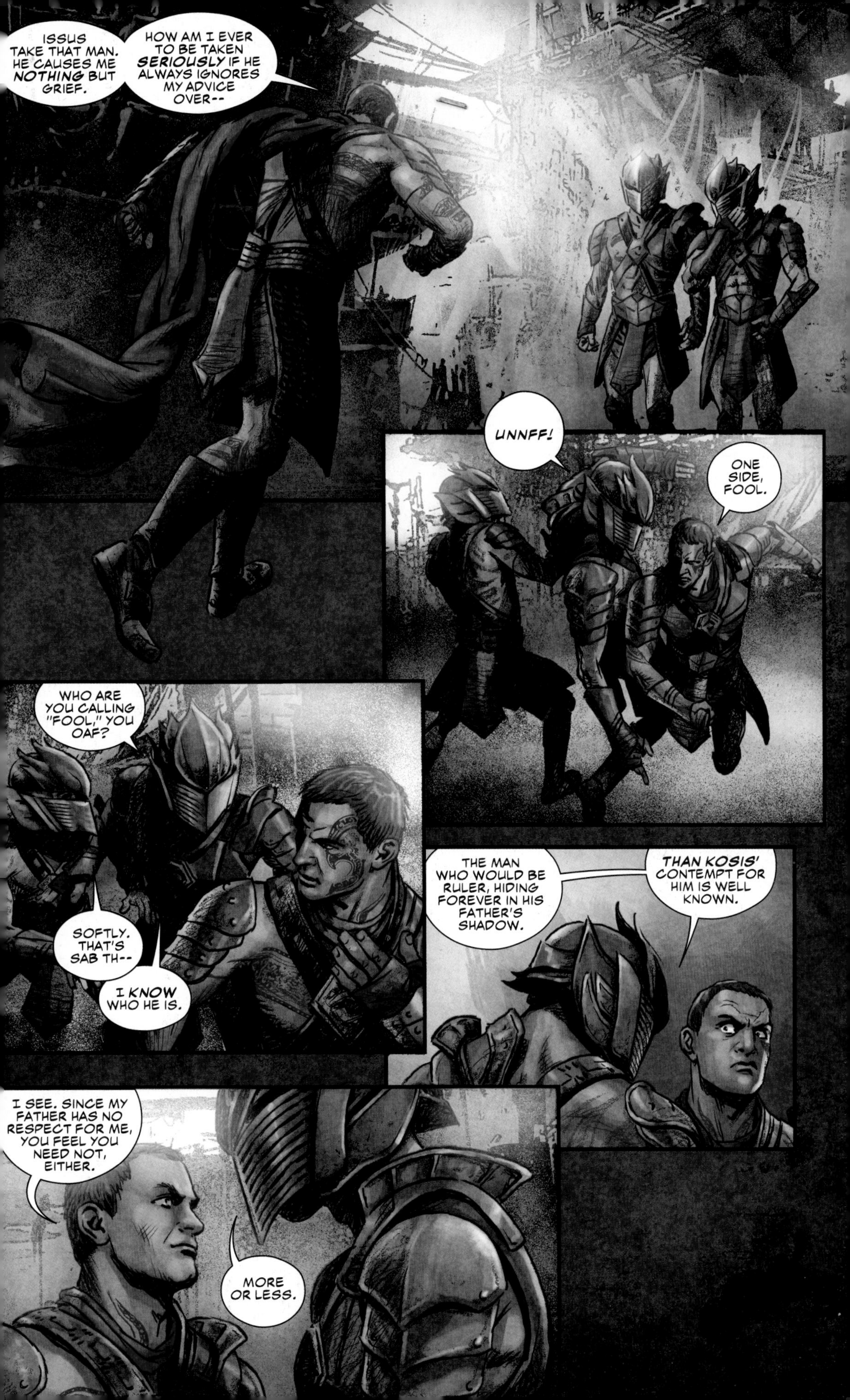
ISSUS TAKE THAT MAN. HE CAUSES ME NOTHING BUT GRIEF.
HOW AM I EVER TO BE TAKEN SERIOUSLY IF HE ALWAYS IGNORES MY ADVICE OVER--
UNNFF!
ONE SIDE, FOOL.
WHO ARE YOU CALLING "FOOL," YOU OAF?
SOFTLY. THAT'S SAB TH--
I KNOW WHO HE IS.
THE MAN WHO WOULD BE RULER, HIDING FOREVER IN HIS FATHER'S SHADOW.
THAN KOSIS' CONTEMPT FOR HIM IS WELL KNOWN.
I SEE. SINCE MY FATHER HAS NO RESPECT FOR ME, YOU FEEL YOU NEED NOT, EITHER.
MORE OR LESS.

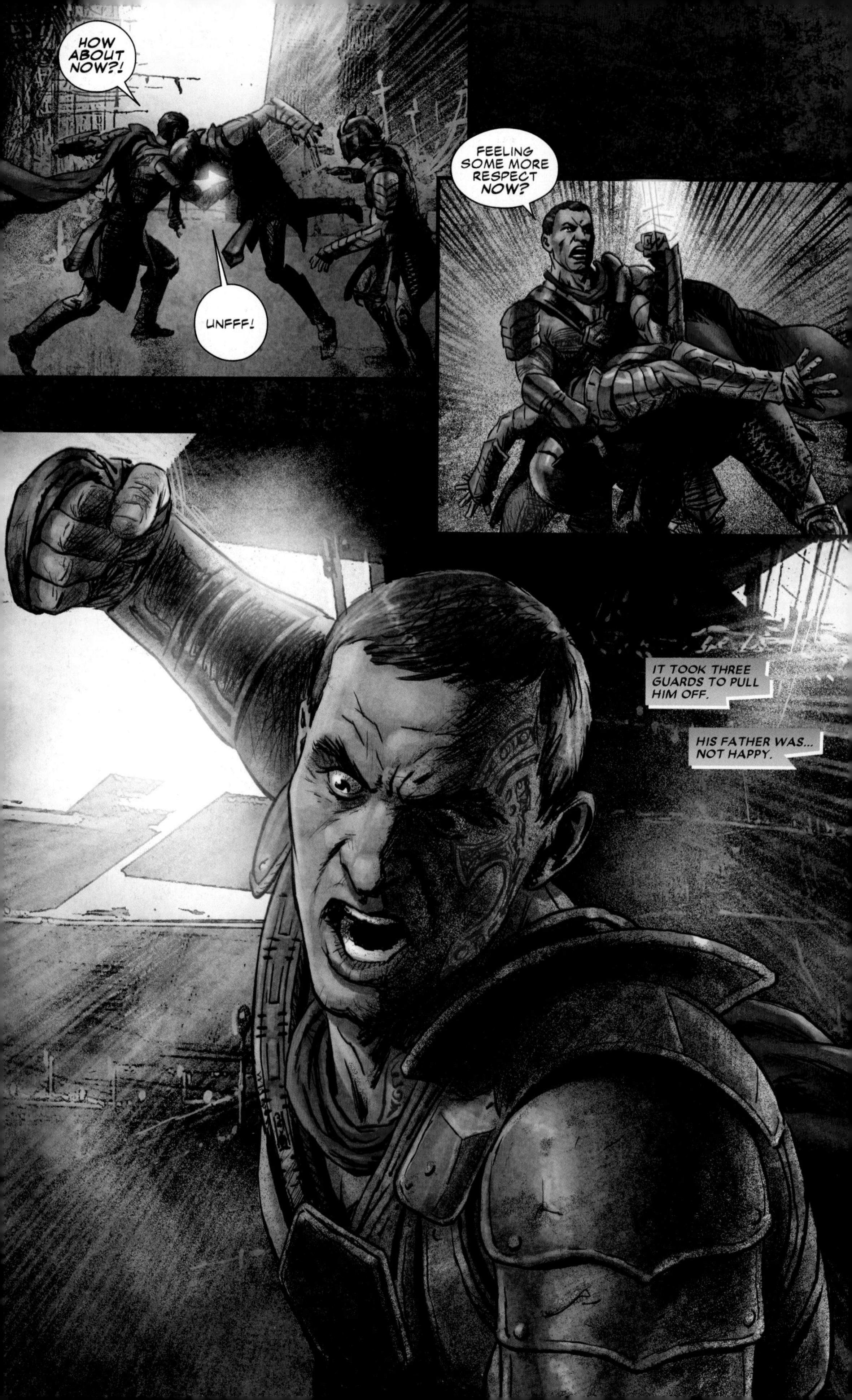
HOW ABOUT NOW?!
UNFFF!
FEELING SOME MORE RESPECT NOW?
IT TOOK THREE GUARDS TO PULL HIM OFF.
HIS FATHER WAS... NOT HAPPY.

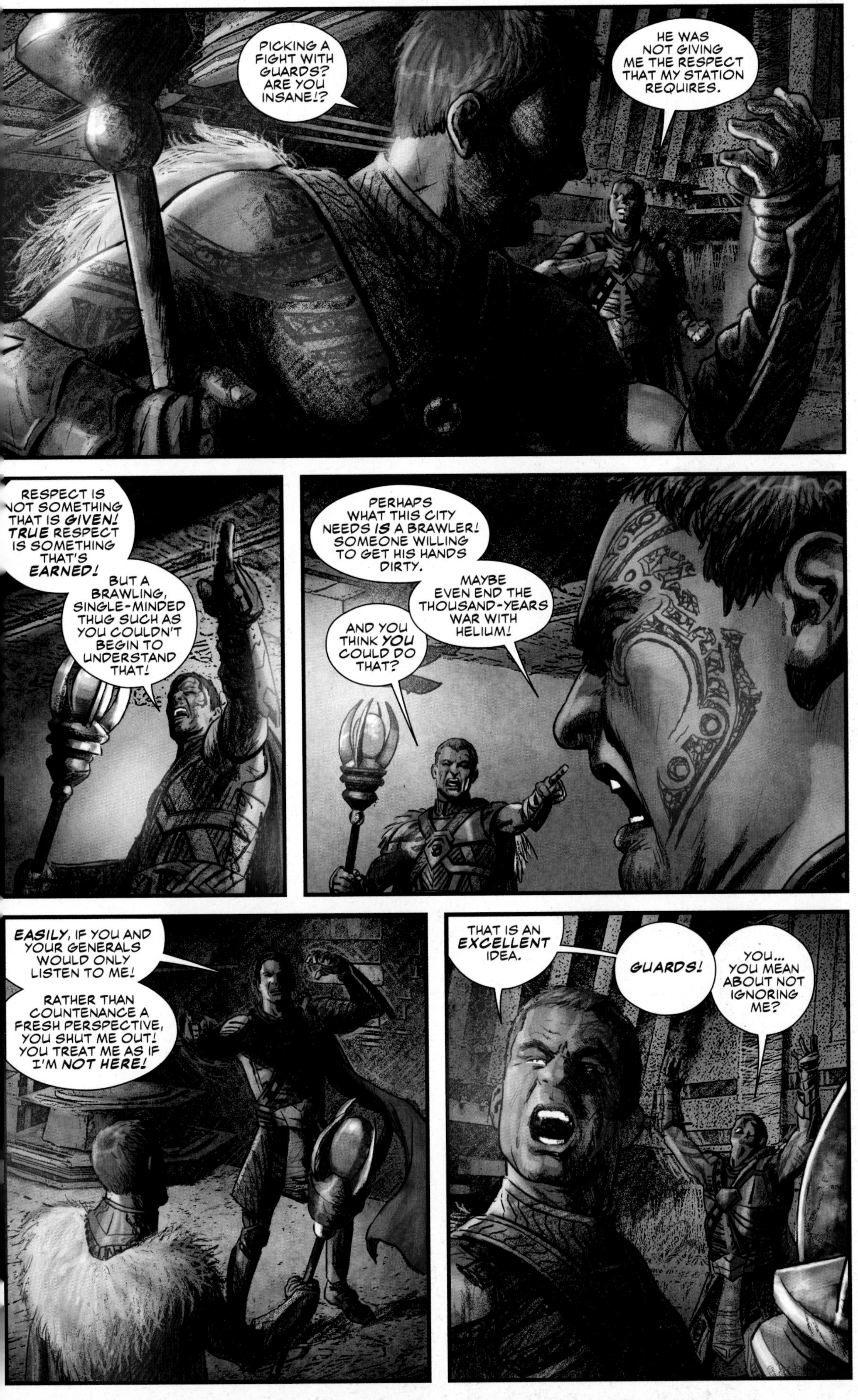
PICKING A FIGHT WITH GUARDS? ARE YOU INSANE!?
HE WAS NOT GIVING ME THE RESPECT THAT MY STATION REQUIRES.
RESPECT IS NOT SOMETHING THAT IS GIVEN! TRUE RESPECT IS SOMETHING THAT'S EARNED!
BUT A BRAWLING, SINGLE-MINDED THUG SUCH AS YOU COULDN'T BEGIN TO UNDERSTAND THAT!
PERHAPS WHAT THIS CITY NEEDS IS A BRAWLER! SOMEONE WILLING TO GET HIS HANDS DIRTY.
MAYBE EVEN END THE THOUSAND-YEARS WAR WITH HELIUM!
AND YOU THINK YOU COULD DO THAT?
EASILY, IF YOU AND YOUR GENERALS WOULD ONLY LISTEN TO ME!
RATHER THAN COUNTENANCE A FRESH PERSPECTIVE, YOU SHUT ME OUT! YOU TREAT ME AS IF I'M NOT HERE!
THAT IS AN EXCELLENT IDEA.
GUARDS!
YOU... YOU MEAN ABOUT NOT IGNORING ME?

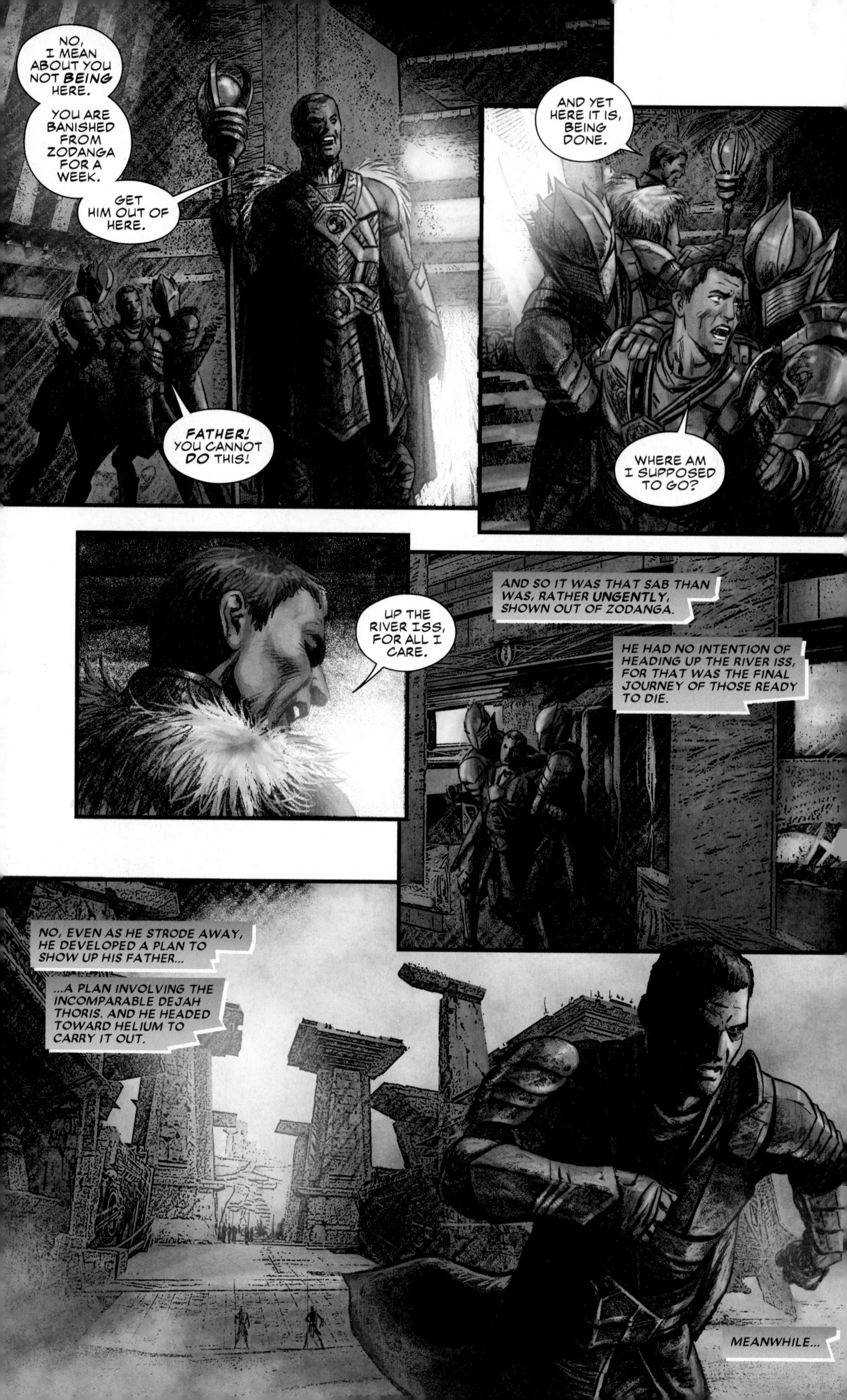
NO, I MEAN ABOUT YOU NOT BEING HERE.
YOU ARE BANISHED FROM ZODANGA FOR A WEEK.
GET HIM OUT OF HERE.
FATHER! YOU CANNOT DO THIS!
AND YET HERE IT IS, BEING DONE.
WHERE AM I SUPPOSED TO GO?
UP THE RIVER ISS, FOR ALL I CARE.
AND SO IT WAS THAT SAB THAN WAS, RATHER UNGENTLY, SHOWN OUT OF ZODANGA.
HE HAD NO INTENTION OF HEADING UP THE RIVER ISS, FOR THAT WAS THE FINAL JOURNEY OF THOSE READY TO DIE.
NO, EVEN AS HE STRODE AWAY, HE DEVELOPED A PLAN TO SHOW UP HIS FATHER...
...A PLAN INVOLVING THE INCOMPARABLE DEJAH THORIS. AND HE HEADED TOWARD HELIUM TO CARRY IT OUT.
MEANWHILE...

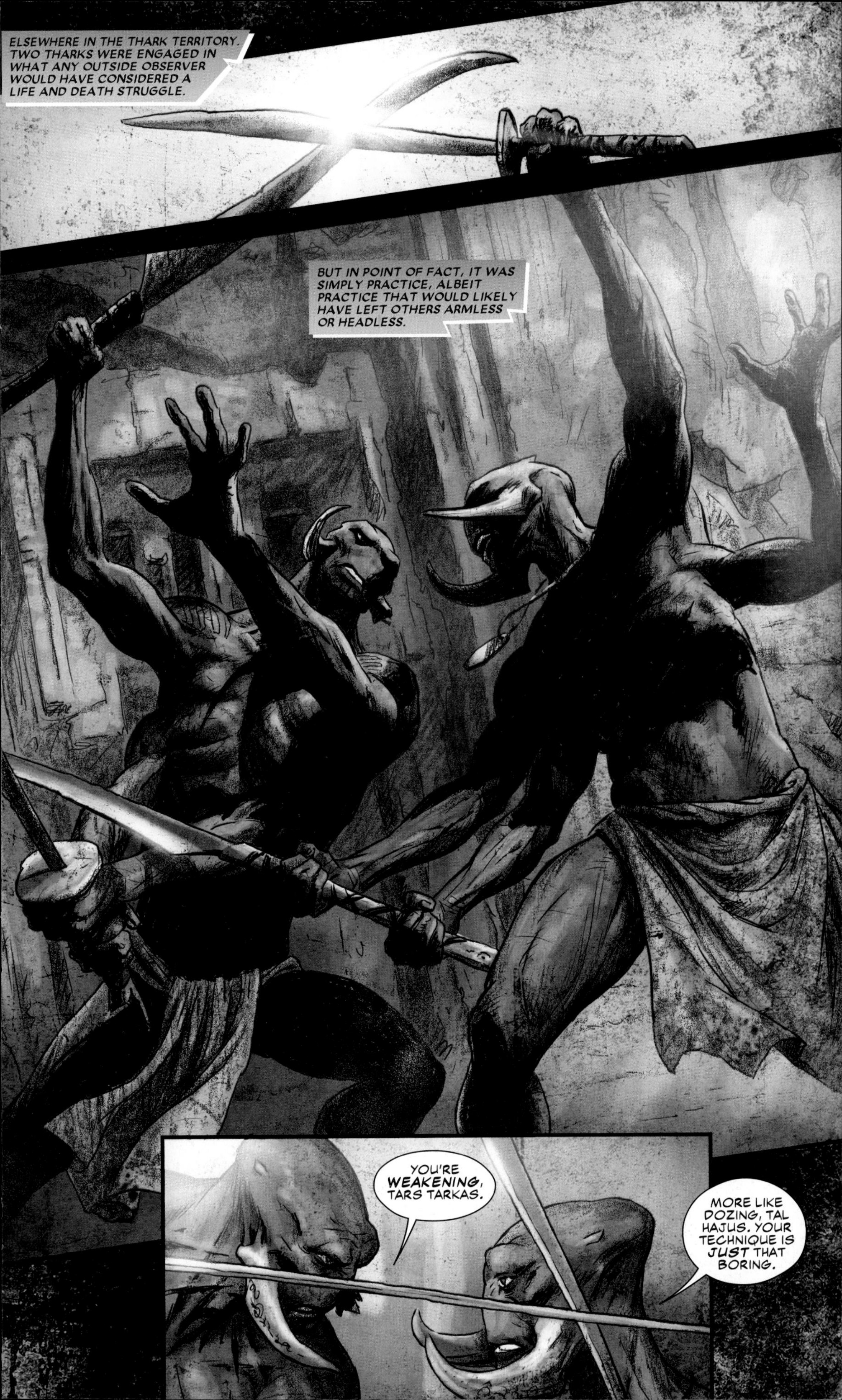
ELSEWHERE IN THE THARK TERRITORY. TWO THARKS WERE ENGAGED IN WHAT ANY OUTSIDE OBSERVER WOULD HAVE CONSIDERED A LIFE AND DEATH STRUGGLE.
BUT IN POINT OF FACT, IT WAS SIMPLY PRACTICE, ALBEIT PRACTICE THAT WOULD LIKELY HAVE LEFT OTHERS ARMLESS OR HEADLESS.
YOU'RE WEAKENING, TARS TARKAS.
MORE LIKE DOZING, TAL HAJUS. YOUR TECHNIQUE IS JUST THAT BORING.

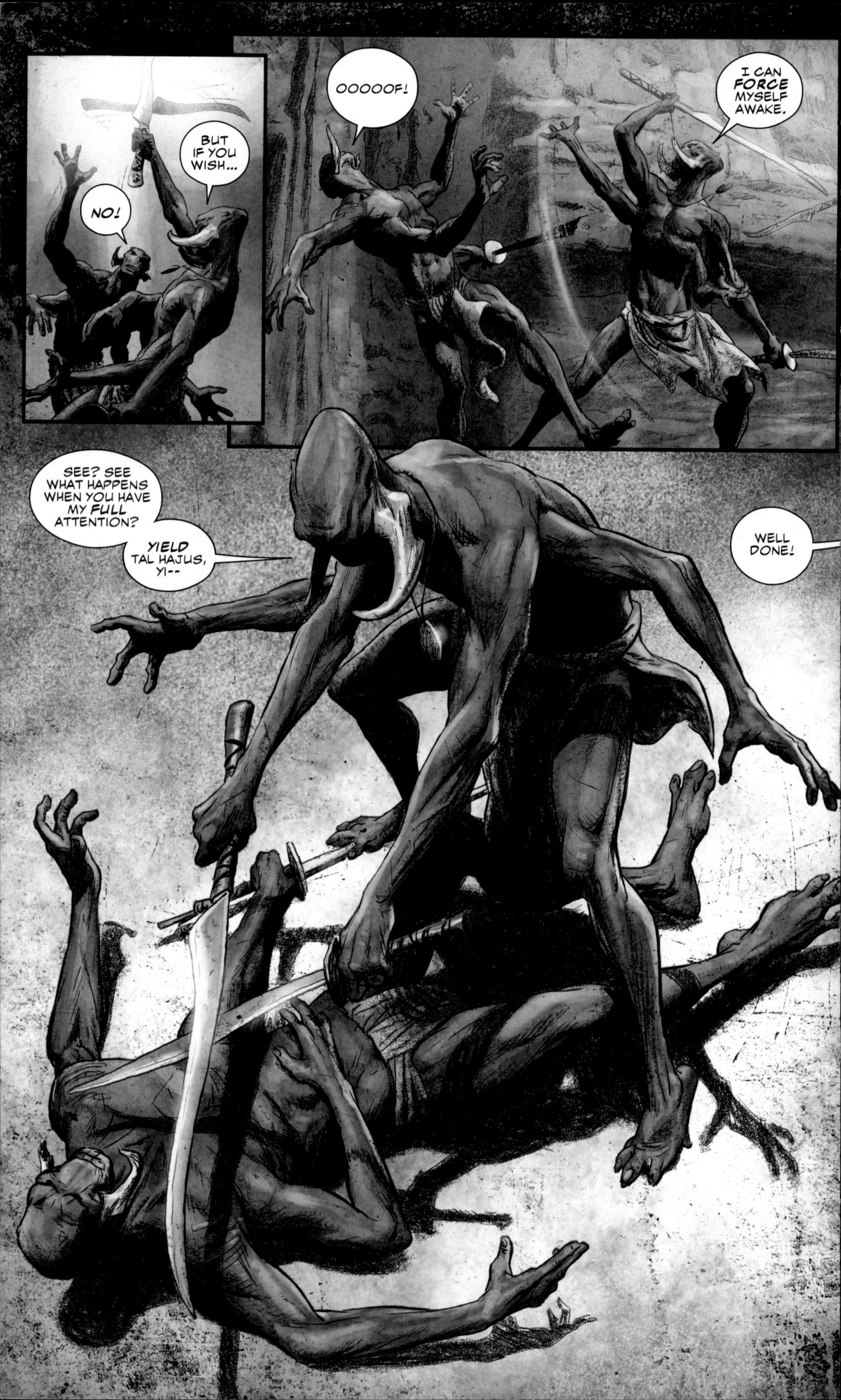
BUT IF YOU WISH...
NO!
OOOOOF!
I CAN FORCE MYSELF AWAKE.
SEE? SEE WHAT HAPPENS WHEN YOU HAVE MY FULL ATTENTION?
YIELD TAL HAJUS, YI--
WELL DONE!

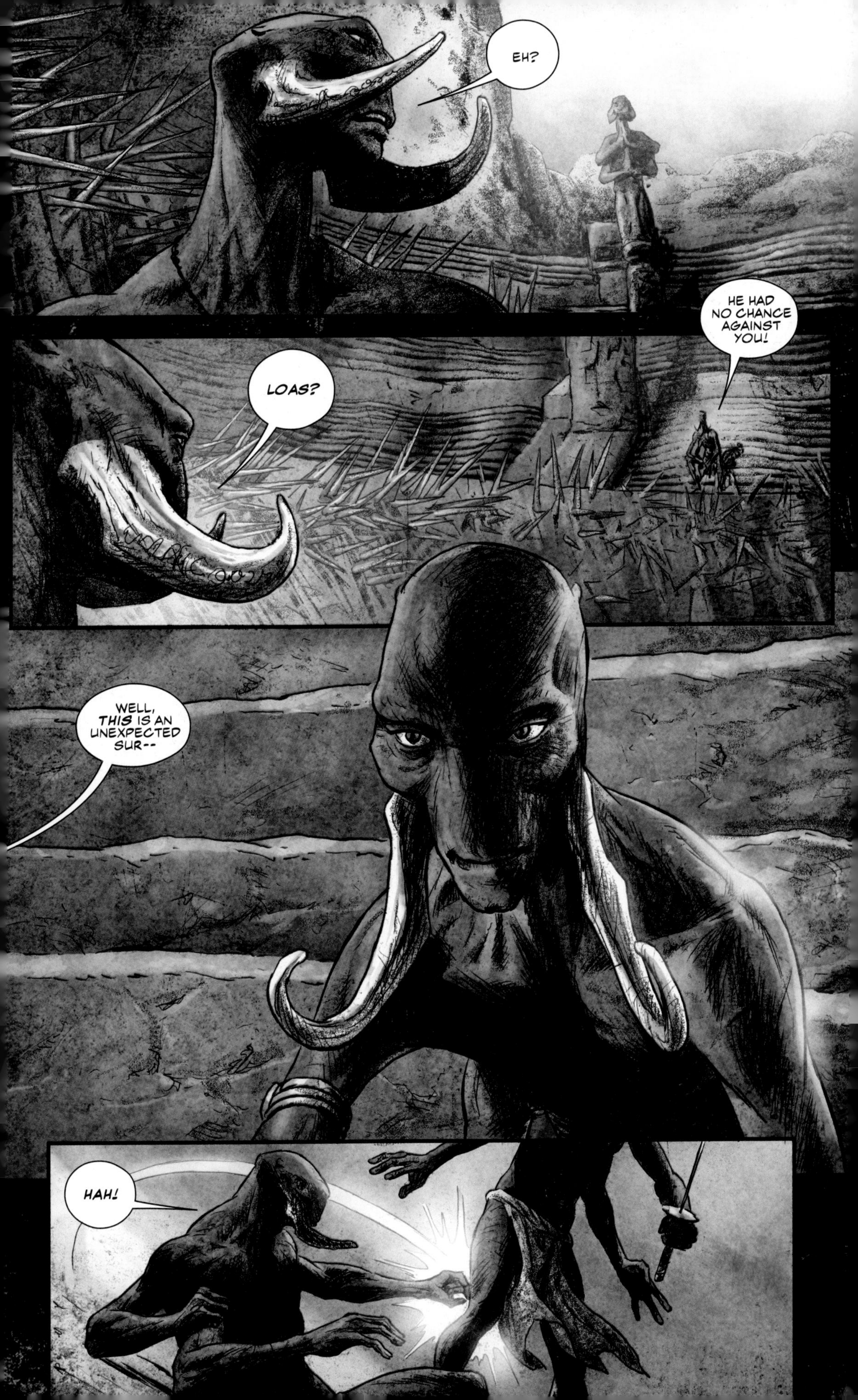
EH?
LOAS?
HE HAD NO CHANCE AGAINST YOU!
WELL, THIS IS AN UNEXPECTED SUR--
HAH!

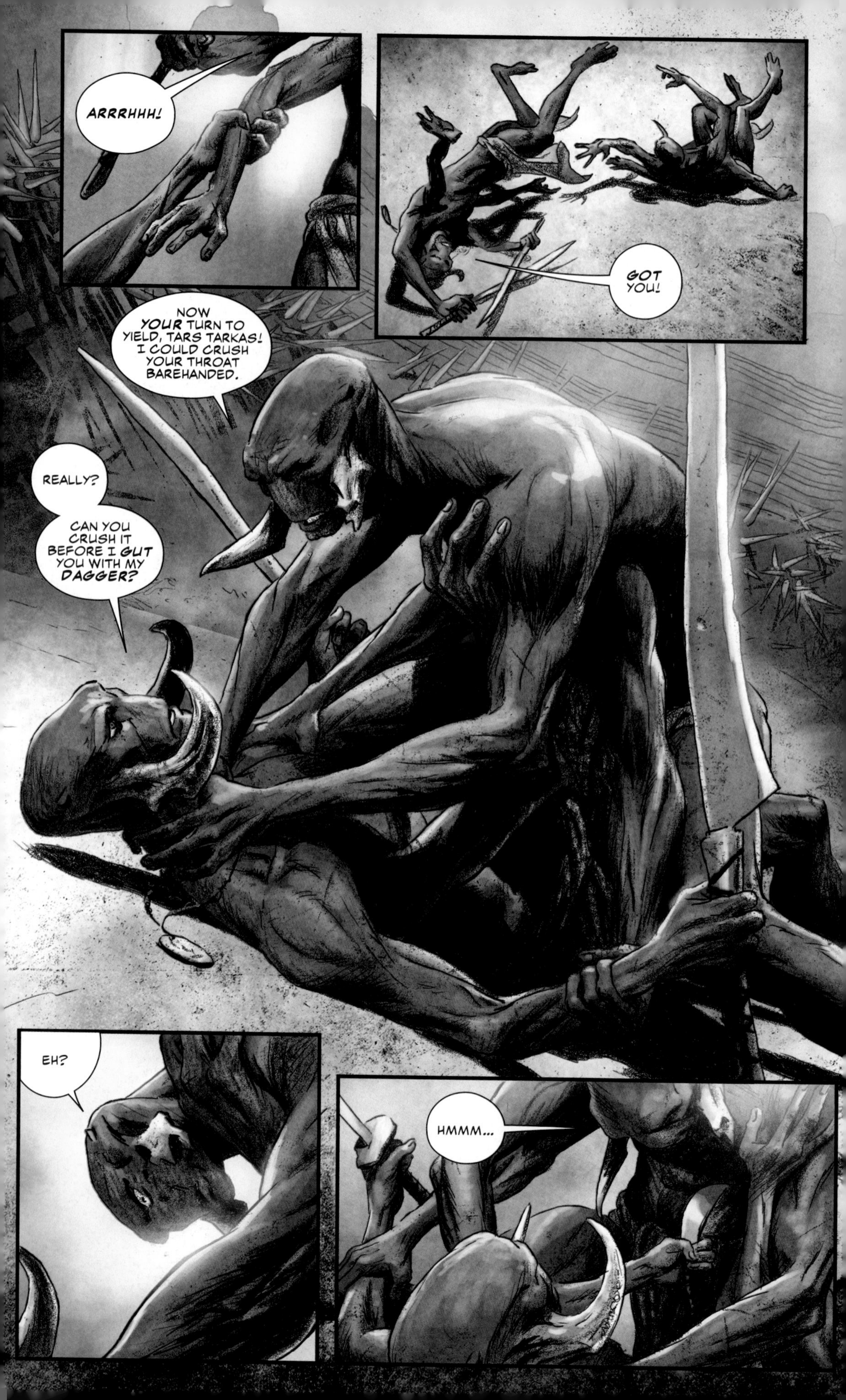
ARRRHHH!
GOT YOU!
NOW YOUR TURN TO YIELD, TARS TARKAS! I COULD CRUSH YOUR THROAT BAREHANDED.
REALLY?
CAN YOU CRUSH IT BEFORE I GUT YOU WITH MY DAGGER?
EH?
HMMM...

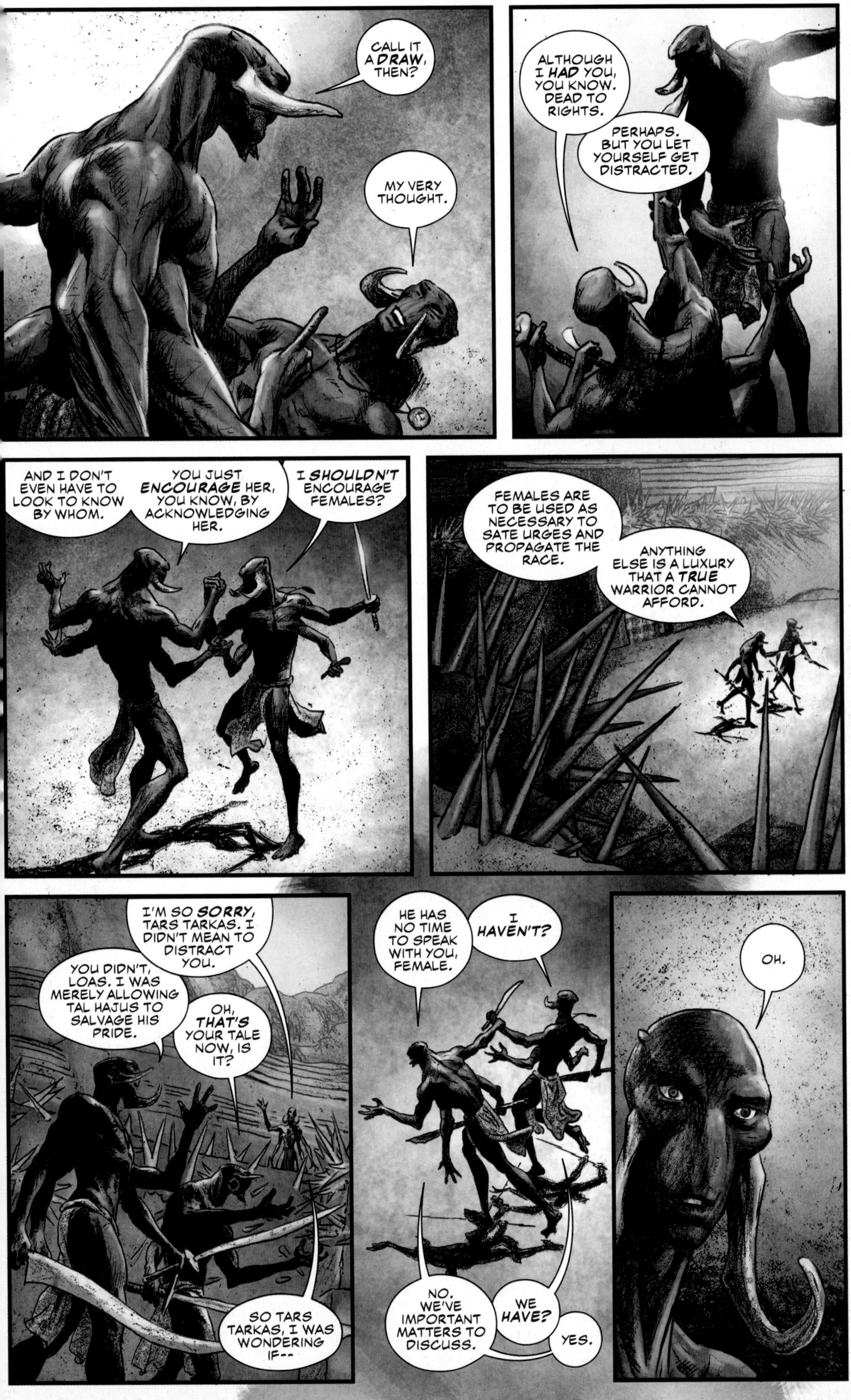
CALL IT A DRAW, THEN?
MY VERY THOUGHT.
ALTHOUGH I HAD YOU, YOU KNOW. DEAD TO RIGHTS.
PERHAPS. BUT YOU LET YOURSELF GET DISTRACTED.
AND I DON'T EVEN HAVE TO LOOK TO KNOW BY WHOM.
YOU JUST ENCOURAGE HER, YOU KNOW, BY ACKNOWLEDGING HER.
I SHOULDN'T ENCOURAGE FEMALES?
FEMALES ARE TO BE USED AS NECESSARY TO SATE URGES AND PROPAGATE THE RACE.
ANYTHING ELSE IS A LUXURY THAT A TRUE WARRIOR CANNOT AFFORD.
I'M SO SORRY, TARS TARKAS. I DIDN'T MEAN TO DISTRACT YOU.
YOU DIDN'T, LOAS. I WAS MERELY ALLOWING TAL HAJUS TO SALVAGE HIS PRIDE.
OH, THAT'S YOUR TALE NOW, IS IT?
SO TARS TARKAS, I WAS WONDERING IF--
HE HAS NO TIME TO SPEAK WITH YOU, FEMALE.
I HAVEN'T?
NO. WE'VE IMPORTANT MATTERS TO DISCUSS.
WE HAVE?
YES.
OH.

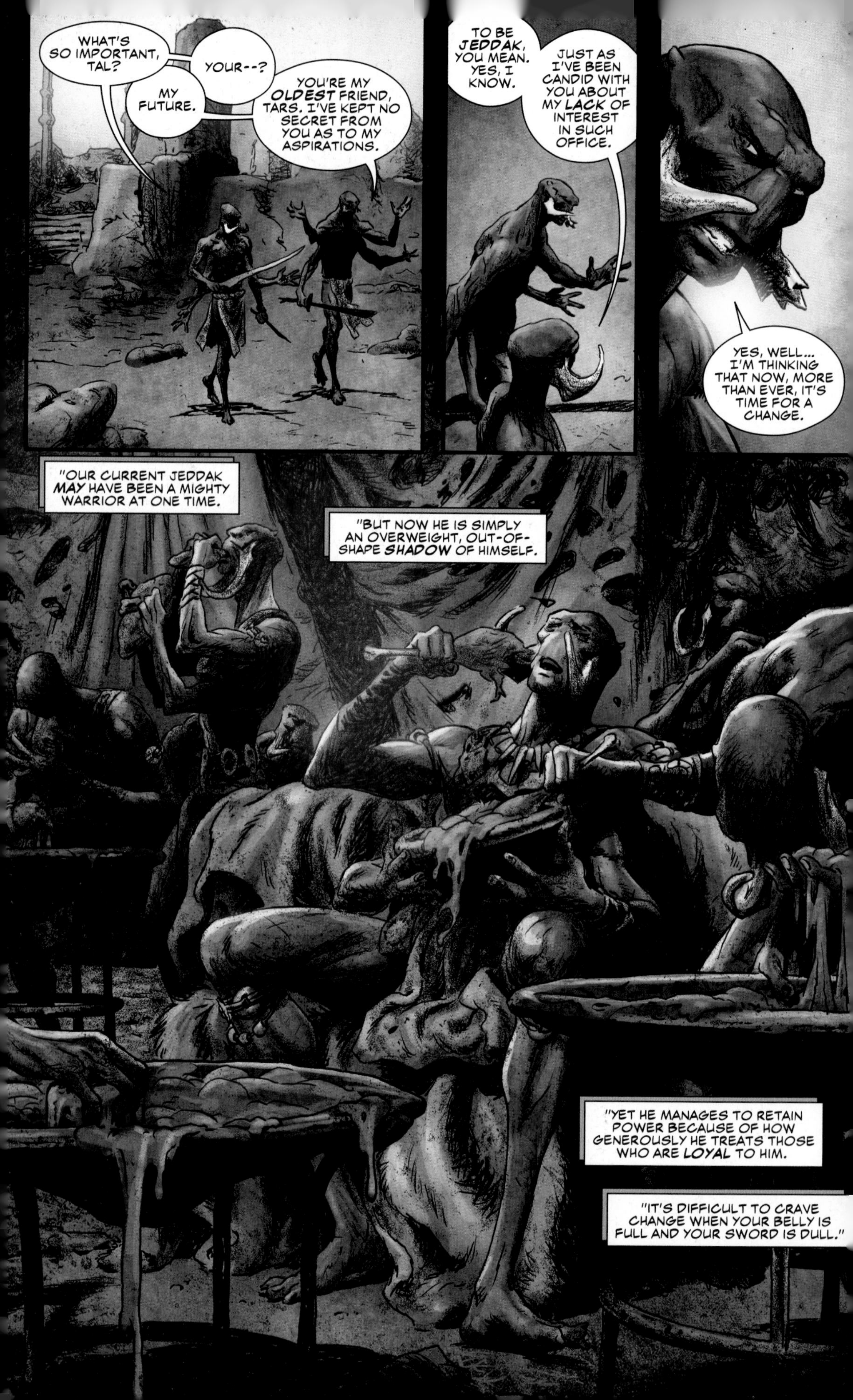

WHAT'S SO IMPORTANT, TAL?
YOUR--?
MY FUTURE.
YOU'RE MY OLDEST FRIEND, TARS. I'VE KEPT NO SECRET FROM YOU AS TO MY ASPIRATIONS.
TO BE JEDDAK, YOU MEAN. YES, I KNOW.
JUST AS I'VE BEEN CANDID WITH YOU ABOUT MY LACK OF INTEREST IN SUCH OFFICE.
YES, WELL... I'M THINKING THAT NOW, MORE THAN EVER, IT'S TIME FOR A CHANGE.
"OUR CURRENT JEDDAK MAY HAVE BEEN A MIGHTY WARRIOR AT ONE TIME.
"BUT NOW HE IS SIMPLY AN OVERWEIGHT, OUT-OF-SHAPE SHADOW OF HIMSELF.
"YET HE MANAGES TO RETAIN POWER BECAUSE OF HOW GENEROUSLY HE TREATS THOSE WHO ARE LOYAL TO HIM.
"IT'S DIFFICULT TO CRAVE CHANGE WHEN YOUR BELLY IS FULL AND YOUR SWORD IS DULL."

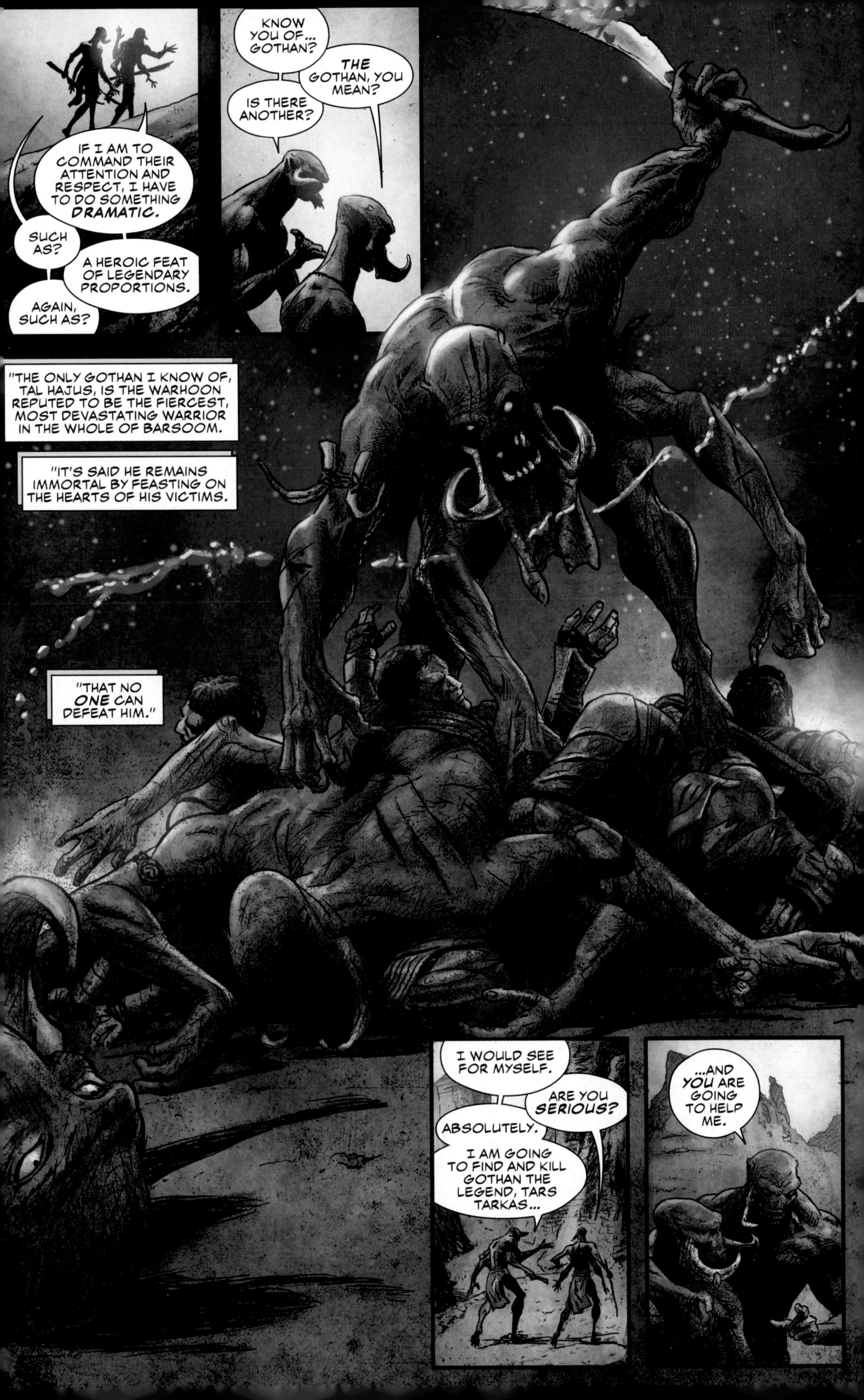

IF I AM TO COMMAND THEIR ATTENTION AND RESPECT, I HAVE TO DO SOMETHING DRAMATIC.
SUCH AS?
A HEROIC FEAT OF LEGENDARY PROPORTIONS.
AGAIN, SUCH AS?
KNOW YOU OF... GOTHAN?
IS THERE ANOTHER?
THE GOTHAN, YOU MEAN?
"THE ONLY GOTHAN I KNOW OF, TAL HAJUS, IS THE WARHOON REPUTED TO BE THE FIERCEST, MOST DEVASTATING WARRIOR IN THE WHOLE OF BARSOOM.
"IT'S SAID HE REMAINS IMMORTAL BY FEASTING ON THE HEARTS OF HIS VICTIMS.
"THAT NO ONE CAN DEFEAT HIM."
I WOULD SEE FOR MYSELF.
ARE YOU SERIOUS?
ABSOLUTELY.
I AM GOING TO FIND AND KILL GOTHAN THE LEGEND, TARS TARKAS...
...AND YOU ARE GOING TO HELP ME.

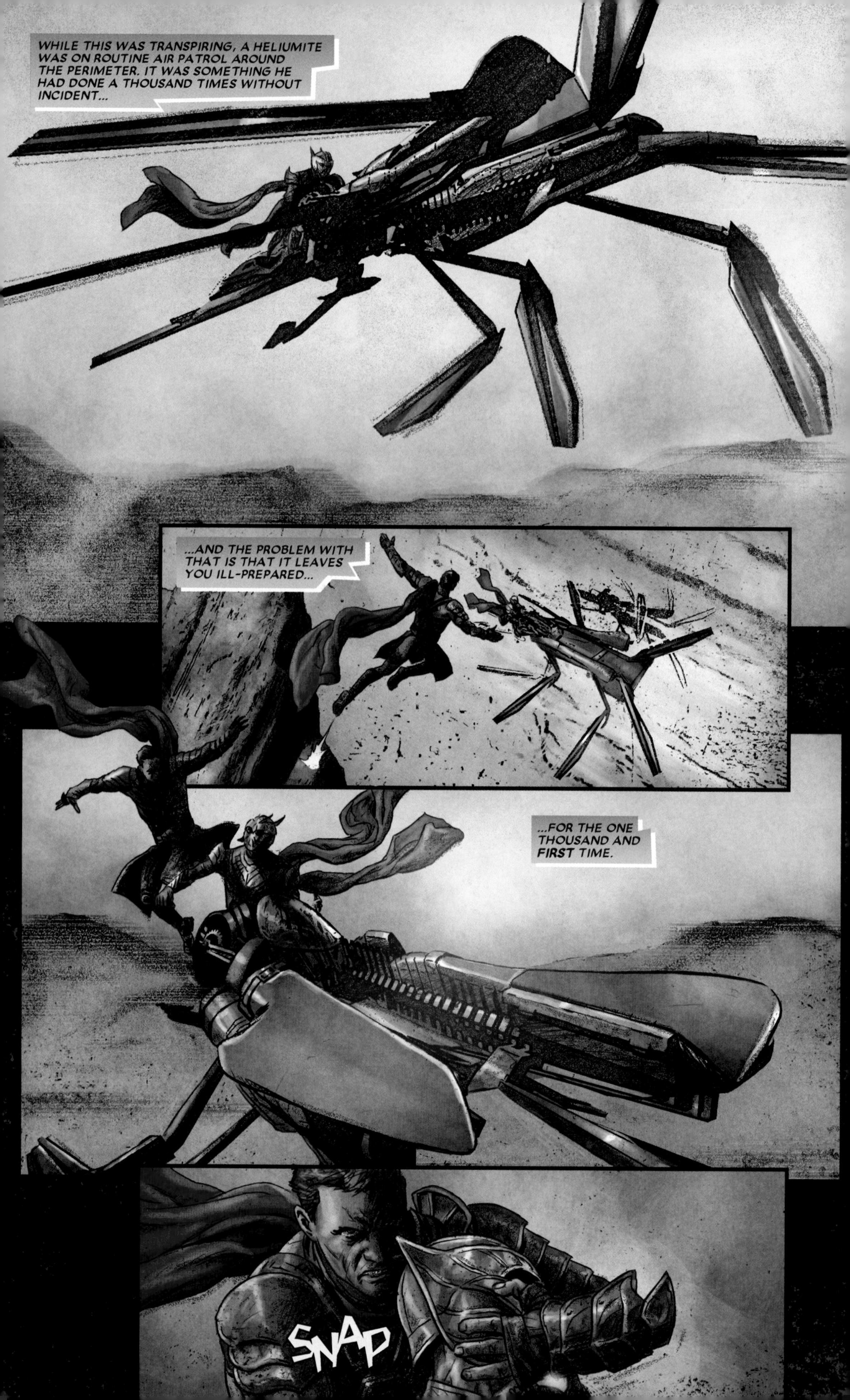
WHILE THIS WAS TRANSPIRING, A HELIUMITE WAS ON ROUTINE AIR PATROL AROUND THE PERIMETER. IT WAS SOMETHING HE HAD DONE A THOUSAND TIMES WITHOUT INCIDENT...
...AND THE PROBLEM WITH THAT IS THAT IT LEAVES YOU ILL-PREPARED...
...FOR THE ONE THOUSAND AND FIRST TIME.
SNAP

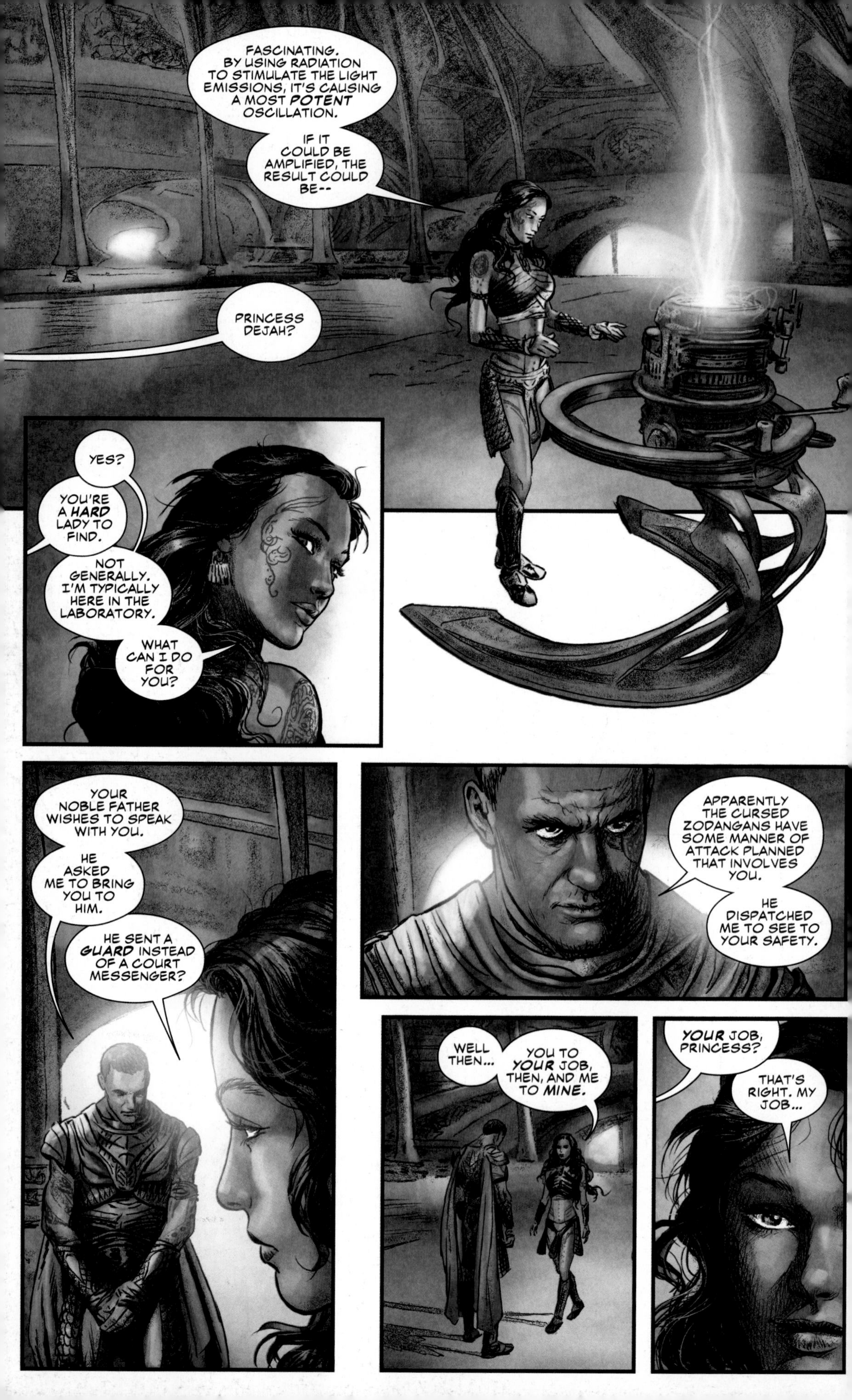
FASCINATING. BY USING RADIATION TO STIMULATE THE LIGHT EMISSIONS, IT'S CAUSING A MOST POTENT OSCILLATION.
IF IT COULD BE AMPLIFIED, THE RESULT COULD BE--
PRINCESS DEJAH?
YES?
YOU'RE A HARD LADY TO FIND.
NOT GENERALLY. I'M TYPICALLY HERE IN THE LABORATORY.
WHAT CAN I DO FOR YOU?
YOUR NOBLE FATHER WISHES TO SPEAK WITH YOU.
HE ASKED ME TO BRING YOU TO HIM.
HE SENT A GUARD INSTEAD OF A COURT MESSENGER?
APPARENTLY THE CURSED ZODANGANS HAVE SOME MANNER OF ATTACK PLANNED THAT INVOLVES YOU.
HE DISPATCHED ME TO SEE TO YOUR SAFETY.
WELL THEN...
YOU TO YOUR JOB, THEN, AND ME TO MINE.
YOUR JOB, PRINCESS?
THAT'S RIGHT. MY JOB...

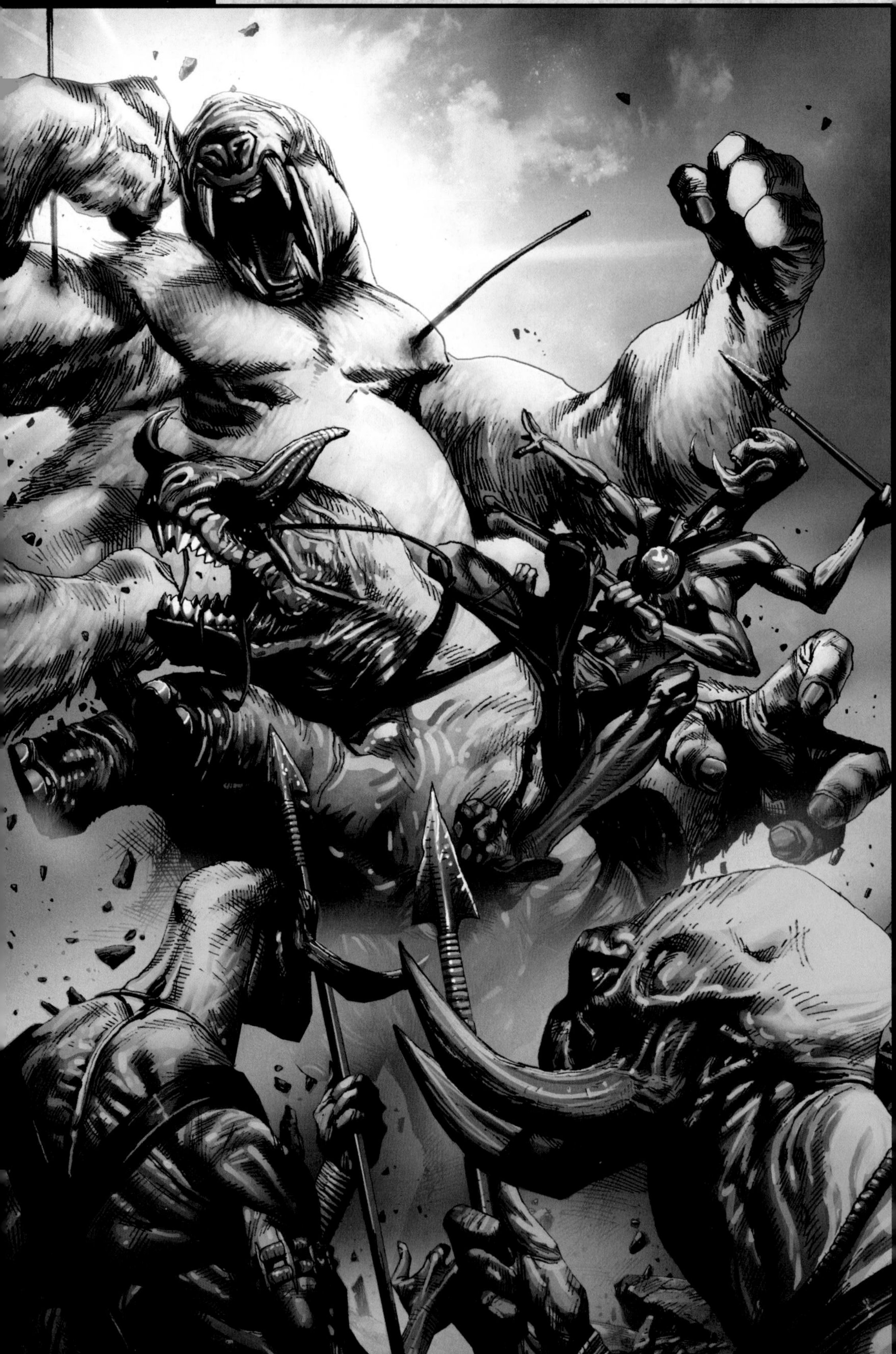

TWO

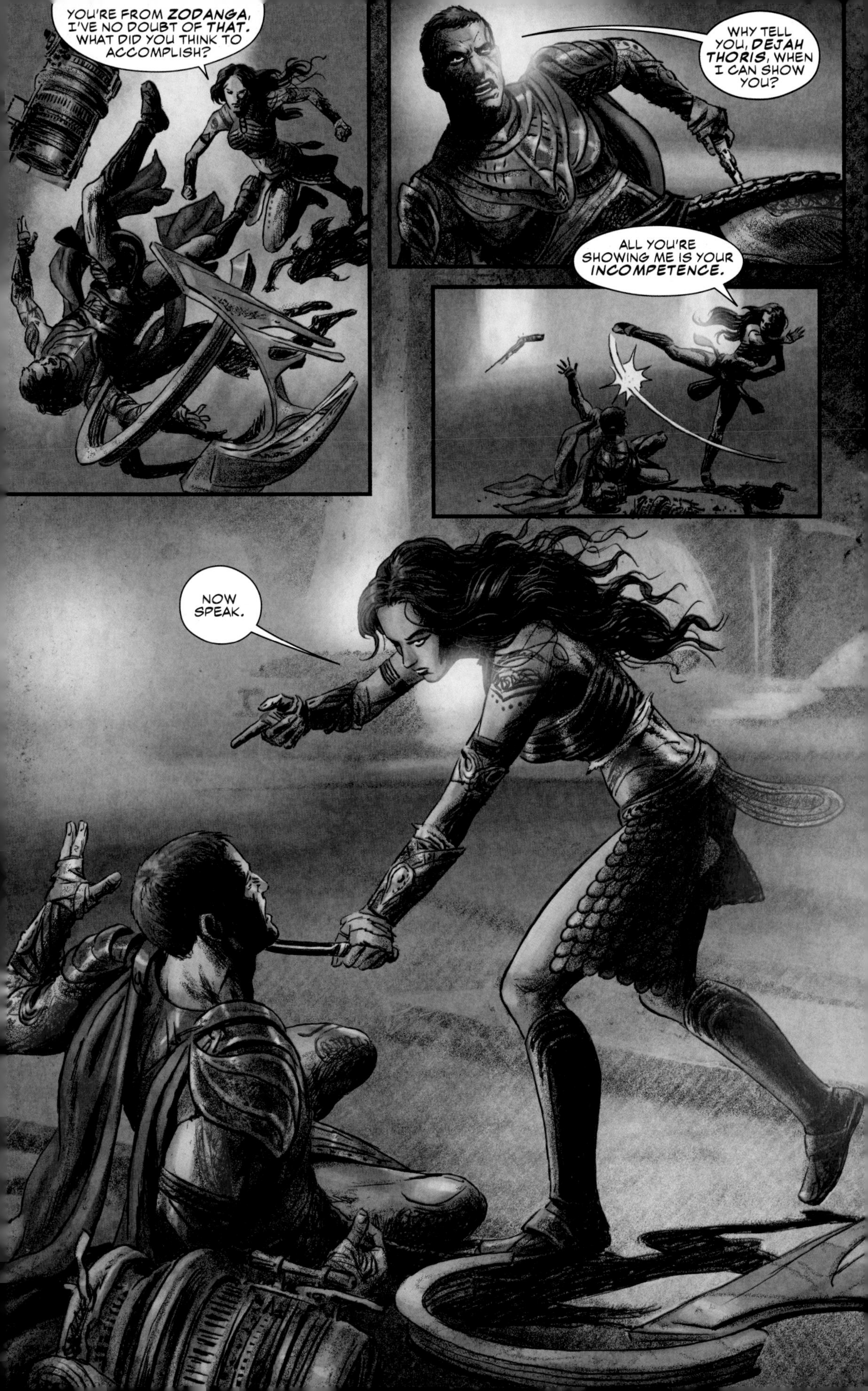
YOU'RE FROM ZODANGA, I'VE NO DOUBT OF THAT. WHAT DID YOU THINK TO ACCOMPLISH?
WHY TELL YOU, DEJAH THORIS, WHEN I CAN SHOW YOU?
ALL YOU'RE SHOWING ME IS YOUR INCOMPETENCE.
NOW SPEAK.

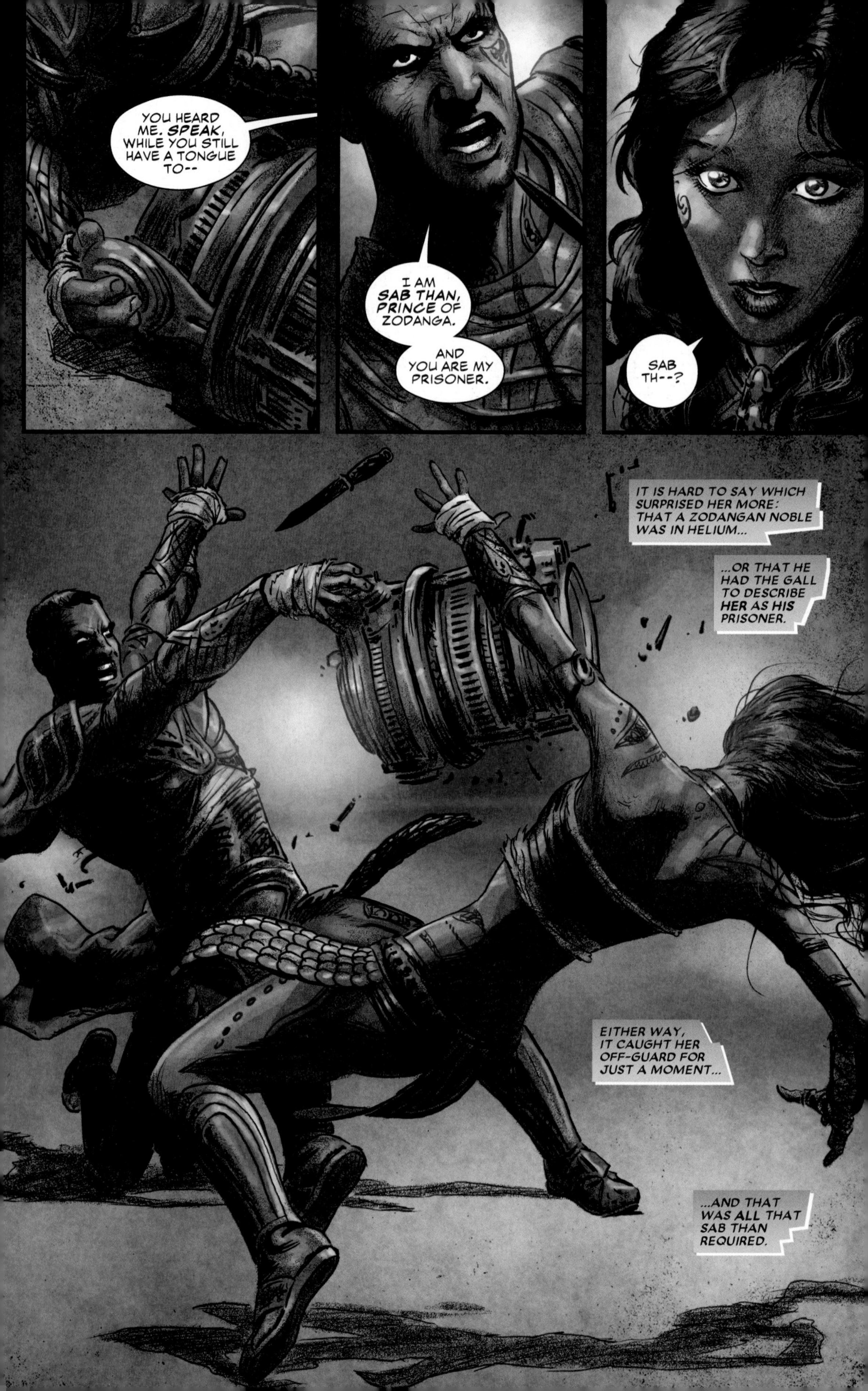
YOU HEARD ME. **SPEAK**, WHILE YOU STILL HAVE A TONGUE TO--
I AM **SAB THAN, PRINCE** OF ZODANGA.
AND YOU ARE MY PRISONER.
SAB TH--?
IT IS HARD TO SAY WHICH SURPRISED HER MORE: THAT A ZODANGAN NOBLE WAS IN HELIUM...
...OR THAT HE HAD THE GALL TO DESCRIBE **HER** AS **HIS** PRISONER.
EITHER WAY, IT CAUGHT HER OFF-GUARD FOR JUST A MOMENT...
...AND THAT WAS **ALL** THAT SAB THAN REQUIRED.

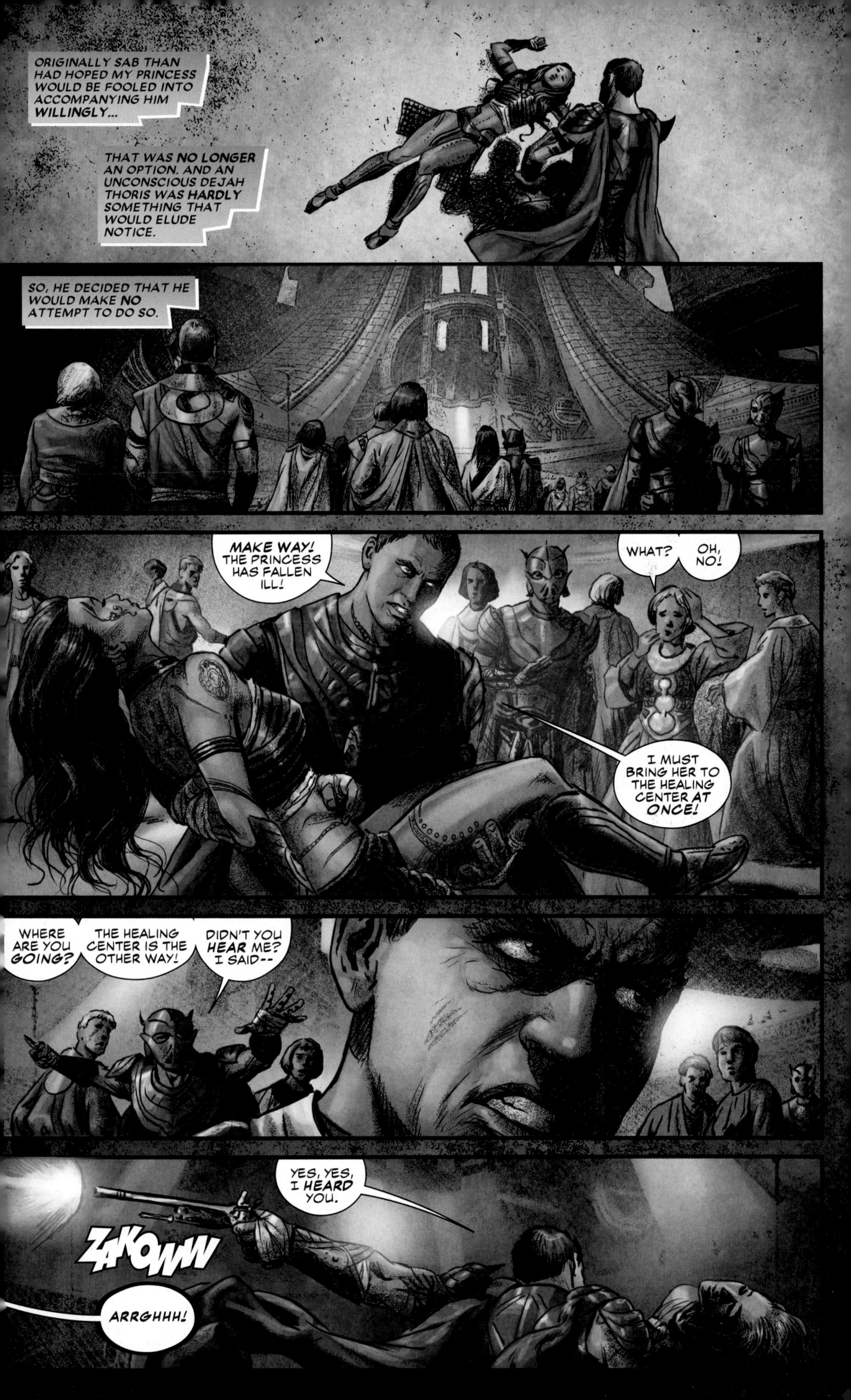
ORIGINALLY SAB THAN HAD HOPED MY PRINCESS WOULD BE FOOLED INTO ACCOMPANYING HIM WILLINGLY...
THAT WAS NO LONGER AN OPTION. AND AN UNCONSCIOUS DEJAH THORIS WAS HARDLY SOMETHING THAT WOULD ELUDE NOTICE.
SO, HE DECIDED THAT HE WOULD MAKE NO ATTEMPT TO DO SO.
MAKE WAY! THE PRINCESS HAS FALLEN ILL!
WHAT?
OH, NO!
I MUST BRING HER TO THE HEALING CENTER AT ONCE!
WHERE ARE YOU GOING?
THE HEALING CENTER IS THE OTHER WAY!
DIDN'T YOU HEAR ME? I SAID--
YES, YES, I HEARD YOU.
ZAKOWW
ARRGHHH!

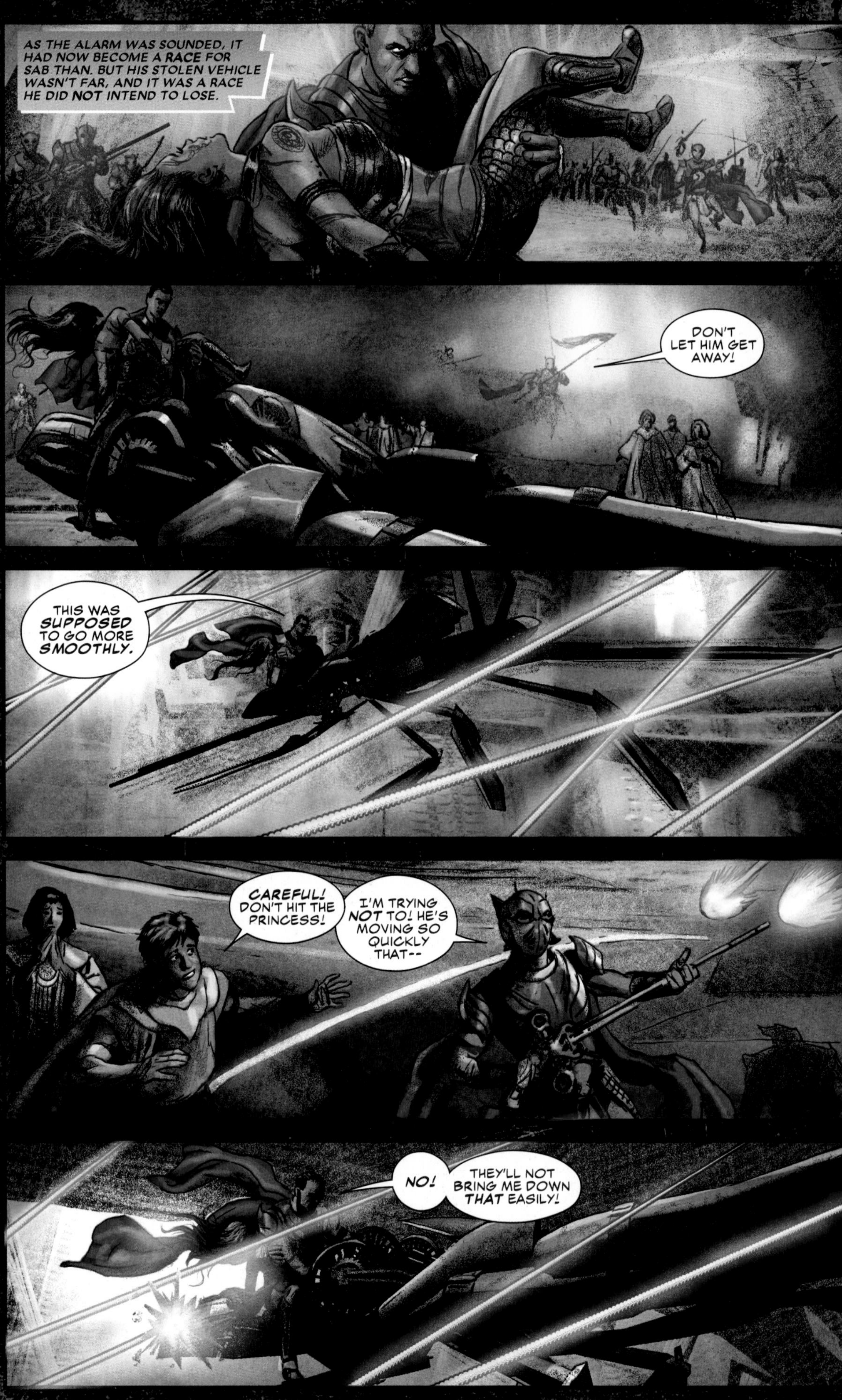
AS THE ALARM WAS SOUNDED, IT HAD NOW BECOME A RACE FOR SAB THAN. BUT HIS STOLEN VEHICLE WASN'T FAR, AND IT WAS A RACE HE DID NOT INTEND TO LOSE.
DON'T LET HIM GET AWAY!
THIS WAS SUPPOSED TO GO MORE SMOOTHLY.
CAREFUL! DON'T HIT THE PRINCESS!
I'M TRYING NOT TO! HE'S MOVING SO QUICKLY THAT--
NO!
THEY'LL NOT BRING ME DOWN THAT EASILY!

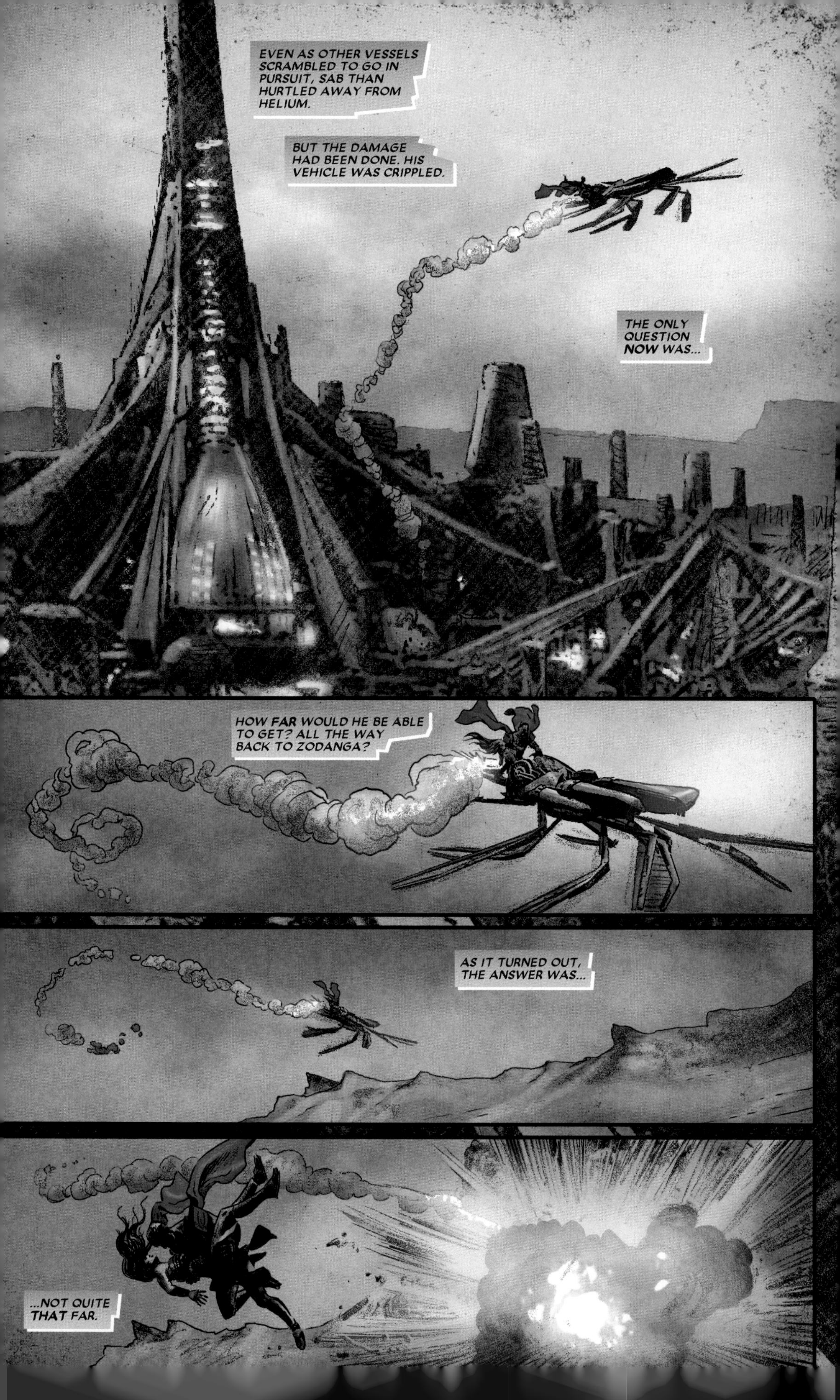
EVEN AS OTHER VESSELS SCRAMBLED TO GO IN PURSUIT, SAB THAN HURTLED AWAY FROM HELIUM.
BUT THE DAMAGE HAD BEEN DONE. HIS VEHICLE WAS CRIPPLED.
THE ONLY QUESTION NOW WAS...
HOW FAR WOULD HE BE ABLE TO GET? ALL THE WAY BACK TO ZODANGA?
AS IT TURNED OUT, THE ANSWER WAS...
...NOT QUITE THAT FAR.

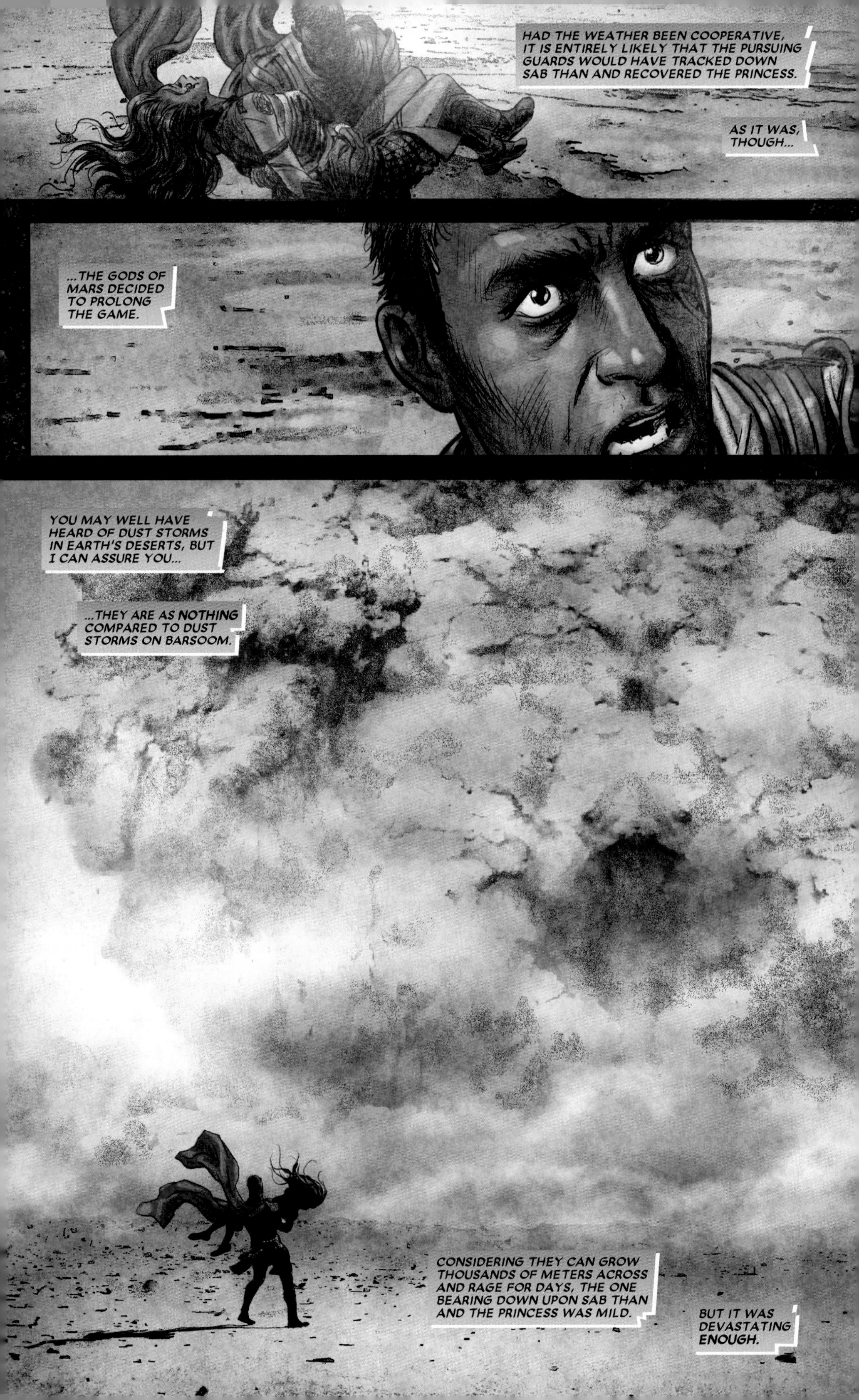
HAD THE WEATHER BEEN COOPERATIVE, IT IS ENTIRELY LIKELY THAT THE PURSUING GUARDS WOULD HAVE TRACKED DOWN SAB THAN AND RECOVERED THE PRINCESS.
AS IT WAS, THOUGH...
...THE GODS OF MARS DECIDED TO PROLONG THE GAME.
YOU MAY WELL HAVE HEARD OF DUST STORMS IN EARTH'S DESERTS, BUT I CAN ASSURE YOU...
...THEY ARE AS NOTHING COMPARED TO DUST STORMS ON BARSOOM.
CONSIDERING THEY CAN GROW THOUSANDS OF METERS ACROSS AND RAGE FOR DAYS, THE ONE BEARING DOWN UPON SAB THAN AND THE PRINCESS WAS MILD.
BUT IT WAS DEVASTATING ENOUGH.

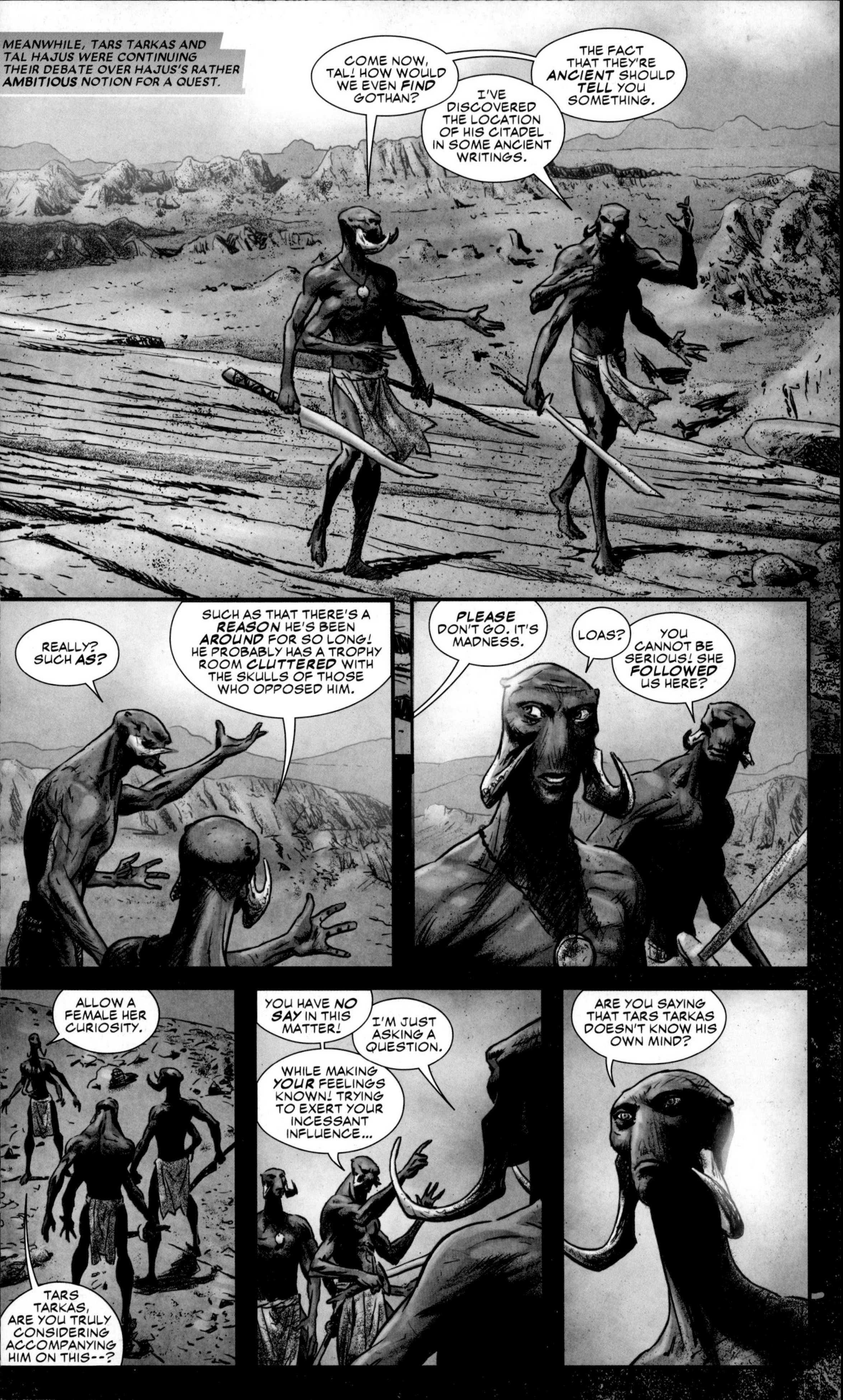
MEANWHILE, TARS TARKAS AND TAL HAJUS WERE CONTINUING THEIR DEBATE OVER HAJUS'S RATHER AMBITIOUS NOTION FOR A QUEST.
COME NOW, TAL! HOW WOULD WE EVEN FIND GOTHAN?
I'VE DISCOVERED THE LOCATION OF HIS CITADEL IN SOME ANCIENT WRITINGS.
THE FACT THAT THEY'RE ANCIENT SHOULD TELL YOU SOMETHING.
REALLY? SUCH AS?
SUCH AS THAT THERE'S A REASON HE'S BEEN AROUND FOR SO LONG! HE PROBABLY HAS A TROPHY ROOM CLUTTERED WITH THE SKULLS OF THOSE WHO OPPOSED HIM.
PLEASE DON'T GO. IT'S MADNESS.
LOAS?
YOU CANNOT BE SERIOUS! SHE FOLLOWED US HERE?
ALLOW A FEMALE HER CURIOSITY.
TARS TARKAS, ARE YOU TRULY CONSIDERING ACCOMPANYING HIM ON THIS--?
YOU HAVE NO SAY IN THIS MATTER!
I'M JUST ASKING A QUESTION.
WHILE MAKING YOUR FEELINGS KNOWN! TRYING TO EXERT YOUR INCESSANT INFLUENCE...
ARE YOU SAYING THAT TARS TARKAS DOESN'T KNOW HIS OWN MIND?

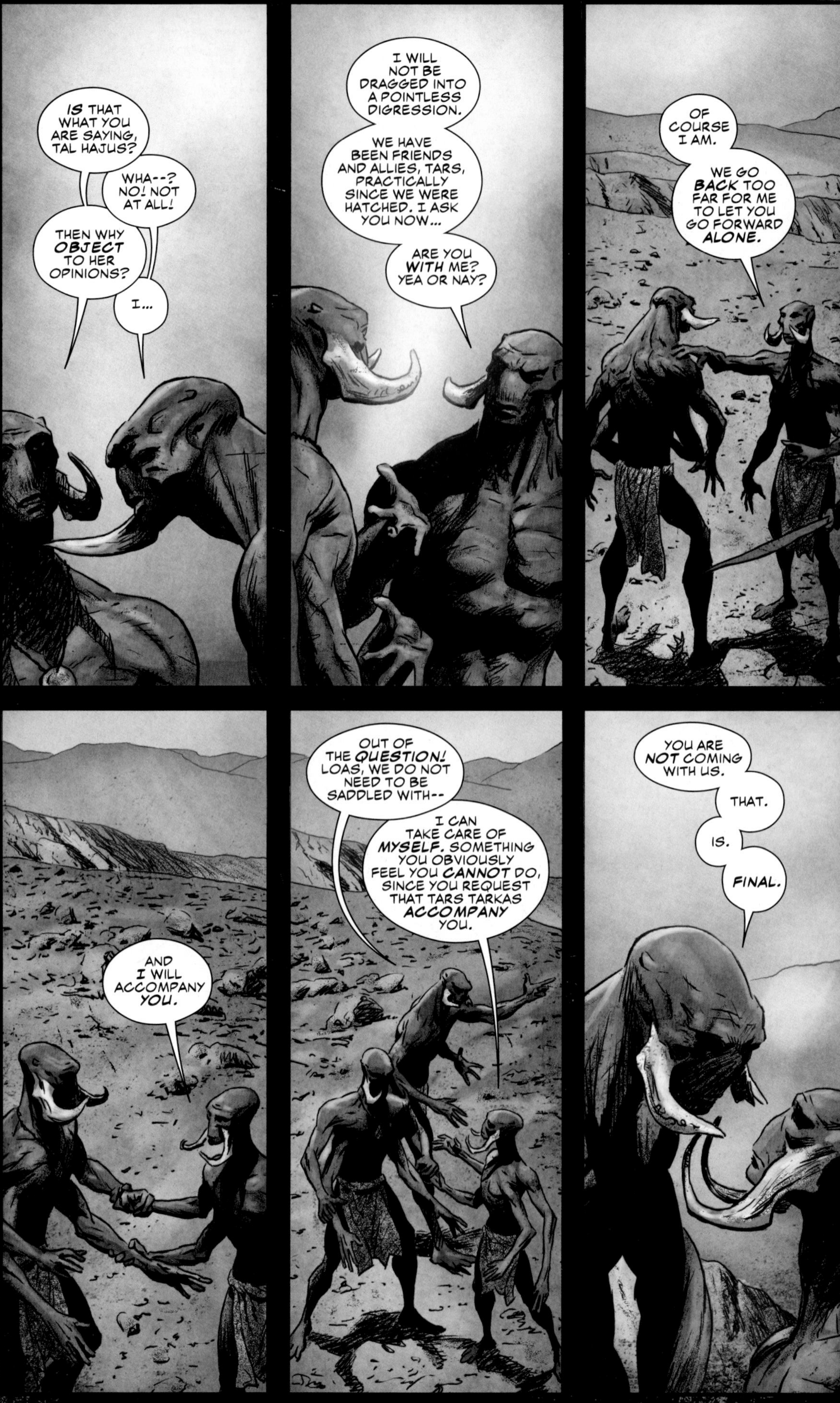
IS THAT WHAT YOU ARE SAYING, TAL HAJUS?
WHA--? NO! NOT AT ALL!
THEN WHY OBJECT TO HER OPINIONS?
I...
I WILL NOT BE DRAGGED INTO A POINTLESS DIGRESSION.
WE HAVE BEEN FRIENDS AND ALLIES, TARS, PRACTICALLY SINCE WE WERE HATCHED. I ASK YOU NOW...
ARE YOU WITH ME? YEA OR NAY?
OF COURSE I AM.
WE GO BACK TOO FAR FOR ME TO LET YOU GO FORWARD ALONE.
AND I WILL ACCOMPANY YOU.
OUT OF THE QUESTION! LOAS, WE DO NOT NEED TO BE SADDLED WITH--
I CAN TAKE CARE OF MYSELF. SOMETHING YOU OBVIOUSLY FEEL YOU CANNOT DO, SINCE YOU REQUEST THAT TARS TARKAS ACCOMPANY YOU.
YOU ARE NOT COMING WITH US.
THAT.
IS.
FINAL.

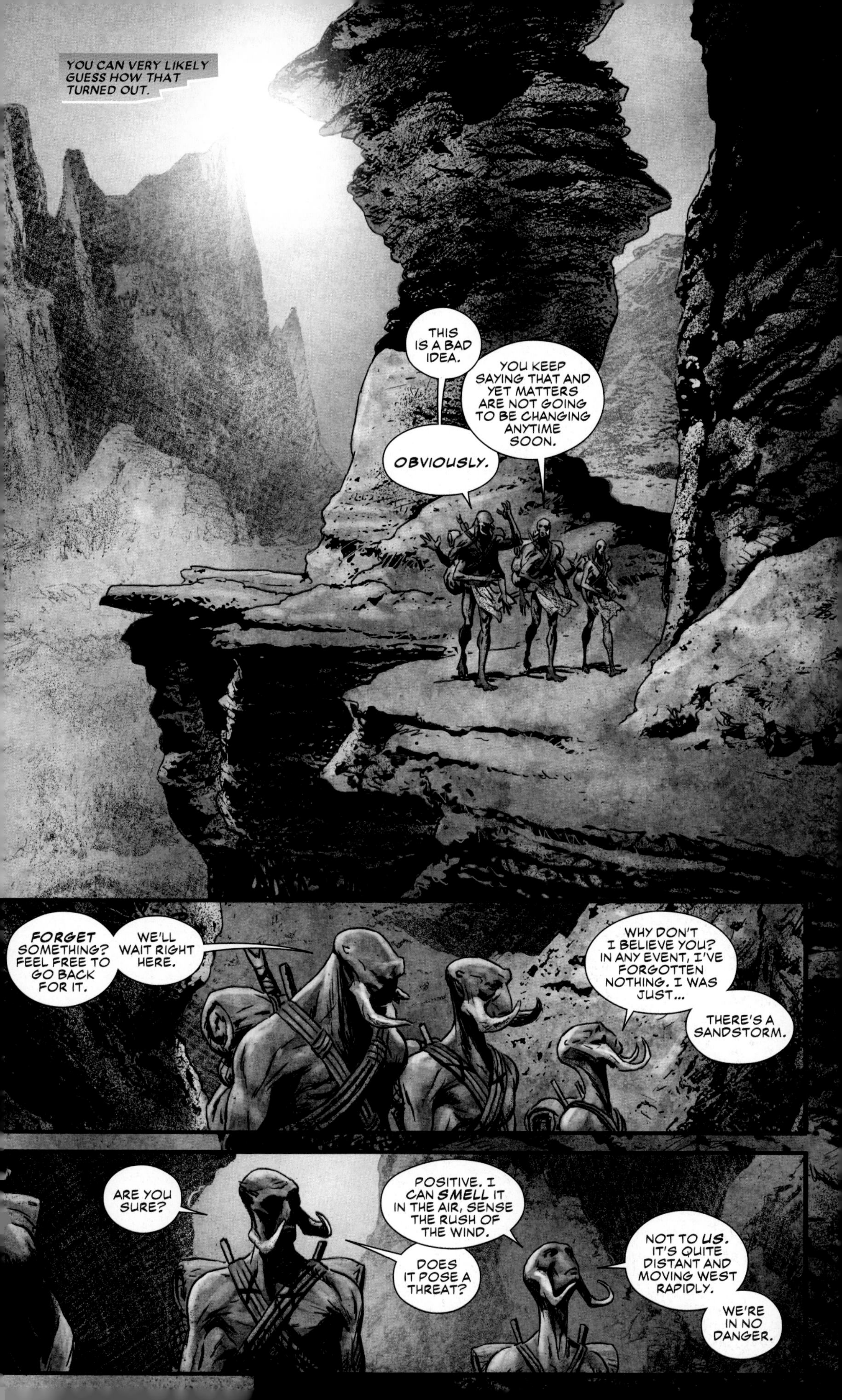
YOU CAN VERY LIKELY GUESS HOW THAT TURNED OUT.
THIS IS A BAD IDEA.
YOU KEEP SAYING THAT AND YET MATTERS ARE NOT GOING TO BE CHANGING ANYTIME SOON.
OBVIOUSLY.
FORGET SOMETHING? FEEL FREE TO GO BACK FOR IT.
WE'LL WAIT RIGHT HERE.
WHY DON'T I BELIEVE YOU? IN ANY EVENT, I'VE FORGOTTEN NOTHING. I WAS JUST...
THERE'S A SANDSTORM.
ARE YOU SURE?
POSITIVE. I CAN SMELL IT IN THE AIR, SENSE THE RUSH OF THE WIND.
DOES IT POSE A THREAT?
NOT TO US. IT'S QUITE DISTANT AND MOVING WEST RAPIDLY.
WE'RE IN NO DANGER.

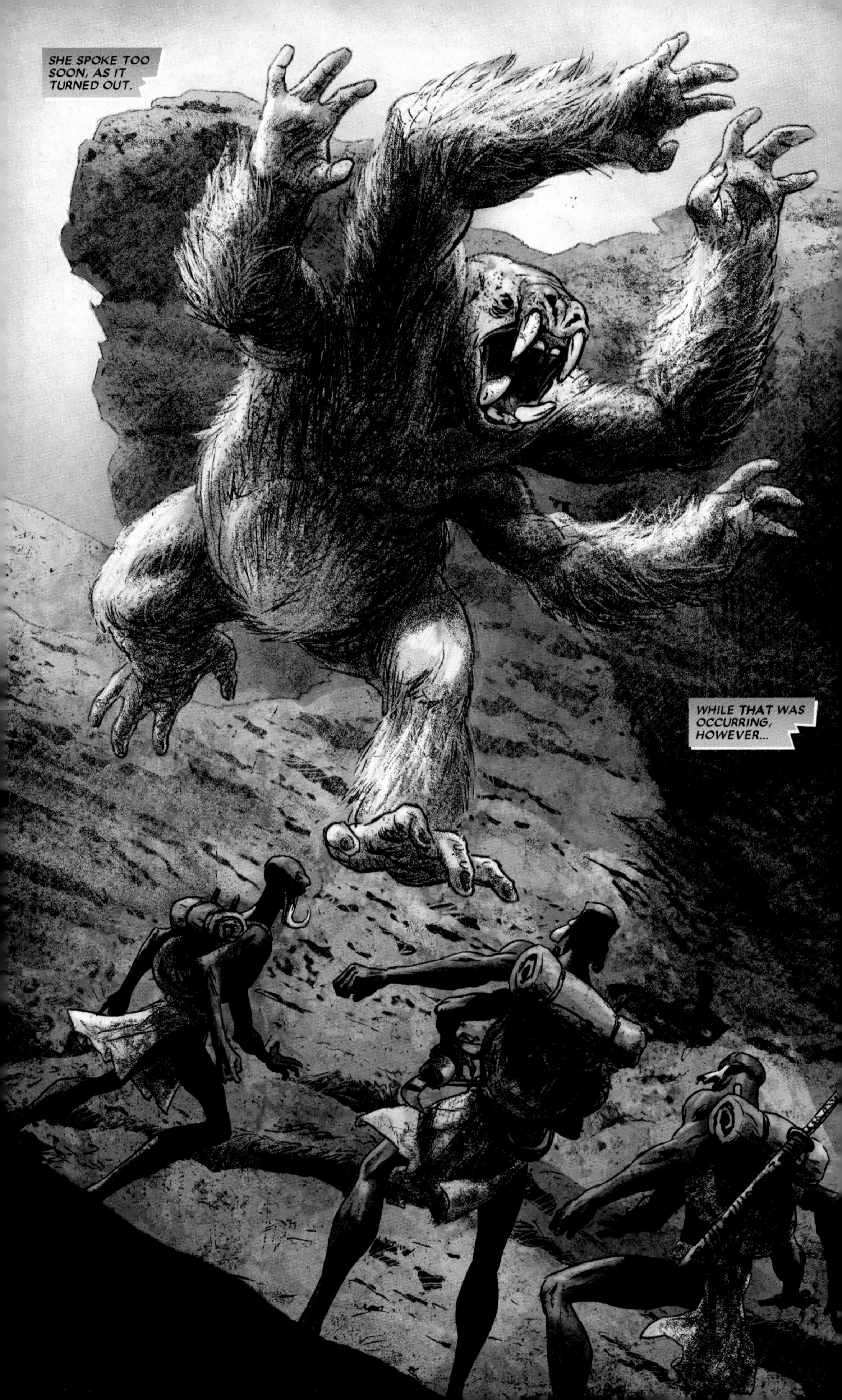
SHE SPOKE TOO SOON, AS IT TURNED OUT.
WHILE THAT WAS OCCURRING, HOWEVER...

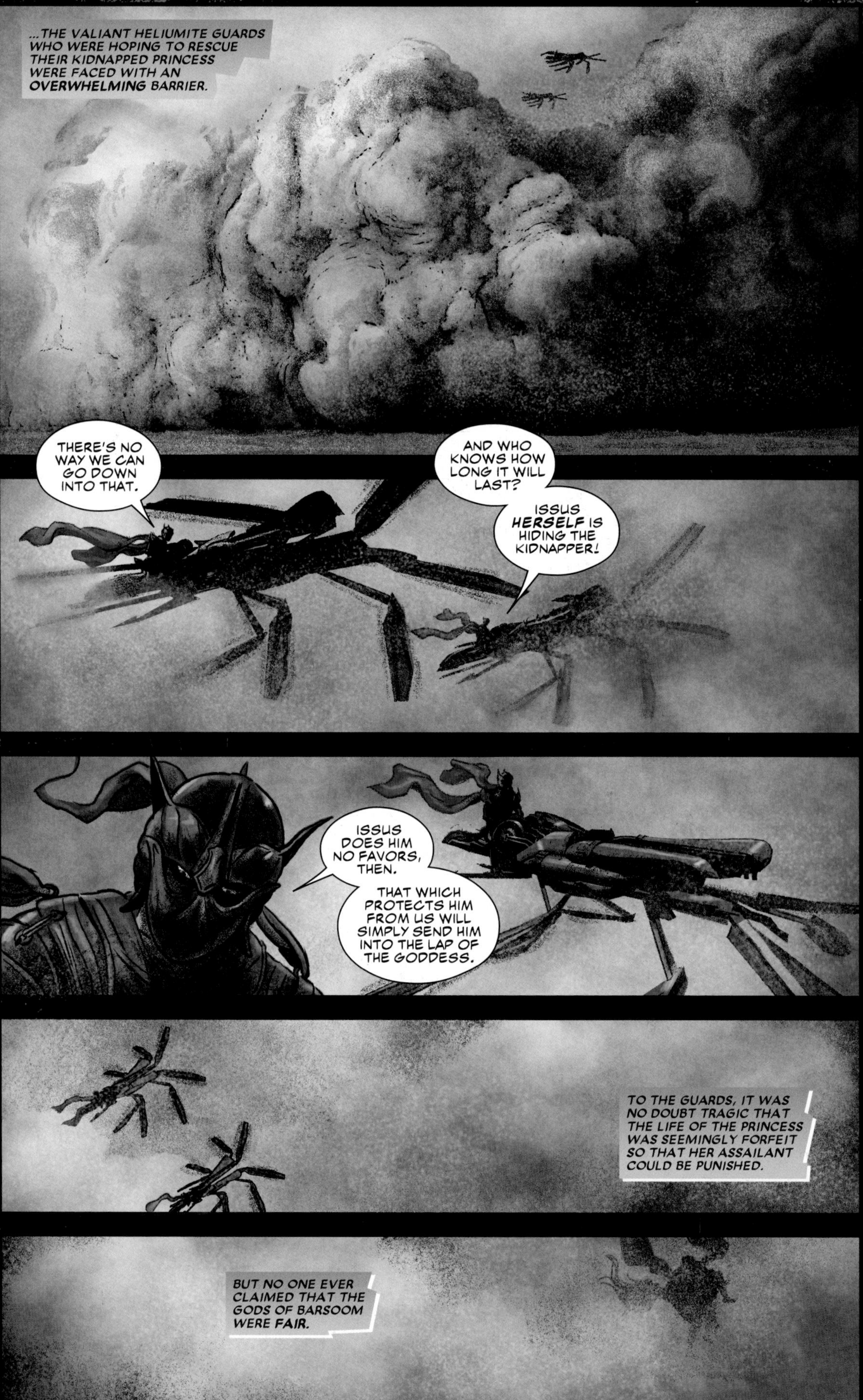

...THE VALIANT HELIUMITE GUARDS WHO WERE HOPING TO RESCUE THEIR KIDNAPPED PRINCESS WERE FACED WITH AN **OVERWHELMING** BARRIER.
THERE'S NO WAY WE CAN GO DOWN INTO THAT.
AND WHO KNOWS HOW LONG IT WILL LAST?
ISSUS **HERSELF** IS HIDING THE KIDNAPPER!
ISSUS DOES HIM NO FAVORS, THEN.
THAT WHICH PROTECTS HIM FROM US WILL SIMPLY SEND HIM INTO THE LAP OF THE GODDESS.
TO THE GUARDS, IT WAS NO DOUBT TRAGIC THAT THE LIFE OF THE PRINCESS WAS SEEMINGLY FORFEIT SO THAT HER ASSAILANT COULD BE PUNISHED.
BUT NO ONE EVER CLAIMED THAT THE GODS OF BARSOOM WERE **FAIR**.

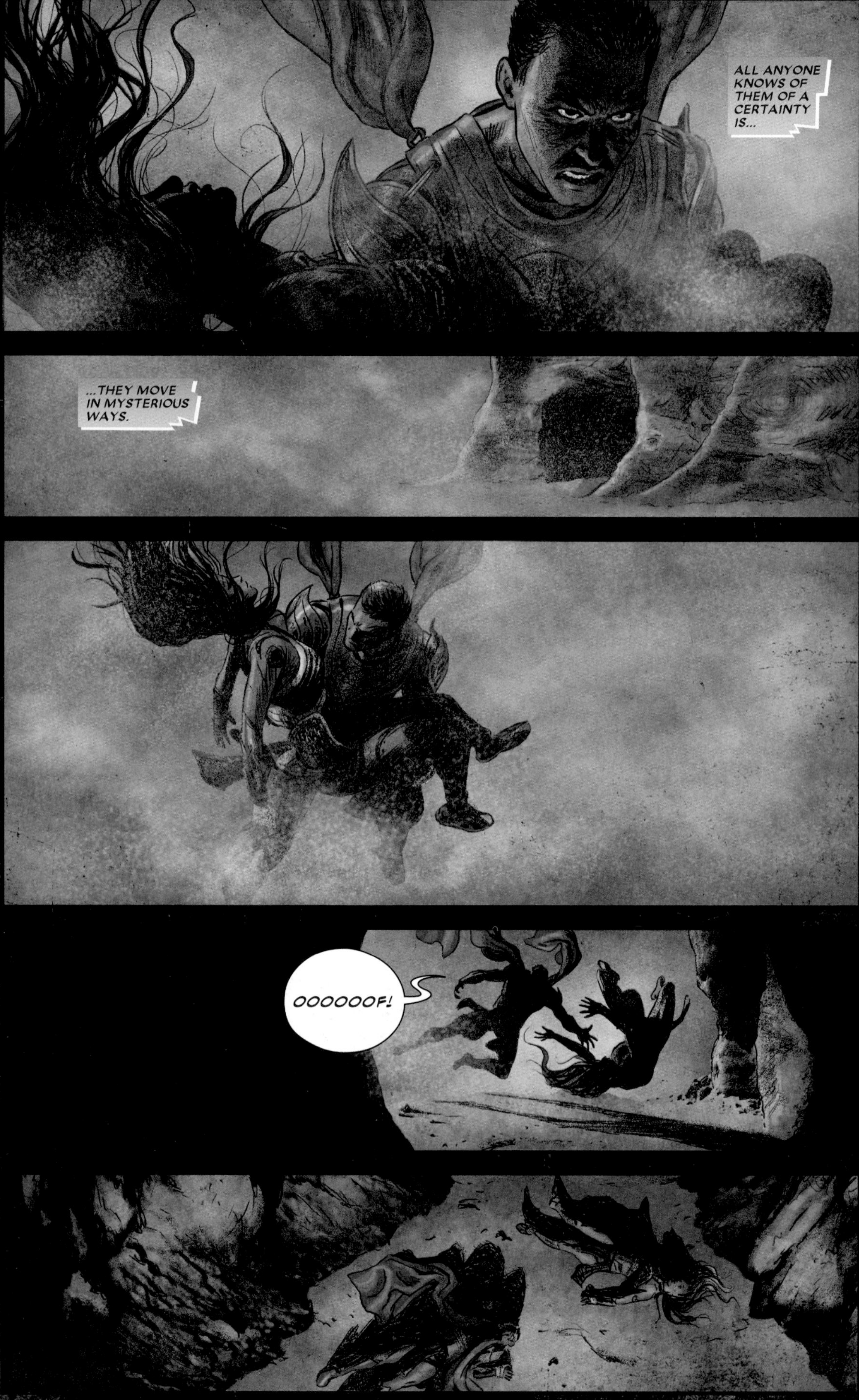
ALL ANYONE KNOWS OF THEM OF A CERTAINTY IS...
...THEY MOVE IN MYSTERIOUS WAYS.
OOOOOOF!

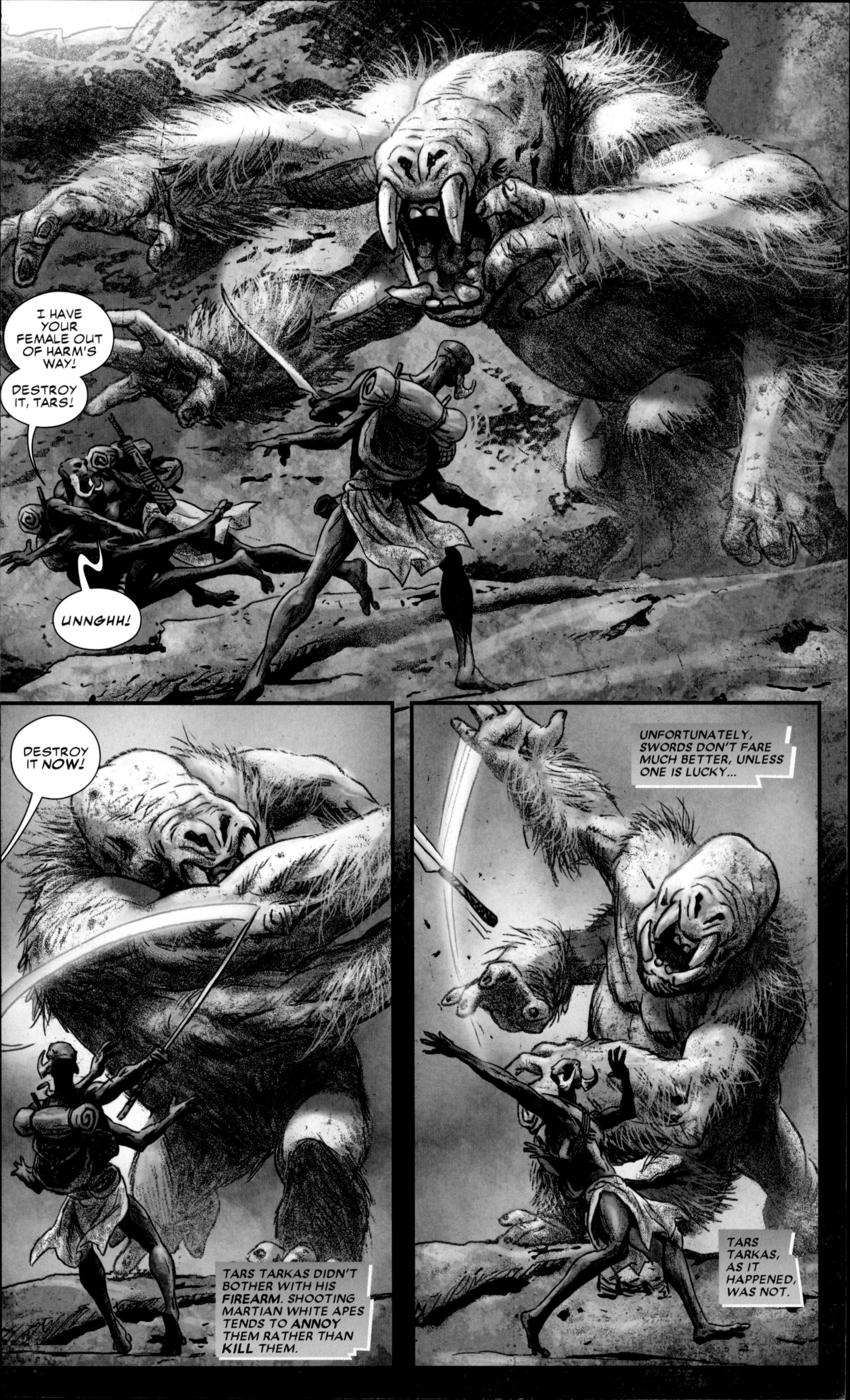
I HAVE YOUR FEMALE OUT OF HARM'S WAY!
DESTROY IT, TARS!
UNNGHH!
DESTROY IT NOW!
TARS TARKAS DIDN'T BOTHER WITH HIS FIREARM. SHOOTING MARTIAN WHITE APES TENDS TO ANNOY THEM RATHER THAN KILL THEM.
UNFORTUNATELY, SWORDS DON'T FARE MUCH BETTER, UNLESS ONE IS LUCKY...
TARS TARKAS, AS IT HAPPENED, WAS NOT.

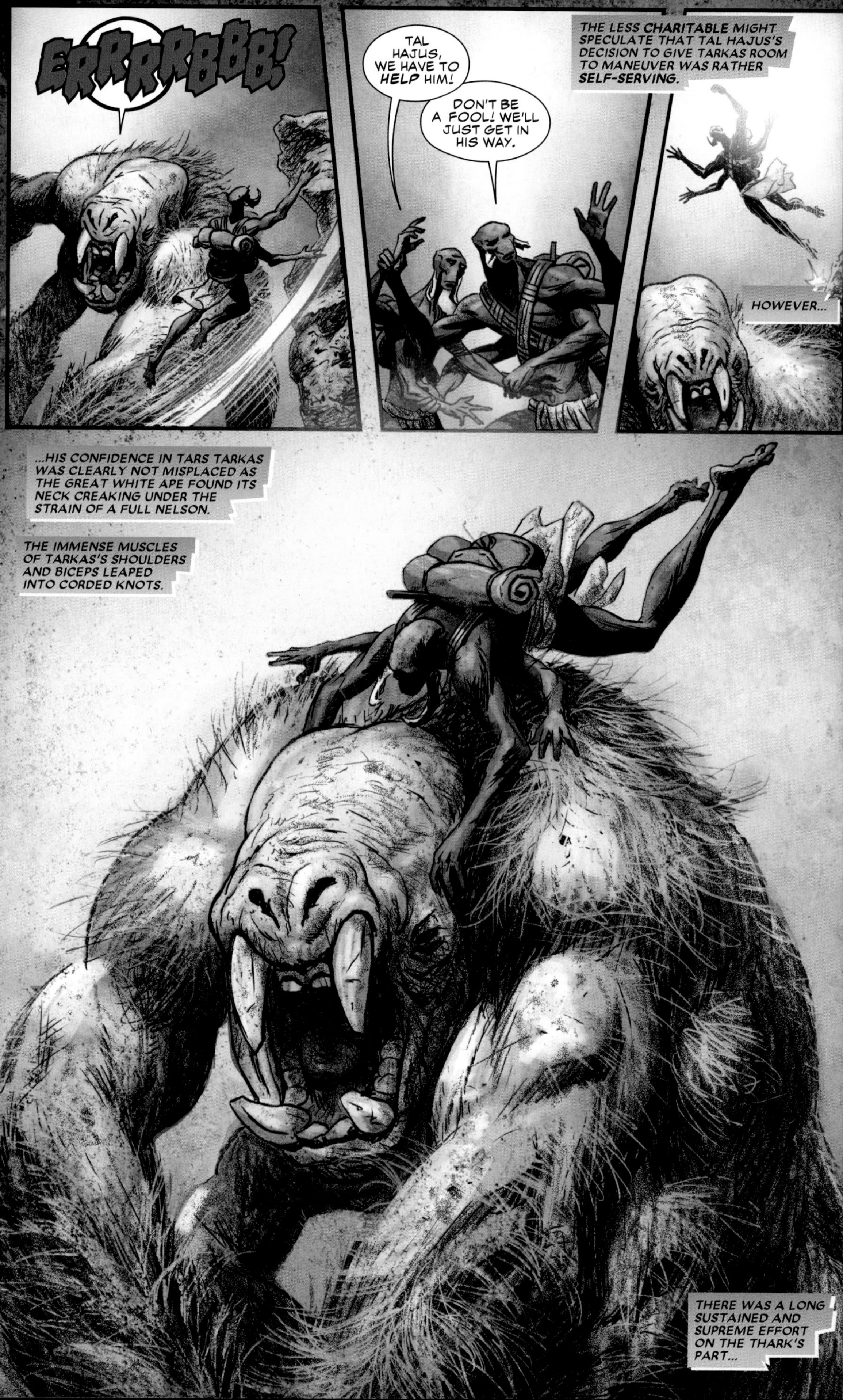
ERRRRBBB!
TAL HAJUS, WE HAVE TO HELP HIM!
DON'T BE A FOOL! WE'LL JUST GET IN HIS WAY.
THE LESS CHARITABLE MIGHT SPECULATE THAT TAL HAJUS'S DECISION TO GIVE TARKAS ROOM TO MANEUVER WAS RATHER SELF-SERVING.
HOWEVER...
...HIS CONFIDENCE IN TARS TARKAS WAS CLEARLY NOT MISPLACED AS THE GREAT WHITE APE FOUND ITS NECK CREAKING UNDER THE STRAIN OF A FULL NELSON.
THE IMMENSE MUSCLES OF TARKAS'S SHOULDERS AND BICEPS LEAPED INTO CORDED KNOTS.
THERE WAS A LONG SUSTAINED AND SUPREME EFFORT ON THE THARK'S PART...

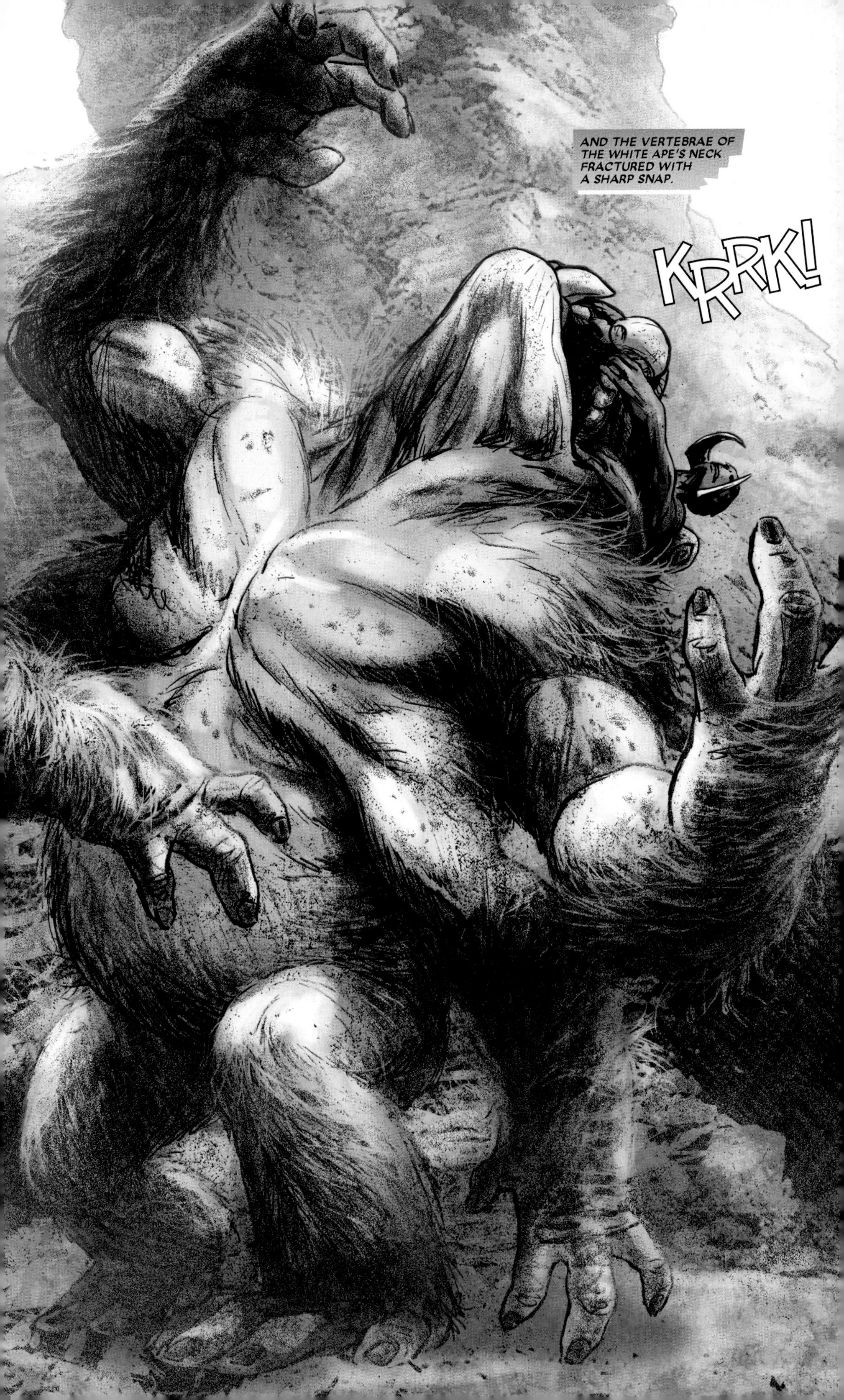
AND THE VERTEBRAE OF THE WHITE APE'S NECK FRACTURED WITH A SHARP SNAP.
KRRK!

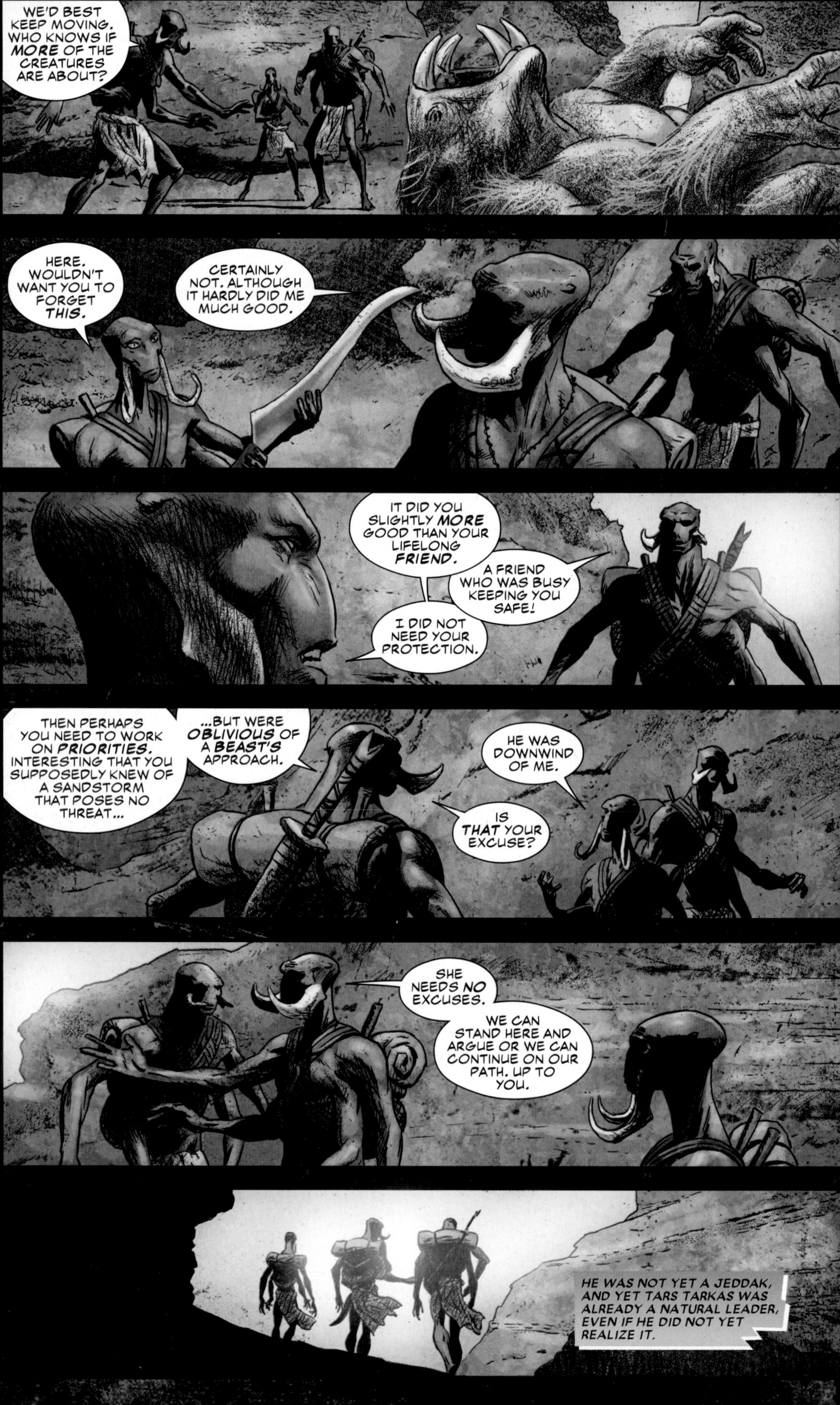
WE'D BEST KEEP MOVING. WHO KNOWS IF MORE OF THE CREATURES ARE ABOUT?
HERE. WOULDN'T WANT YOU TO FORGET THIS.
CERTAINLY NOT. ALTHOUGH IT HARDLY DID ME MUCH GOOD.
IT DID YOU SLIGHTLY MORE GOOD THAN YOUR LIFELONG FRIEND.
A FRIEND WHO WAS BUSY KEEPING YOU SAFE!
I DID NOT NEED YOUR PROTECTION.
THEN PERHAPS YOU NEED TO WORK ON PRIORITIES. INTERESTING THAT YOU SUPPOSEDLY KNEW OF A SANDSTORM THAT POSES NO THREAT...
...BUT WERE OBLIVIOUS OF A BEAST'S APPROACH.
HE WAS DOWNWIND OF ME.
IS THAT YOUR EXCUSE?
SHE NEEDS NO EXCUSES.
WE CAN STAND HERE AND ARGUE OR WE CAN CONTINUE ON OUR PATH. UP TO YOU.
HE WAS NOT YET A JEDDAK, AND YET TARS TARKAS WAS ALREADY A NATURAL LEADER, EVEN IF HE DID NOT YET REALIZE IT.

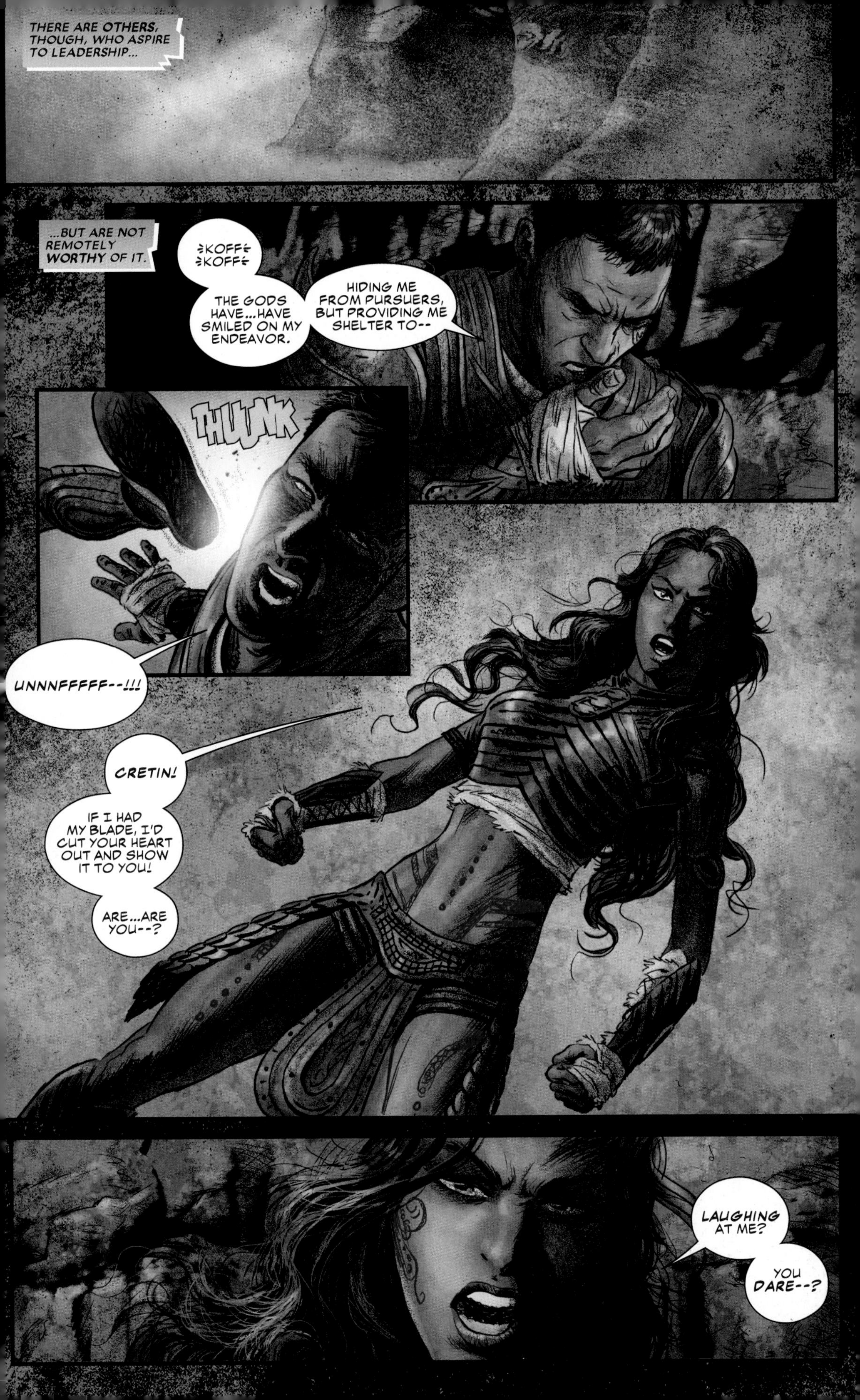
THERE ARE OTHERS, THOUGH, WHO ASPIRE TO LEADERSHIP...
...BUT ARE NOT REMOTELY WORTHY OF IT.
KOFF KOFF
THE GODS HAVE...HAVE SMILED ON MY ENDEAVOR.
HIDING ME FROM PURSUERS, BUT PROVIDING ME SHELTER TO--
THUUNK
UNNNFFFFF--!!!
CRETIN!
IF I HAD MY BLADE, I'D CUT YOUR HEART OUT AND SHOW IT TO YOU!
ARE...ARE YOU--?
LAUGHING AT ME?
YOU DARE--?

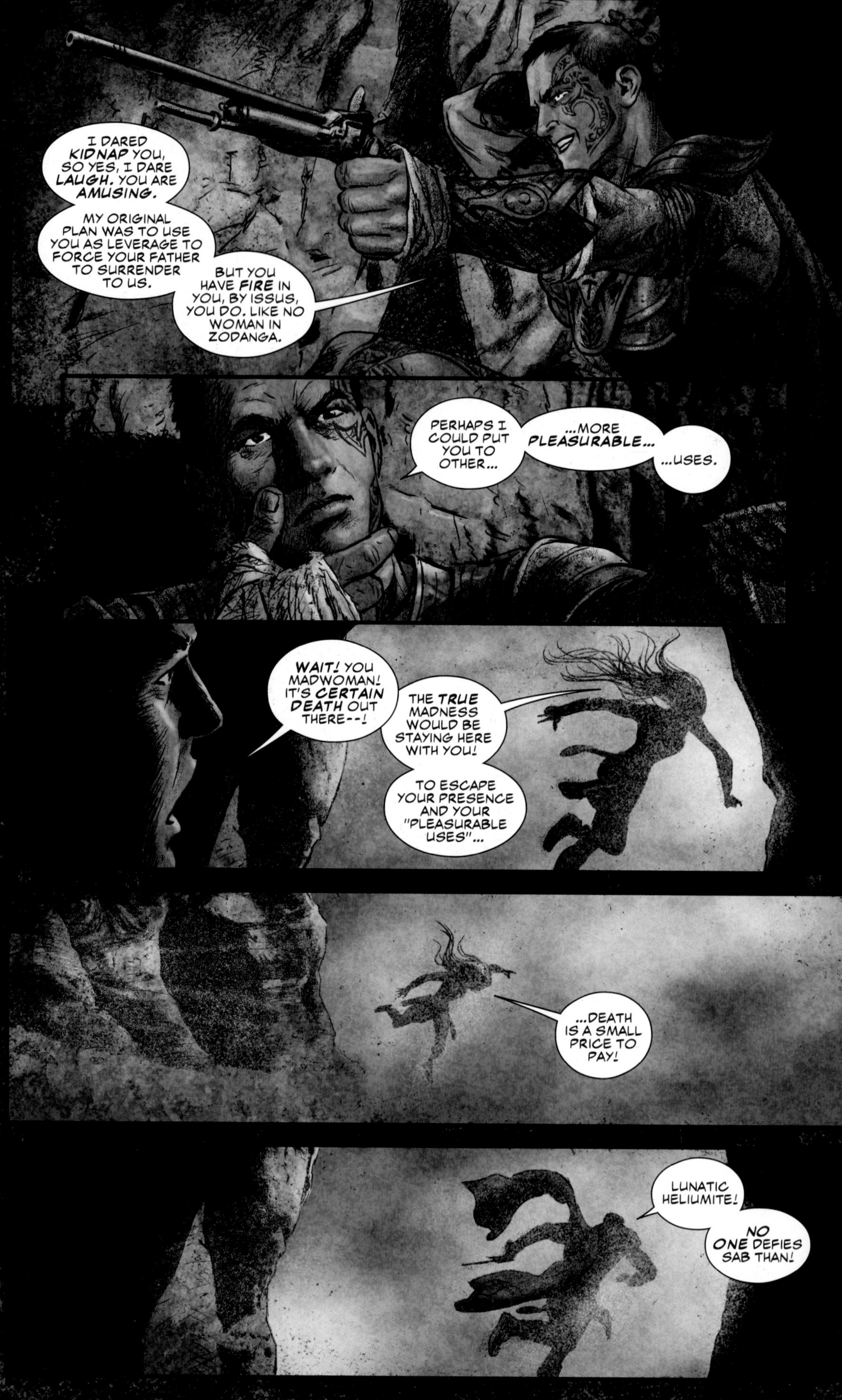
I DARED KIDNAP YOU, SO YES, I DARE LAUGH. YOU ARE AMUSING.
MY ORIGINAL PLAN WAS TO USE YOU AS LEVERAGE TO FORCE YOUR FATHER TO SURRENDER TO US.
BUT YOU HAVE FIRE IN YOU, BY ISSUS, YOU DO. LIKE NO WOMAN IN ZODANGA.
PERHAPS I COULD PUT YOU TO OTHER...
...MORE PLEASURABLE...
...USES.
WAIT! YOU MADWOMAN! IT'S CERTAIN DEATH OUT THERE--!
THE TRUE MADNESS WOULD BE STAYING HERE WITH YOU!
TO ESCAPE YOUR PRESENCE AND YOUR "PLEASURABLE USES"...
...DEATH IS A SMALL PRICE TO PAY!
LUNATIC HELIUMITE!
NO ONE DEFIES SAB THAN!

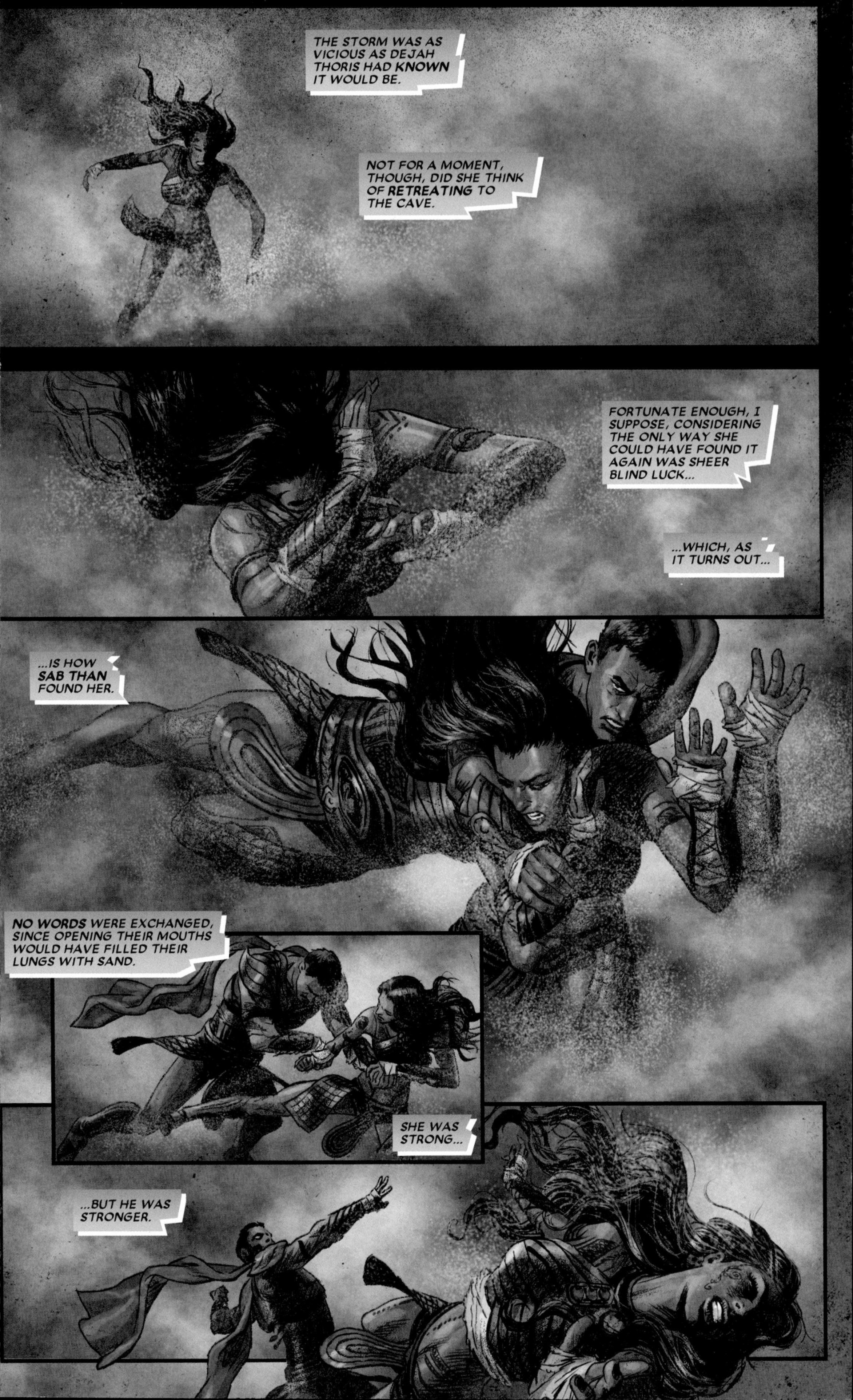
THE STORM WAS AS VICIOUS AS DEJAH THORIS HAD KNOWN IT WOULD BE.
NOT FOR A MOMENT, THOUGH, DID SHE THINK OF RETREATING TO THE CAVE.
FORTUNATE ENOUGH, I SUPPOSE, CONSIDERING THE ONLY WAY SHE COULD HAVE FOUND IT AGAIN WAS SHEER BLIND LUCK...
...WHICH, AS IT TURNS OUT...
...IS HOW SAB THAN FOUND HER.
NO WORDS WERE EXCHANGED, SINCE OPENING THEIR MOUTHS WOULD HAVE FILLED THEIR LUNGS WITH SAND.
SHE WAS STRONG...
...BUT HE WAS STRONGER.

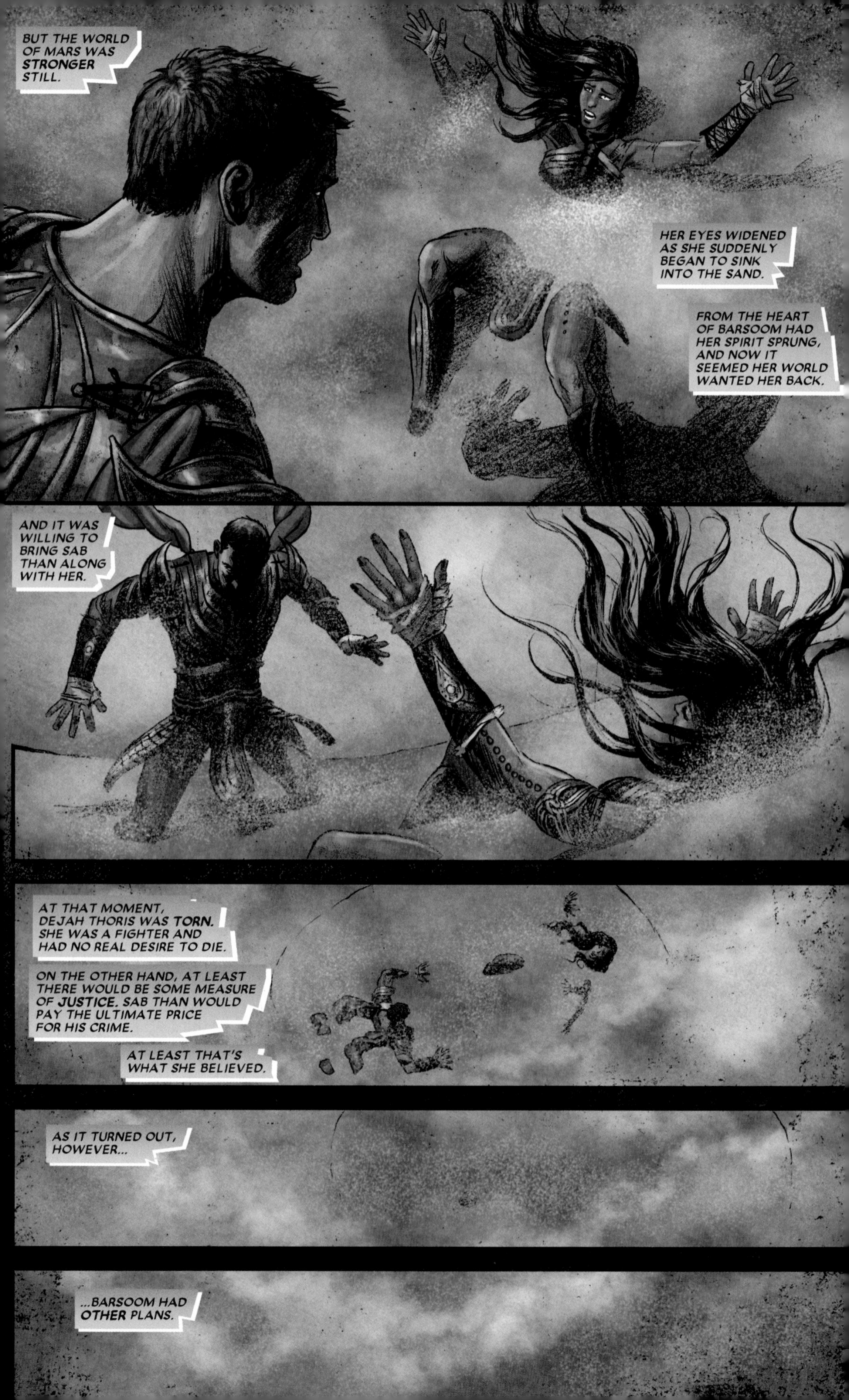
BUT THE WORLD OF MARS WAS STRONGER STILL.
HER EYES WIDENED AS SHE SUDDENLY BEGAN TO SINK INTO THE SAND.
FROM THE HEART OF BARSOOM HAD HER SPIRIT SPRUNG, AND NOW IT SEEMED HER WORLD WANTED HER BACK.
AND IT WAS WILLING TO BRING SAB THAN ALONG WITH HER.
AT THAT MOMENT, DEJAH THORIS WAS TORN. SHE WAS A FIGHTER AND HAD NO REAL DESIRE TO DIE.
ON THE OTHER HAND, AT LEAST THERE WOULD BE SOME MEASURE OF JUSTICE. SAB THAN WOULD PAY THE ULTIMATE PRICE FOR HIS CRIME.
AT LEAST THAT'S WHAT SHE BELIEVED.
AS IT TURNED OUT, HOWEVER...
...BARSOOM HAD OTHER PLANS.

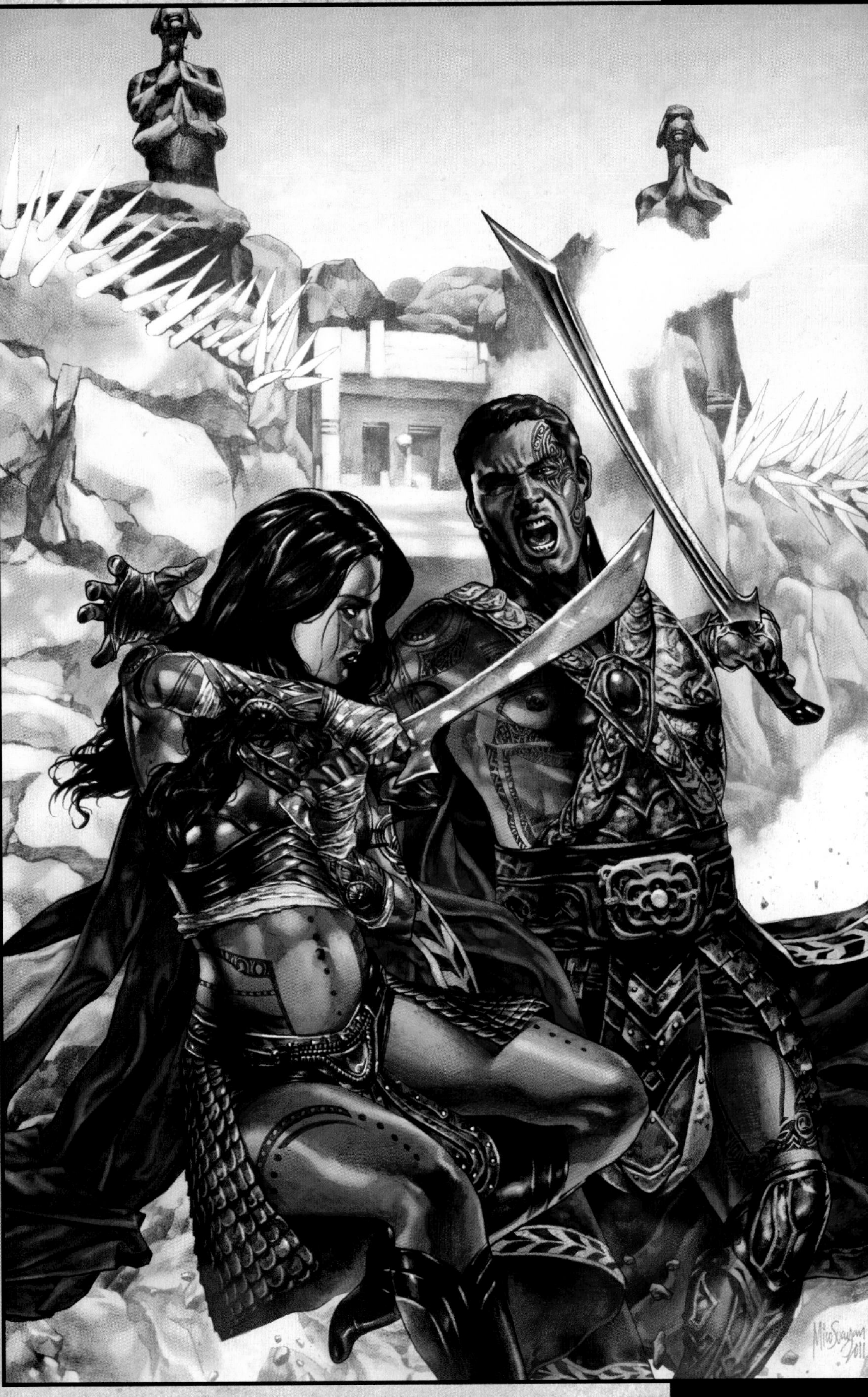

THREE

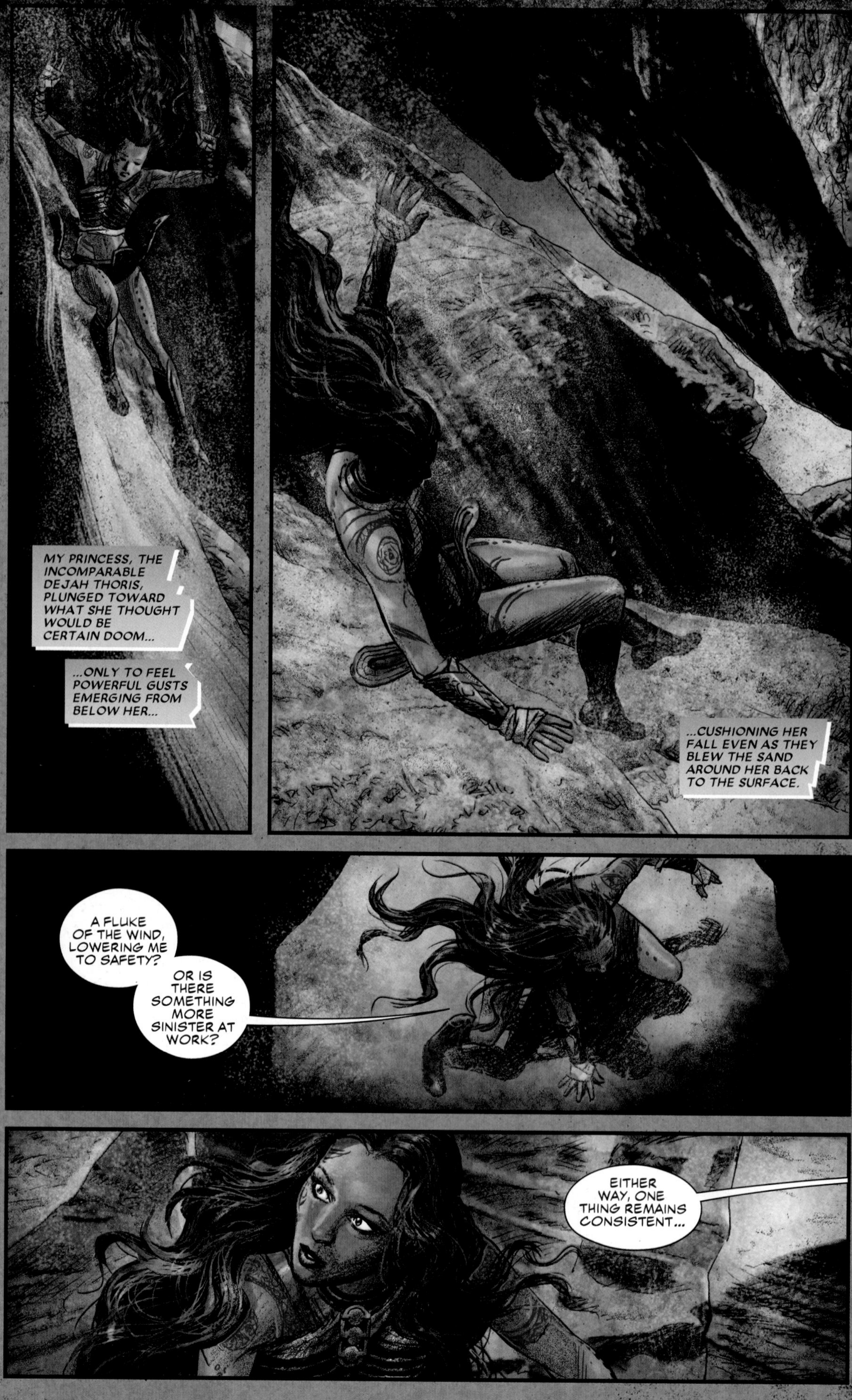
MY PRINCESS, THE INCOMPARABLE DEJAH THORIS, PLUNGED TOWARD WHAT SHE THOUGHT WOULD BE CERTAIN DOOM...
...ONLY TO FEEL POWERFUL GUSTS EMERGING FROM BELOW HER...
...CUSHIONING HER FALL EVEN AS THEY BLEW THE SAND AROUND HER BACK TO THE SURFACE.
A FLUKE OF THE WIND, LOWERING ME TO SAFETY?
OR IS THERE SOMETHING MORE SINISTER AT WORK?
EITHER WAY, ONE THING REMAINS CONSISTENT...

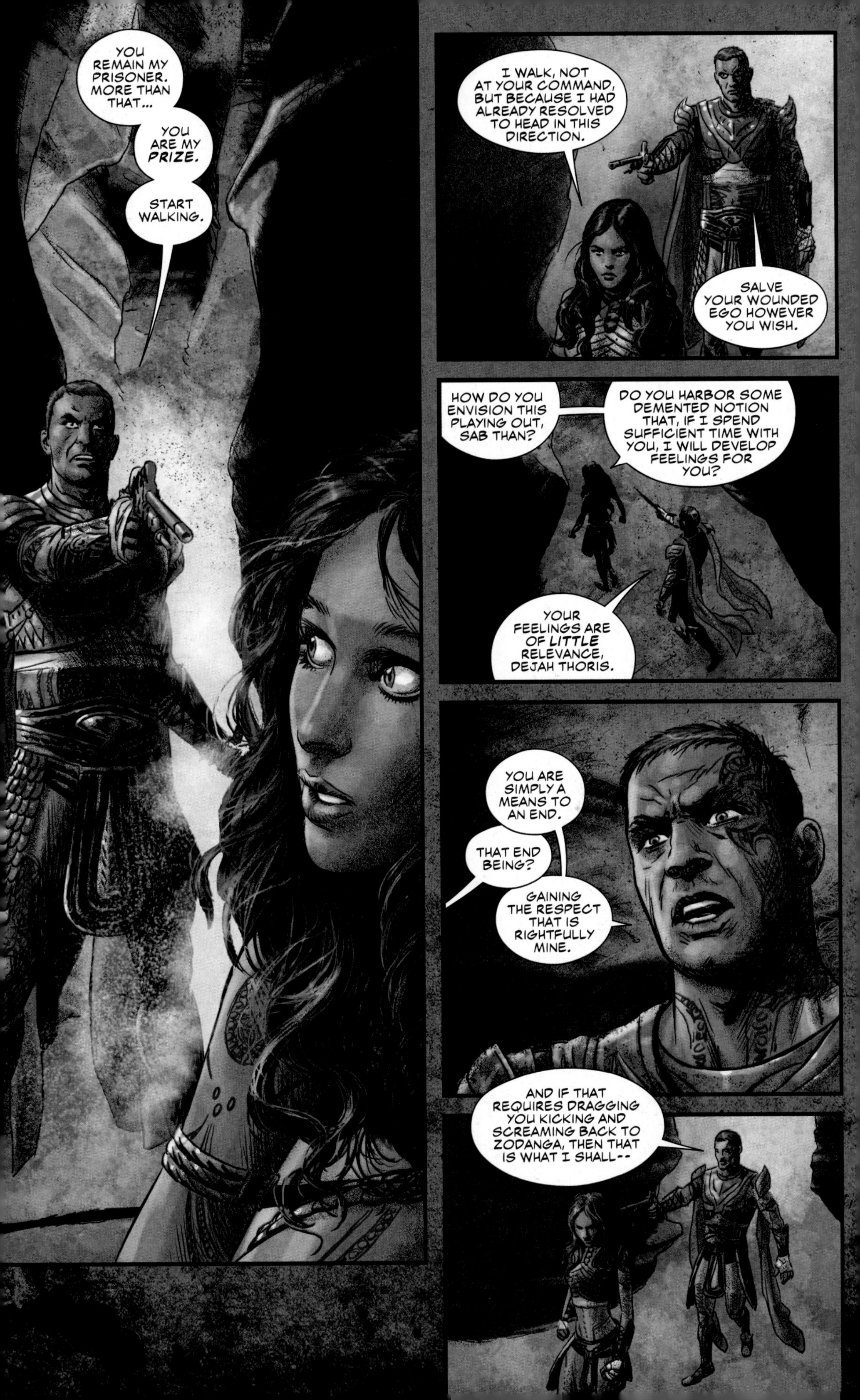
YOU REMAIN MY PRISONER. MORE THAN THAT...
YOU ARE MY PRIZE.
START WALKING.
I WALK, NOT AT YOUR COMMAND, BUT BECAUSE I HAD ALREADY RESOLVED TO HEAD IN THIS DIRECTION.
SALVE YOUR WOUNDED EGO HOWEVER YOU WISH.
HOW DO YOU ENVISION THIS PLAYING OUT, SAB THAN?
DO YOU HARBOR SOME DEMENTED NOTION THAT, IF I SPEND SUFFICIENT TIME WITH YOU, I WILL DEVELOP FEELINGS FOR YOU?
YOUR FEELINGS ARE OF LITTLE RELEVANCE, DEJAH THORIS.
YOU ARE SIMPLY A MEANS TO AN END.
THAT END BEING?
GAINING THE RESPECT THAT IS RIGHTFULLY MINE.
AND IF THAT REQUIRES DRAGGING YOU KICKING AND SCREAMING BACK TO ZODANGA, THEN THAT IS WHAT I SHALL--

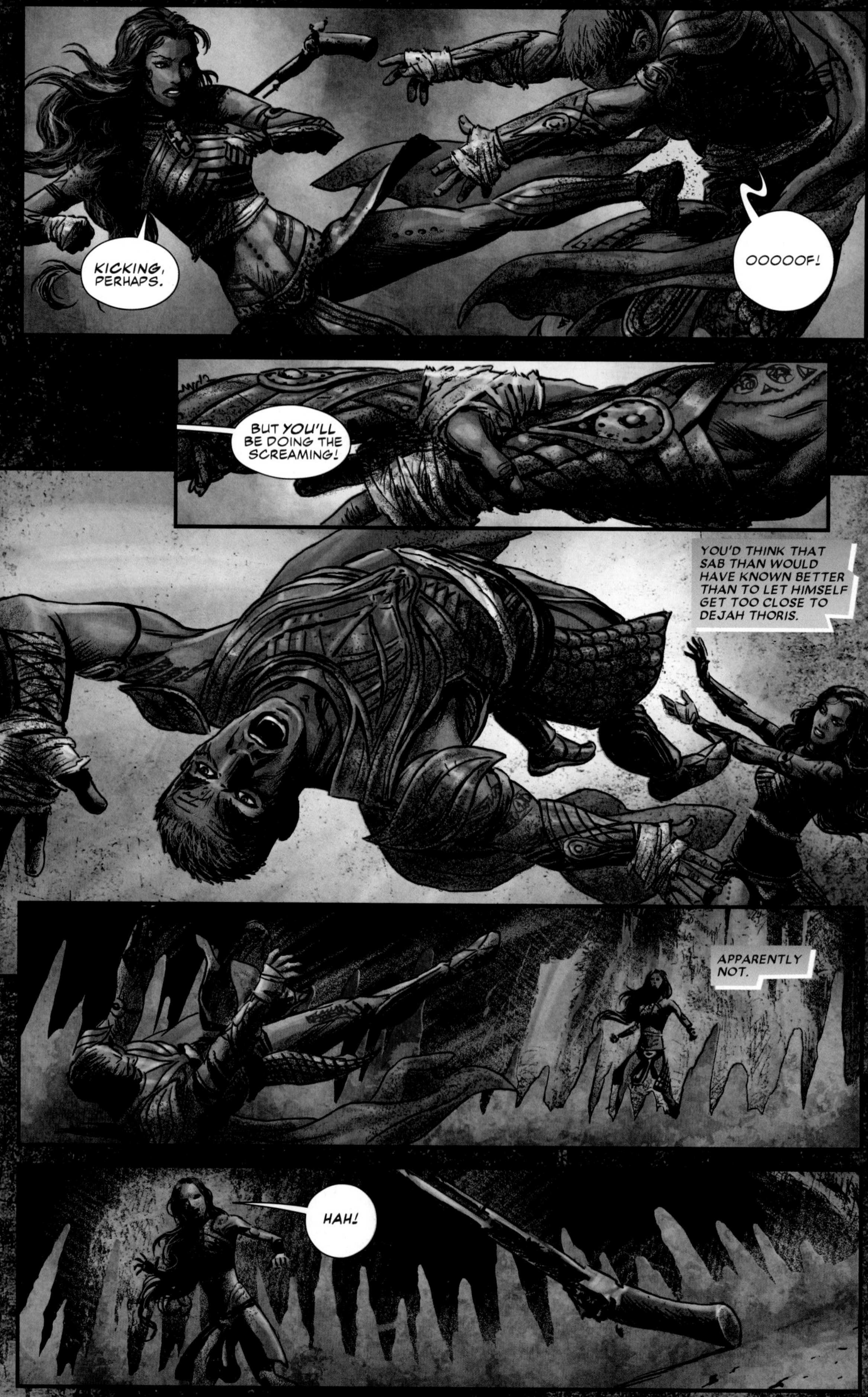
KICKING, PERHAPS.
OOOOOF!
BUT YOU'LL BE DOING THE SCREAMING!
YOU'D THINK THAT SAB THAN WOULD HAVE KNOWN BETTER THAN TO LET HIMSELF GET TOO CLOSE TO DEJAH THORIS.
APPARENTLY NOT.
HAH!

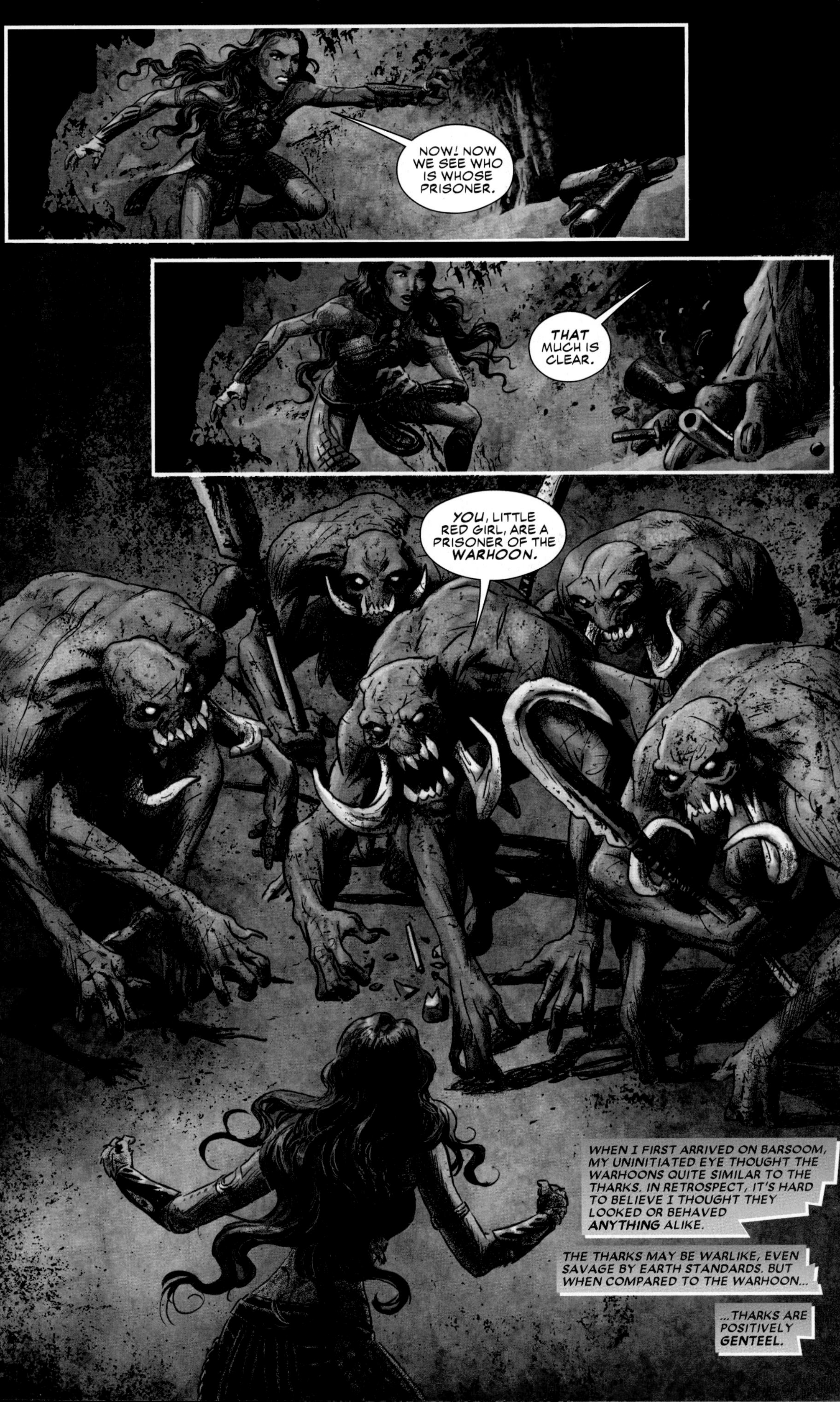

NOW! NOW WE SEE WHO IS WHOSE PRISONER.
THAT MUCH IS CLEAR.
YOU, LITTLE RED GIRL, ARE A PRISONER OF THE WARHOON.
WHEN I FIRST ARRIVED ON BARSOOM, MY UNINITIATED EYE THOUGHT THE WARHOONS QUITE SIMILAR TO THE THARKS. IN RETROSPECT, IT'S HARD TO BELIEVE I THOUGHT THEY LOOKED OR BEHAVED ANYTHING ALIKE.
THE THARKS MAY BE WARLIKE, EVEN SAVAGE BY EARTH STANDARDS. BUT WHEN COMPARED TO THE WARHOON...
...THARKS ARE POSITIVELY GENTEEL.

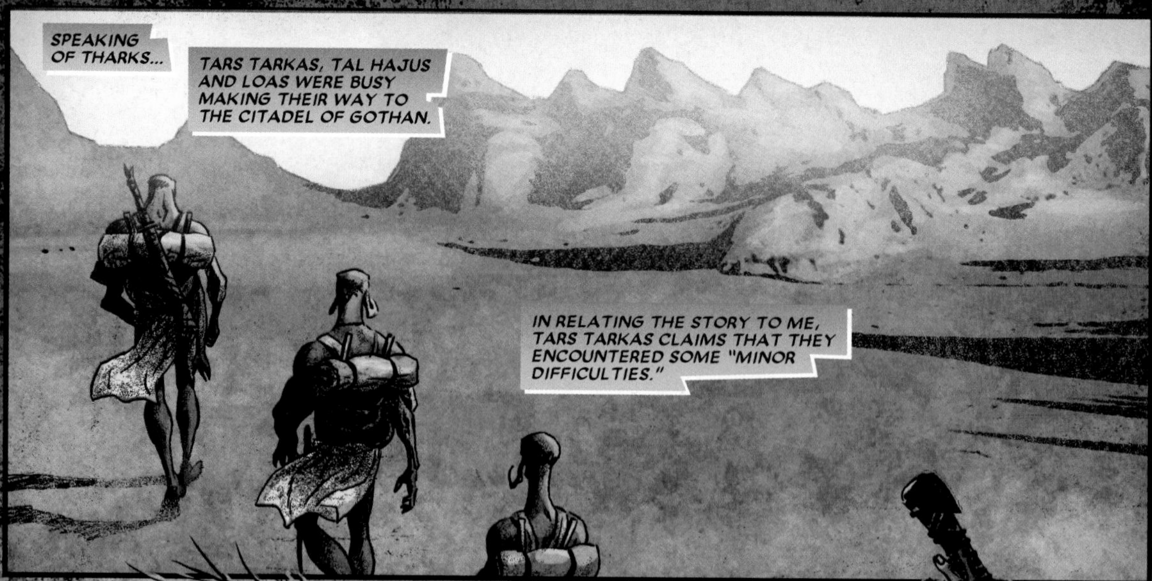
SPEAKING OF THARKS...
TARS TARKAS, TAL HAJUS AND LOAS WERE BUSY MAKING THEIR WAY TO THE CITADEL OF GOTHAN.
IN RELATING THE STORY TO ME, TARS TARKAS CLAIMS THAT THEY ENCOUNTERED SOME "MINOR DIFFICULTIES."

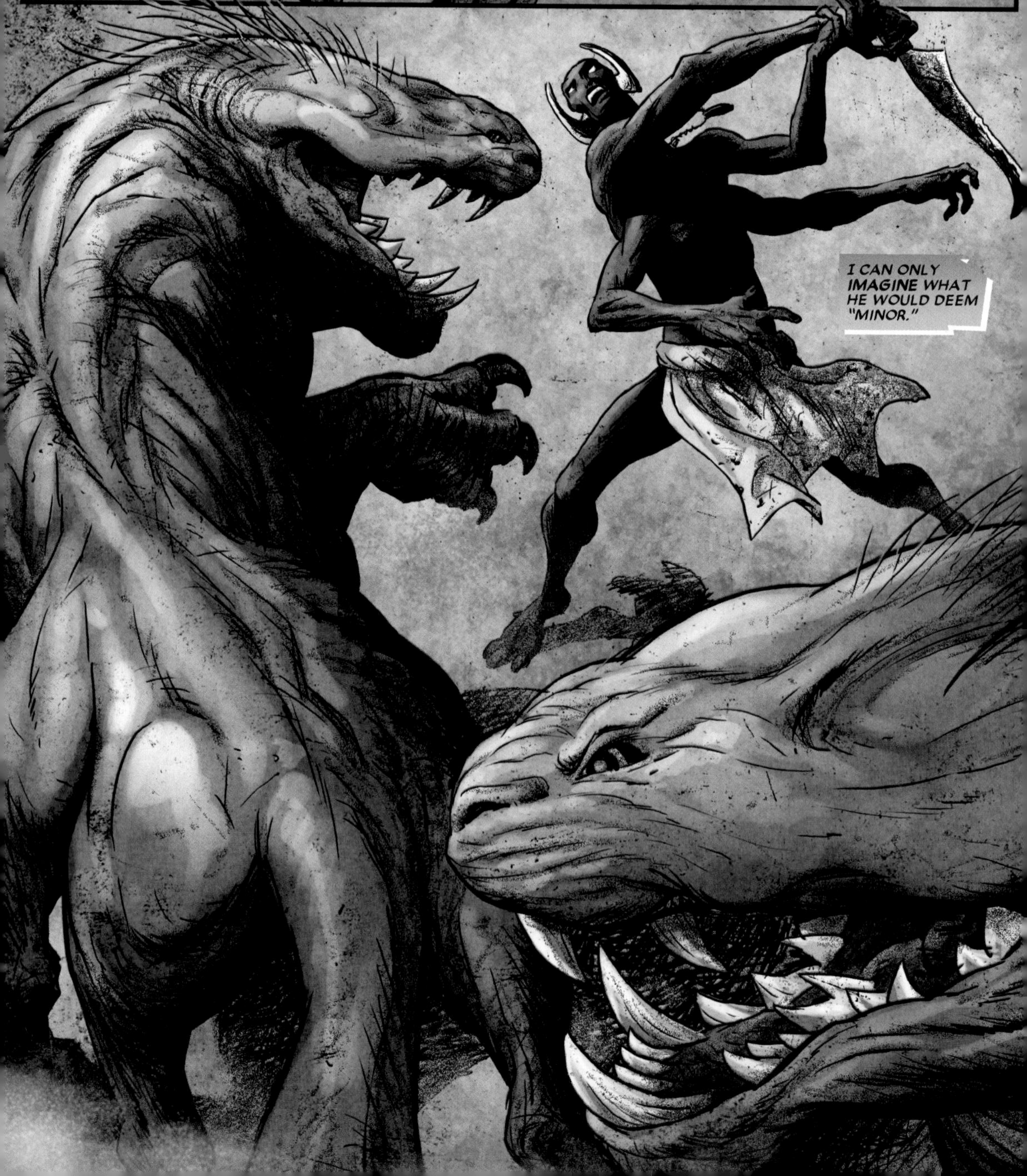
I CAN ONLY IMAGINE WHAT HE WOULD DEEM "MINOR."

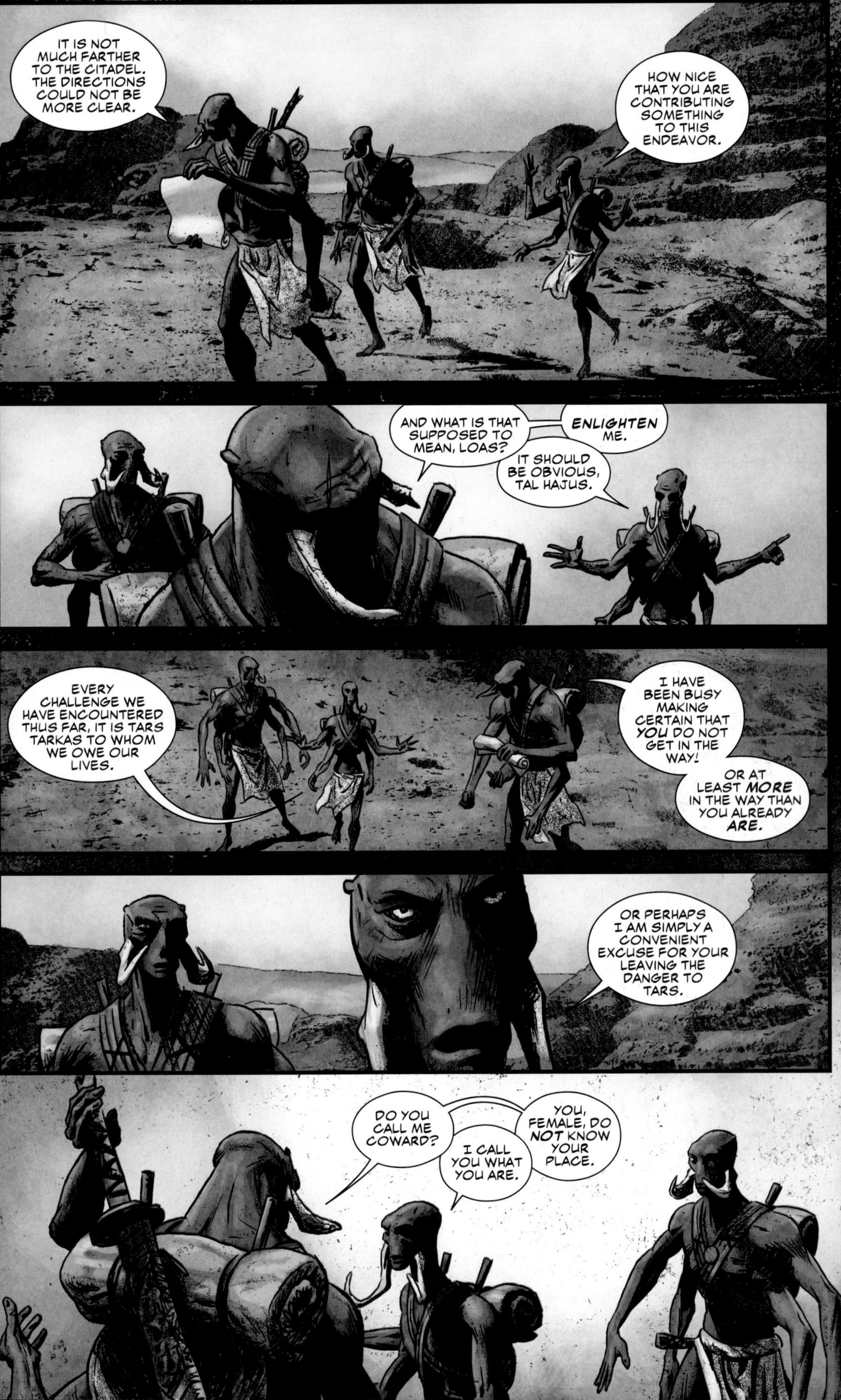
IT IS NOT MUCH FARTHER TO THE CITADEL. THE DIRECTIONS COULD NOT BE MORE CLEAR.
HOW NICE THAT YOU ARE CONTRIBUTING SOMETHING TO THIS ENDEAVOR.
AND WHAT IS THAT SUPPOSED TO MEAN, LOAS?
ENLIGHTEN ME.
IT SHOULD BE OBVIOUS, TAL HAJUS.
EVERY CHALLENGE WE HAVE ENCOUNTERED THUS FAR, IT IS TARS TARKAS TO WHOM WE OWE OUR LIVES.
I HAVE BEEN BUSY MAKING CERTAIN THAT YOU DO NOT GET IN THE WAY!
OR AT LEAST MORE IN THE WAY THAN YOU ALREADY ARE.
OR PERHAPS I AM SIMPLY A CONVENIENT EXCUSE FOR YOUR LEAVING THE DANGER TO TARS.
DO YOU CALL ME COWARD?
I CALL YOU WHAT YOU ARE.
YOU, FEMALE, DO NOT KNOW YOUR PLACE.

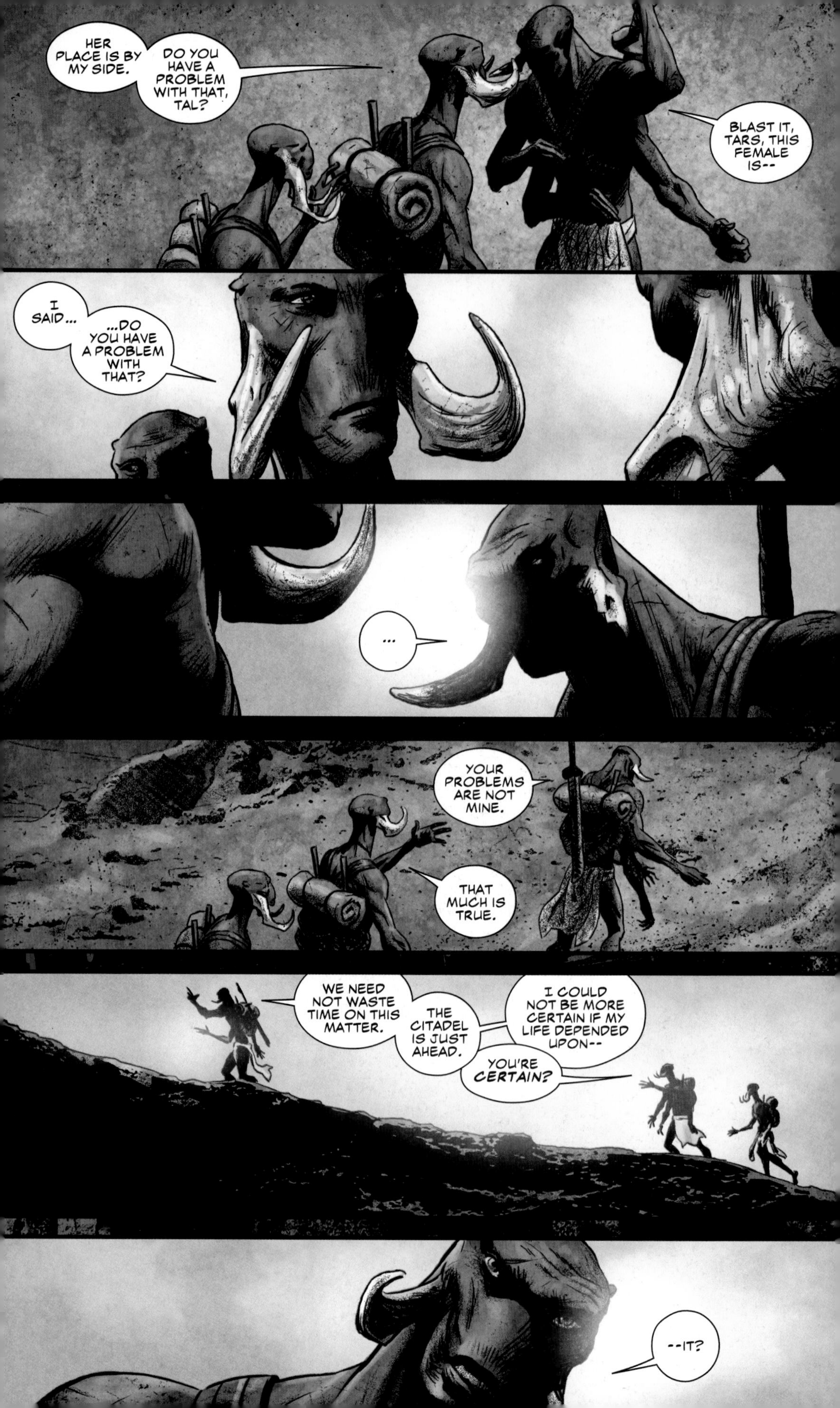
HER PLACE IS BY MY SIDE.
DO YOU HAVE A PROBLEM WITH THAT, TAL?
BLAST IT, TARS, THIS FEMALE IS--
I SAID...
...DO YOU HAVE A PROBLEM WITH THAT?
...
YOUR PROBLEMS ARE NOT MINE.
THAT MUCH IS TRUE.
WE NEED NOT WASTE TIME ON THIS MATTER.
THE CITADEL IS JUST AHEAD.
YOU'RE CERTAIN?
I COULD NOT BE MORE CERTAIN IF MY LIFE DEPENDED UPON--
--IT?

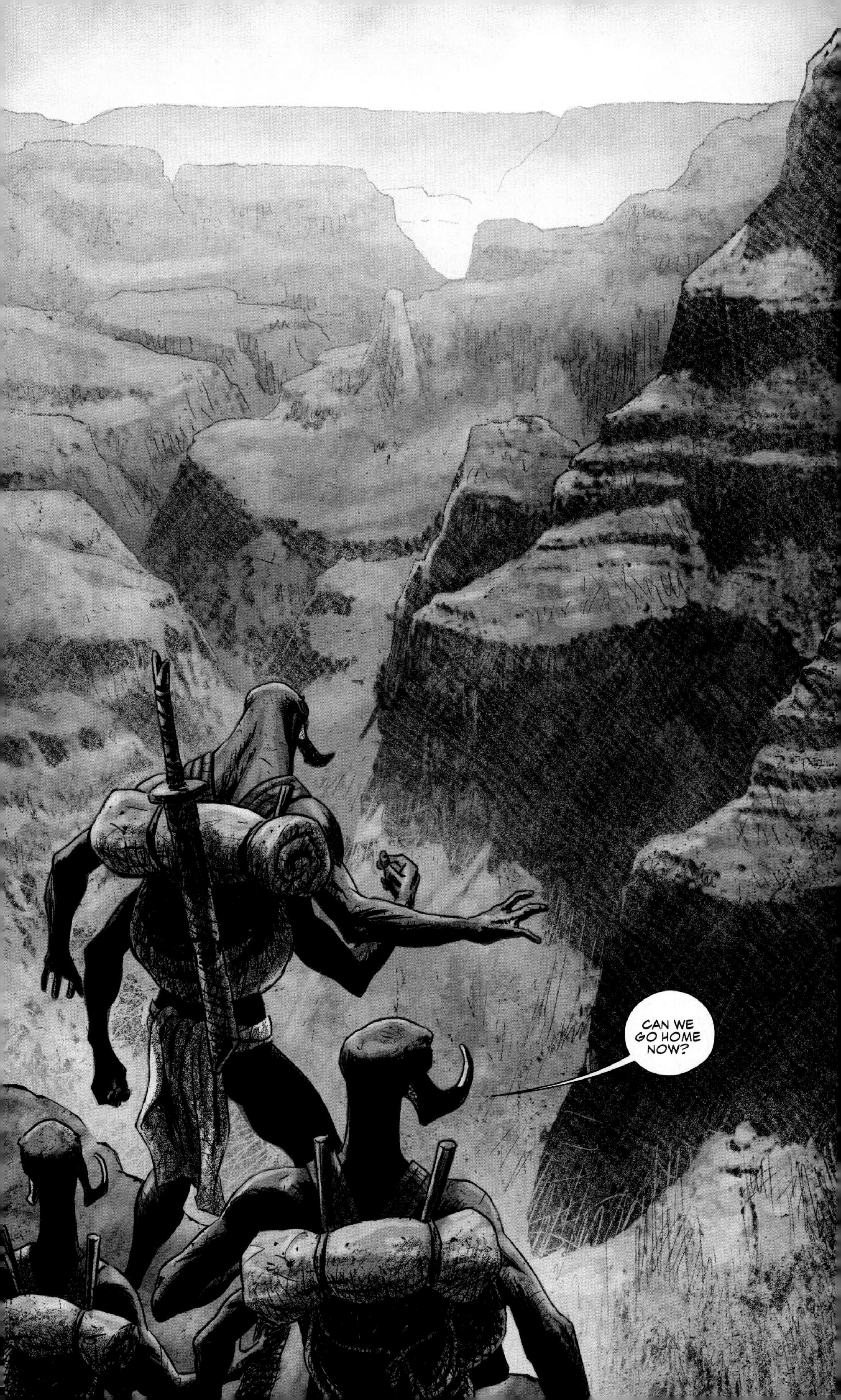
CAN WE
GO HOME
NOW?

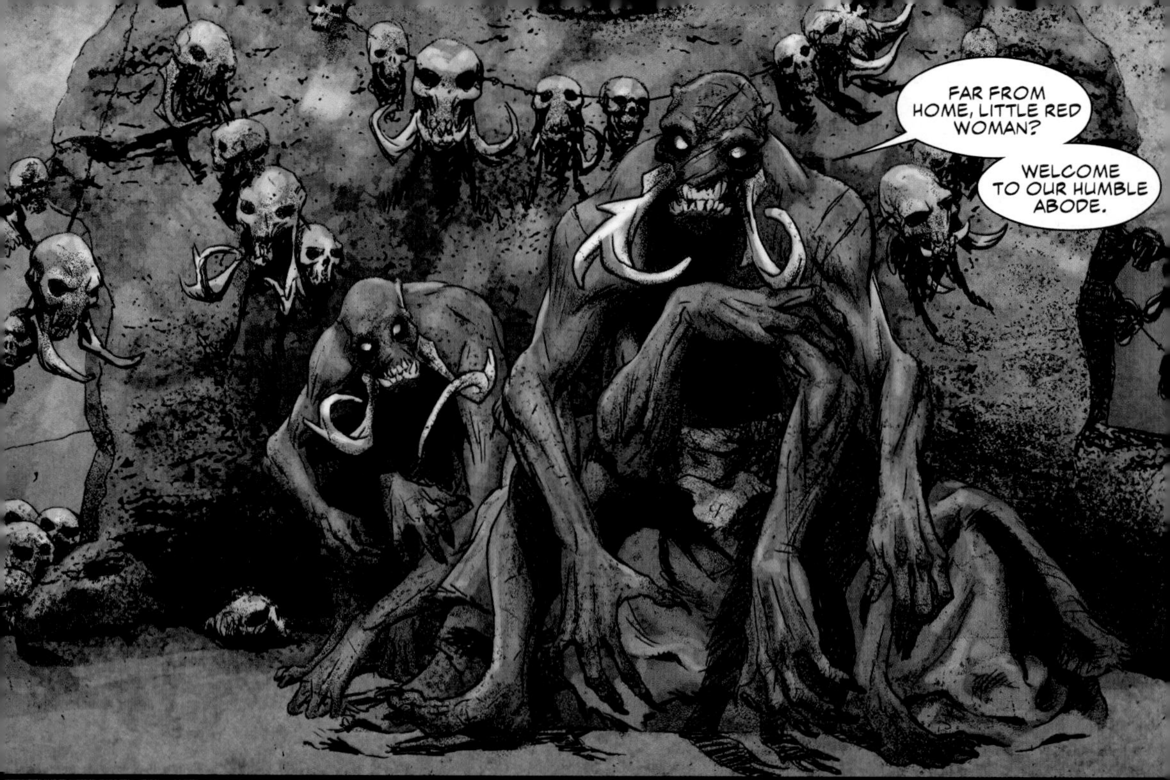
FAR FROM HOME, LITTLE RED WOMAN?
WELCOME TO OUR HUMBLE ABODE.

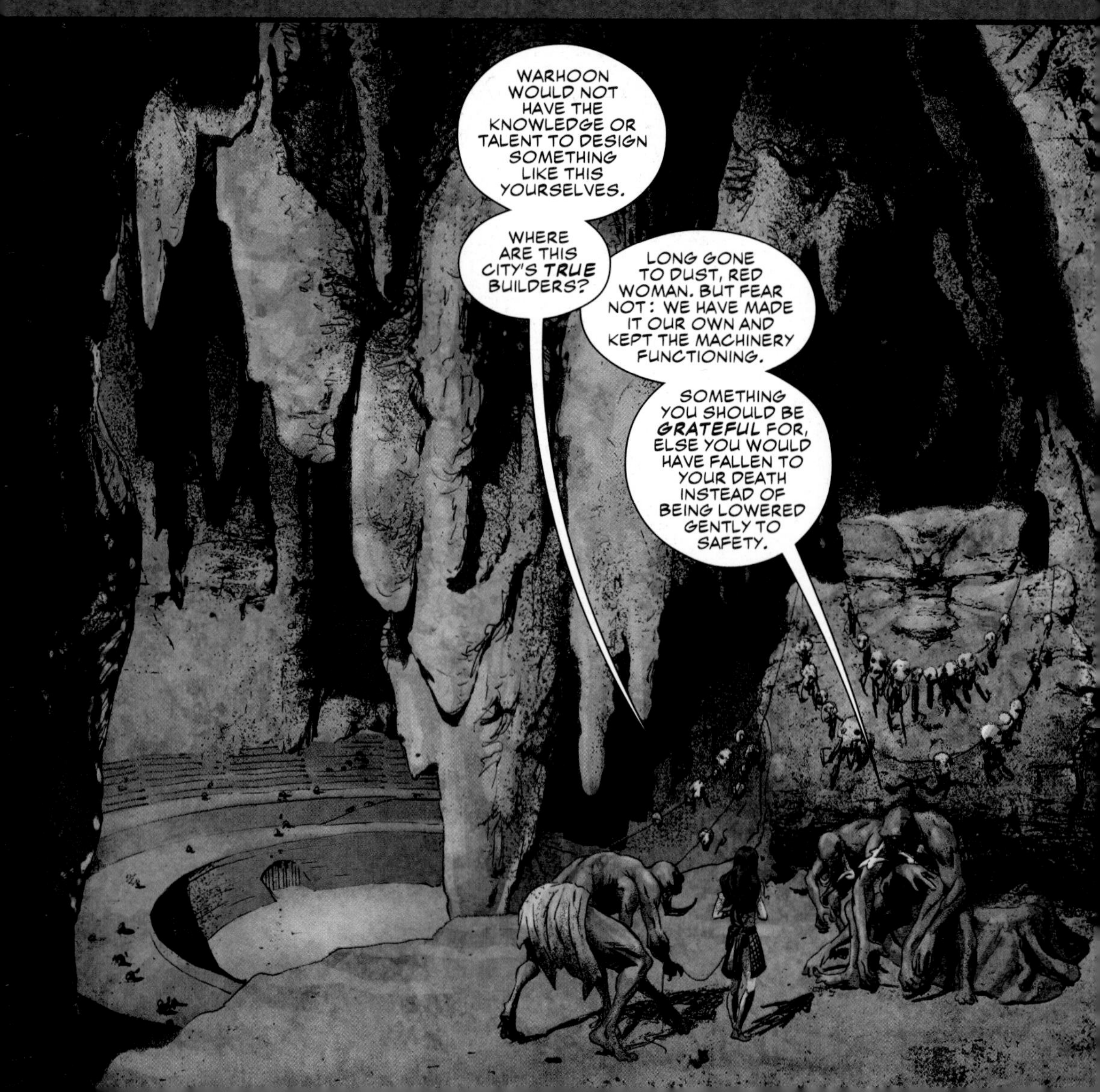
WARHOON WOULD NOT HAVE THE KNOWLEDGE OR TALENT TO DESIGN SOMETHING LIKE THIS YOURSELVES.
WHERE ARE THIS CITY'S TRUE BUILDERS?
LONG GONE TO DUST, RED WOMAN. BUT FEAR NOT: WE HAVE MADE IT OUR OWN AND KEPT THE MACHINERY FUNCTIONING.
SOMETHING YOU SHOULD BE GRATEFUL FOR, ELSE YOU WOULD HAVE FALLEN TO YOUR DEATH INSTEAD OF BEING LOWERED GENTLY TO SAFETY.

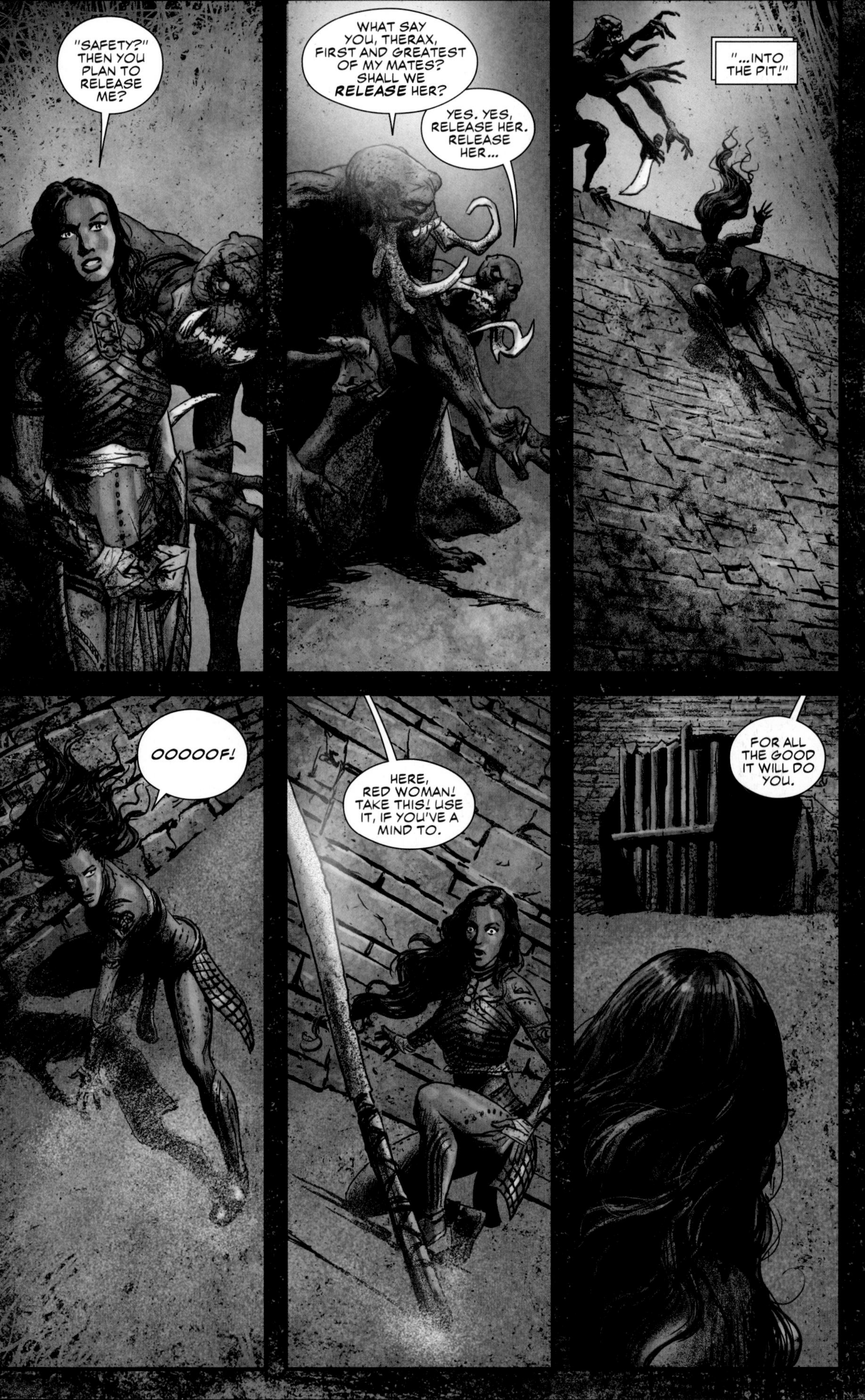
"SAFETY?" THEN YOU PLAN TO RELEASE ME?
WHAT SAY YOU, THERAX, FIRST AND GREATEST OF MY MATES? SHALL WE RELEASE HER?
YES. YES, RELEASE HER. RELEASE HER...
"...INTO THE PIT!"
OOOOOF!
HERE, RED WOMAN! TAKE THIS! USE IT, IF YOU'VE A MIND TO.
FOR ALL THE GOOD IT WILL DO YOU.

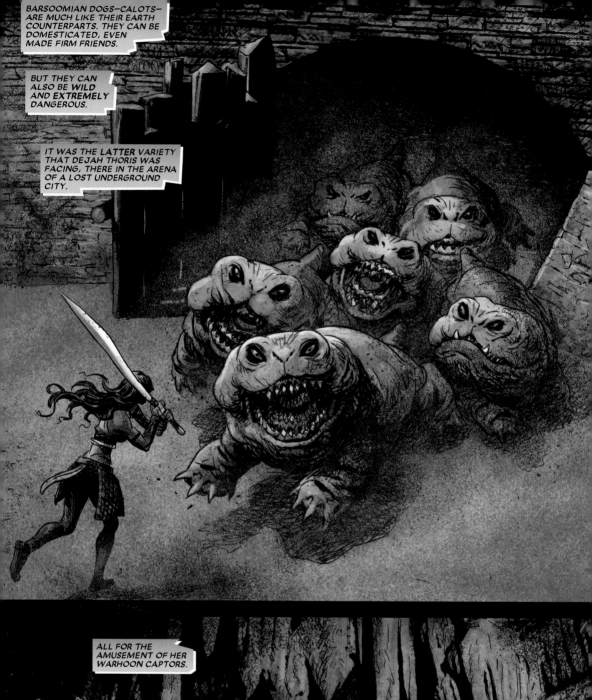

BARSOOMIAN DOGS—CALOTS— ARE MUCH LIKE THEIR EARTH COUNTERPARTS. THEY CAN BE DOMESTICATED, EVEN MADE FIRM FRIENDS.

BUT THEY CAN ALSO BE WILD AND EXTREMELY DANGEROUS.

IT WAS THE LATTER VARIETY THAT DEJAH THORIS WAS FACING, THERE IN THE ARENA OF A LOST UNDERGROUND CITY.

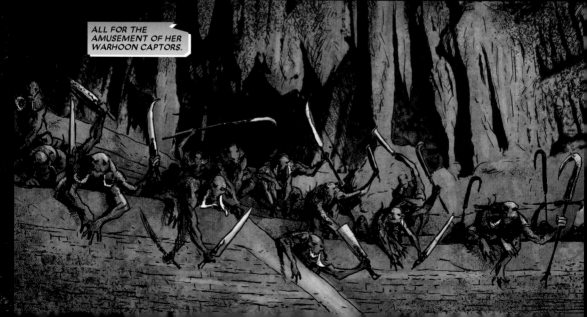

ALL FOR THE AMUSEMENT OF HER WARHOON CAPTORS.

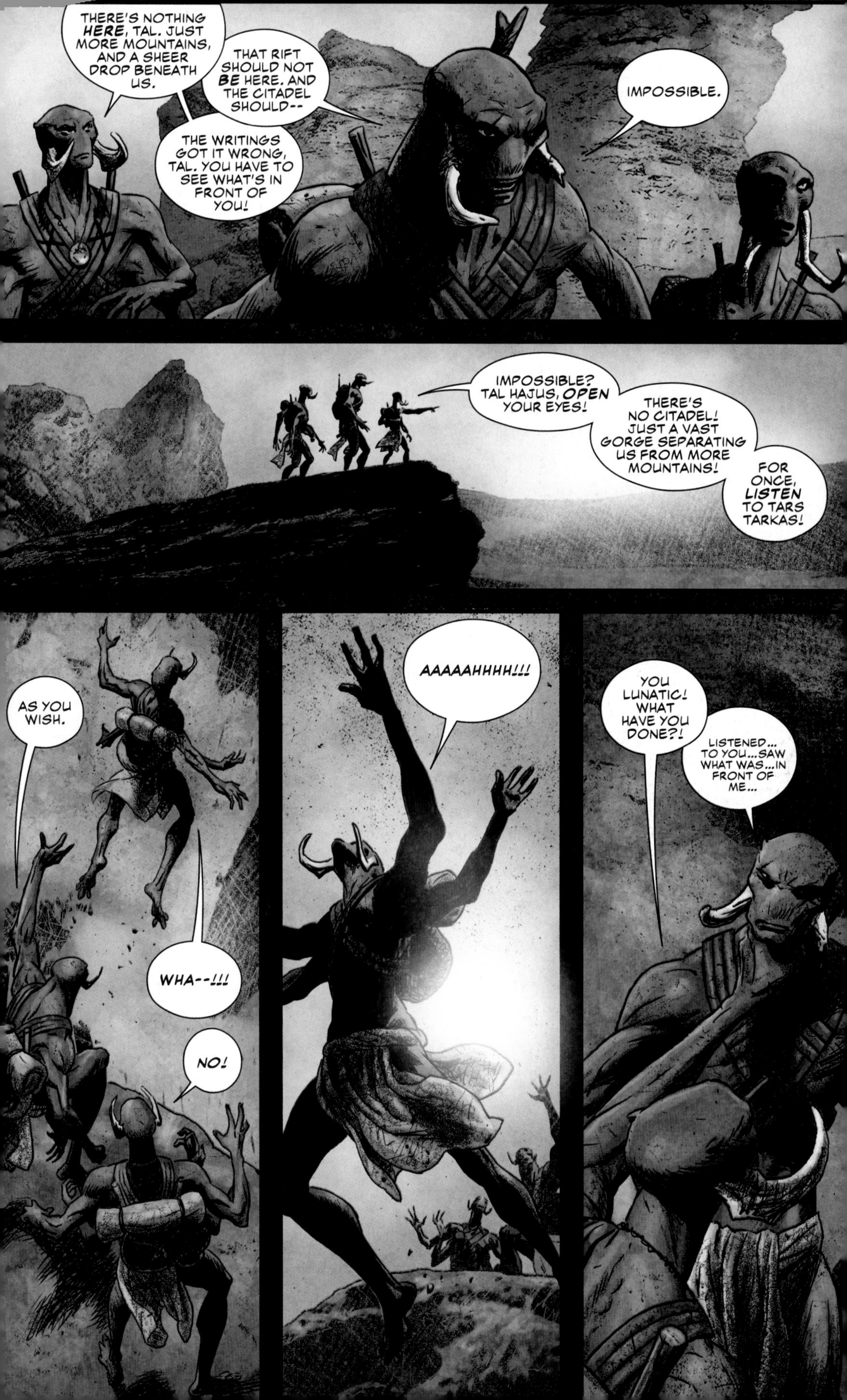

THERE'S NOTHING HERE, TAL. JUST MORE MOUNTAINS, AND A SHEER DROP BENEATH US.
THAT RIFT SHOULD NOT BE HERE. AND THE CITADEL SHOULD--
THE WRITINGS GOT IT WRONG, TAL. YOU HAVE TO SEE WHAT'S IN FRONT OF YOU!
IMPOSSIBLE.
IMPOSSIBLE? TAL HAJUS, OPEN YOUR EYES!
THERE'S NO CITADEL! JUST A VAST GORGE SEPARATING US FROM MORE MOUNTAINS!
FOR ONCE, LISTEN TO TARS TARKAS!
AS YOU WISH.
WHA--!!!
NO!
AAAAAHHHH!!!
YOU LUNATIC! WHAT HAVE YOU DONE?!
LISTENED... TO YOU...SAW WHAT WAS...IN FRONT OF ME...

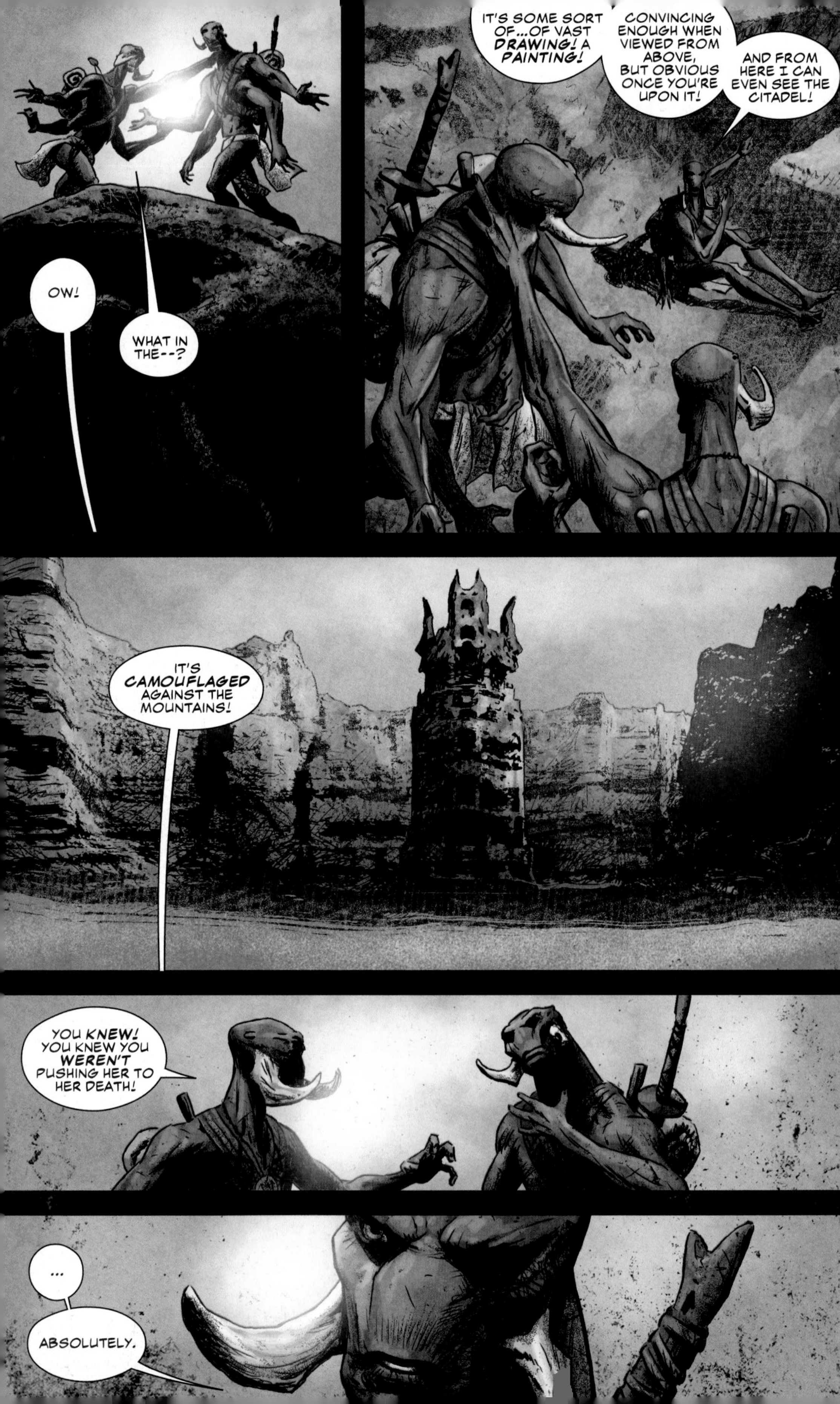
OW!
WHAT IN THE--?
IT'S SOME SORT OF...OF VAST DRAWING! A PAINTING!
CONVINCING ENOUGH WHEN VIEWED FROM ABOVE, BUT OBVIOUS ONCE YOU'RE UPON IT!
AND FROM HERE I CAN EVEN SEE THE CITADEL!
IT'S CAMOUFLAGED AGAINST THE MOUNTAINS!
YOU KNEW! YOU KNEW YOU WEREN'T PUSHING HER TO HER DEATH!
...
ABSOLUTELY.

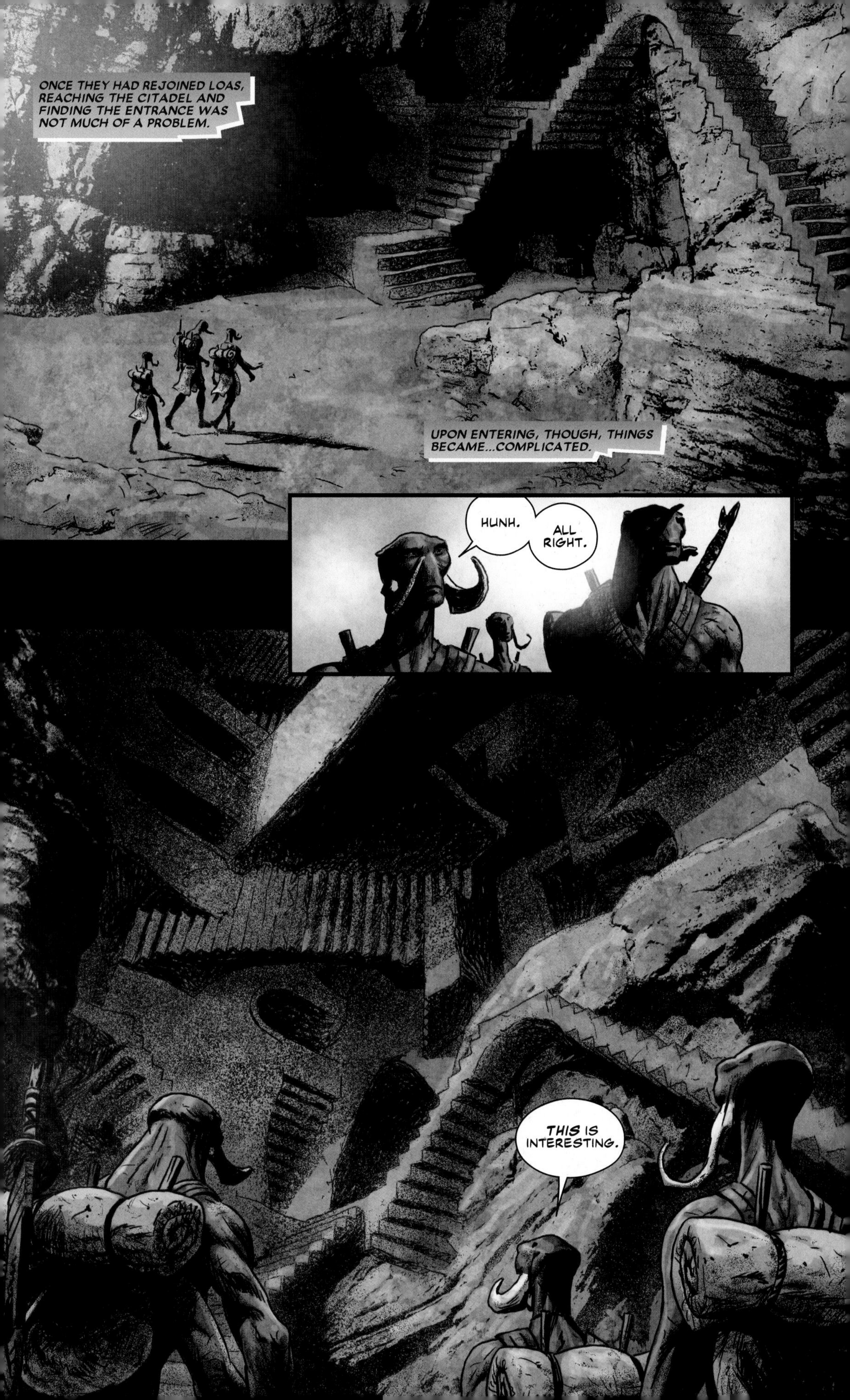
ONCE THEY HAD REJOINED LOAS, REACHING THE CITADEL AND FINDING THE ENTRANCE WAS NOT MUCH OF A PROBLEM.
UPON ENTERING, THOUGH, THINGS BECAME...COMPLICATED.
HUNH.
ALL RIGHT.
THIS IS INTERESTING.

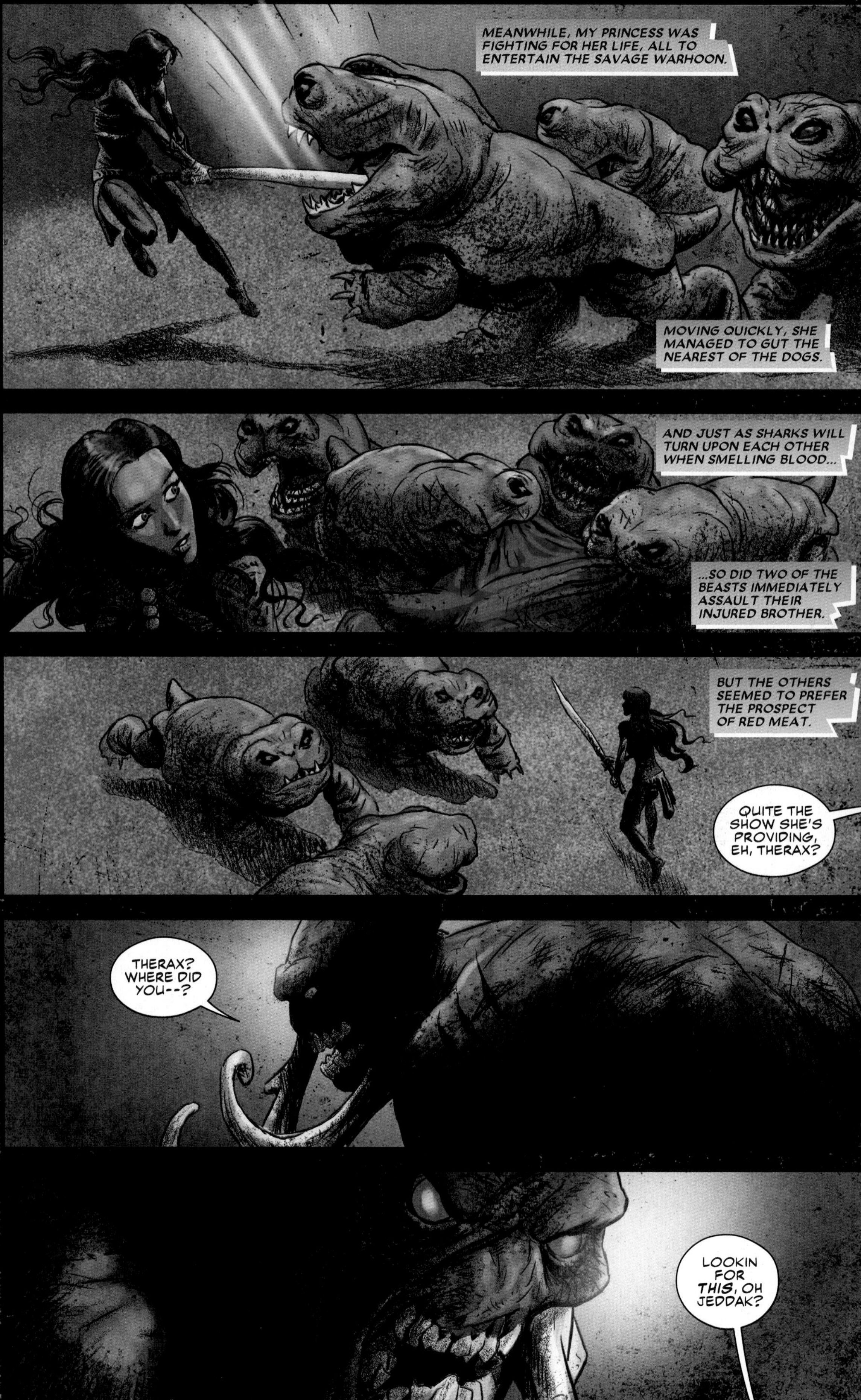

MEANWHILE, MY PRINCESS WAS FIGHTING FOR HER LIFE, ALL TO ENTERTAIN THE SAVAGE WARHOON.
MOVING QUICKLY, SHE MANAGED TO GUT THE NEAREST OF THE DOGS.
AND JUST AS SHARKS WILL TURN UPON EACH OTHER WHEN SMELLING BLOOD...
...SO DID TWO OF THE BEASTS IMMEDIATELY ASSAULT THEIR INJURED BROTHER.
BUT THE OTHERS SEEMED TO PREFER THE PROSPECT OF RED MEAT.
QUITE THE SHOW SHE'S PROVIDING, EH, THERAX?
THERAX? WHERE DID YOU--?
LOOKIN FOR THIS, OH JEDDAK?

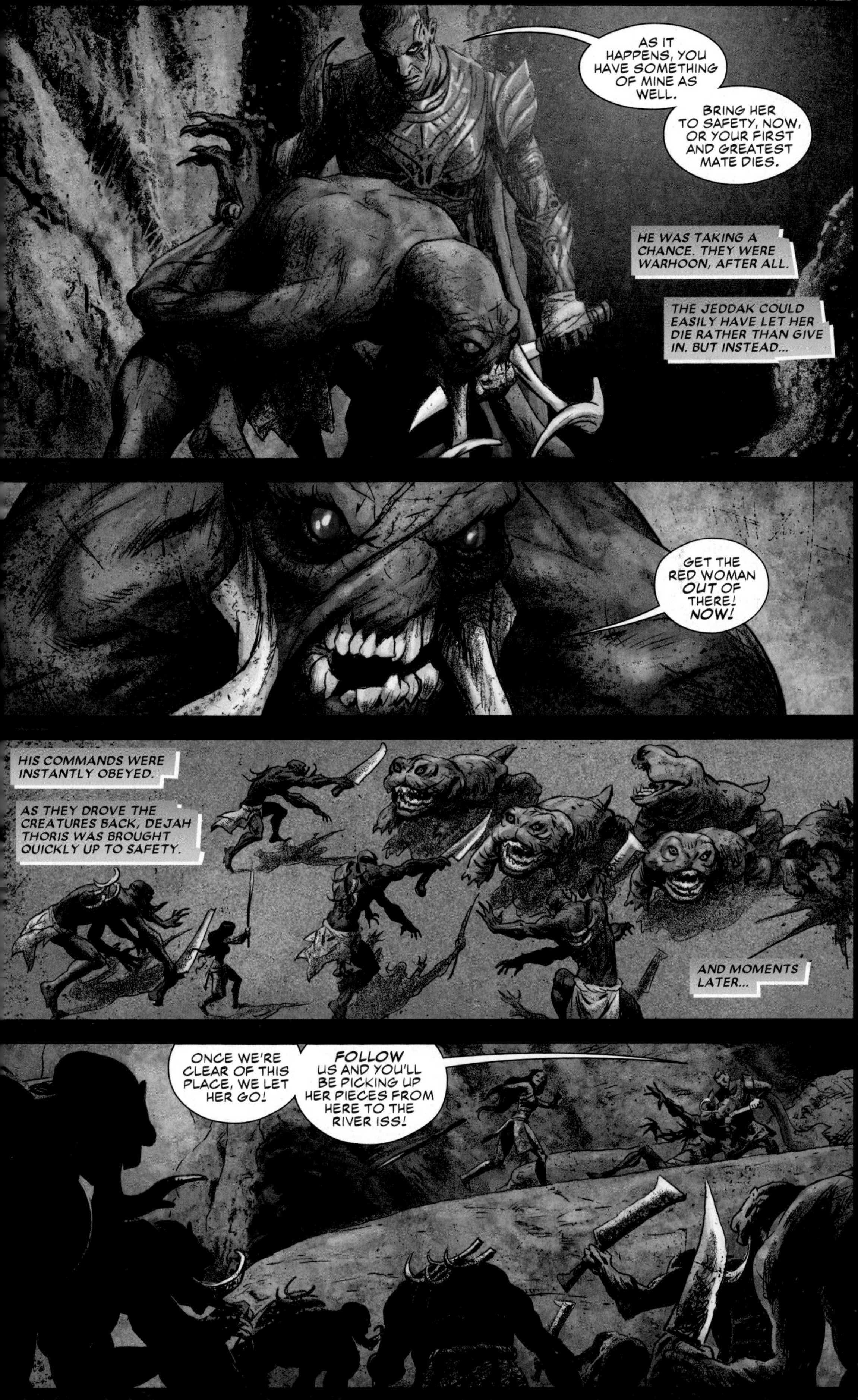
AS IT HAPPENS, YOU HAVE SOMETHING OF MINE AS WELL.
BRING HER TO SAFETY, NOW, OR YOUR FIRST AND GREATEST MATE DIES.
HE WAS TAKING A CHANCE. THEY WERE WARHOON, AFTER ALL.
THE JEDDAK COULD EASILY HAVE LET HER DIE RATHER THAN GIVE IN. BUT INSTEAD...
GET THE RED WOMAN OUT OF THERE! NOW!
HIS COMMANDS WERE INSTANTLY OBEYED.
AS THEY DROVE THE CREATURES BACK, DEJAH THORIS WAS BROUGHT QUICKLY UP TO SAFETY.
AND MOMENTS LATER...
ONCE WE'RE CLEAR OF THIS PLACE, WE LET HER GO!
FOLLOW US AND YOU'LL BE PICKING UP HER PIECES FROM HERE TO THE RIVER ISS!

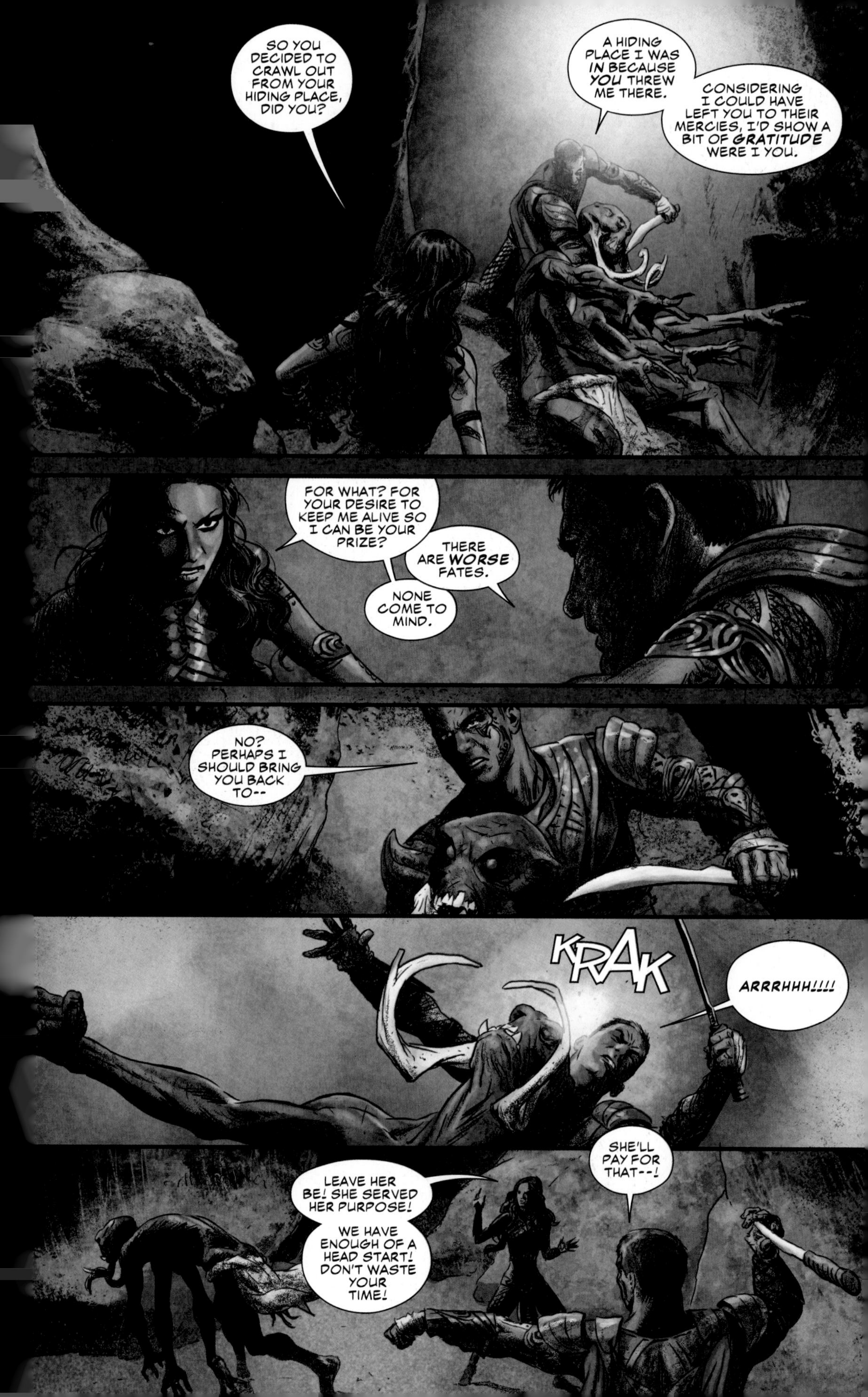
SO YOU DECIDED TO CRAWL OUT FROM YOUR HIDING PLACE, DID YOU?
A HIDING PLACE I WAS *IN* BECAUSE *YOU* THREW ME THERE.
CONSIDERING I COULD HAVE LEFT YOU TO THEIR MERCIES, I'D SHOW A BIT OF *GRATITUDE* WERE I YOU.
FOR WHAT? FOR YOUR DESIRE TO KEEP ME ALIVE SO I CAN BE YOUR PRIZE?
THERE ARE *WORSE* FATES.
NONE COME TO MIND.
NO? PERHAPS I SHOULD BRING YOU BACK TO--
KRAK
ARRRHHH!!!!
LEAVE HER BE! SHE SERVED HER PURPOSE!
WE HAVE ENOUGH OF A HEAD START! DON'T WASTE YOUR TIME!
SHE'LL PAY FOR THAT--!

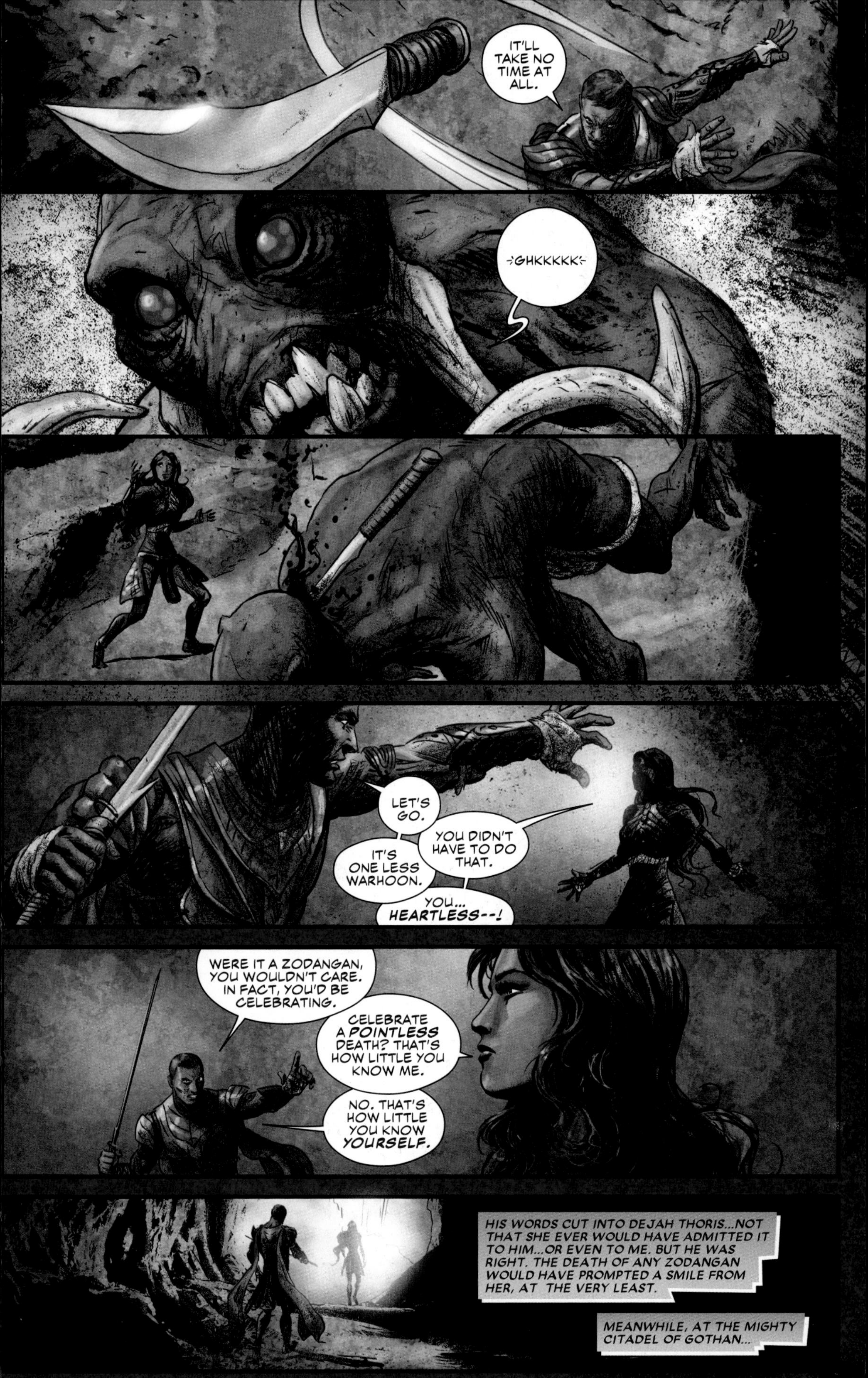
IT'LL TAKE NO TIME AT ALL.
-GHKKKKK-
LET'S GO.
YOU DIDN'T HAVE TO DO THAT.
IT'S ONE LESS WARHOON.
YOU... HEARTLESS--!
WERE IT A ZODANGAN, YOU WOULDN'T CARE. IN FACT, YOU'D BE CELEBRATING.
CELEBRATE A POINTLESS DEATH? THAT'S HOW LITTLE YOU KNOW ME.
NO. THAT'S HOW LITTLE YOU KNOW YOURSELF.
HIS WORDS CUT INTO DEJAH THORIS...NOT THAT SHE EVER WOULD HAVE ADMITTED IT TO HIM...OR EVEN TO ME. BUT HE WAS RIGHT. THE DEATH OF ANY ZODANGAN WOULD HAVE PROMPTED A SMILE FROM HER, AT THE VERY LEAST.
MEANWHILE, AT THE MIGHTY CITADEL OF GOTHAN...

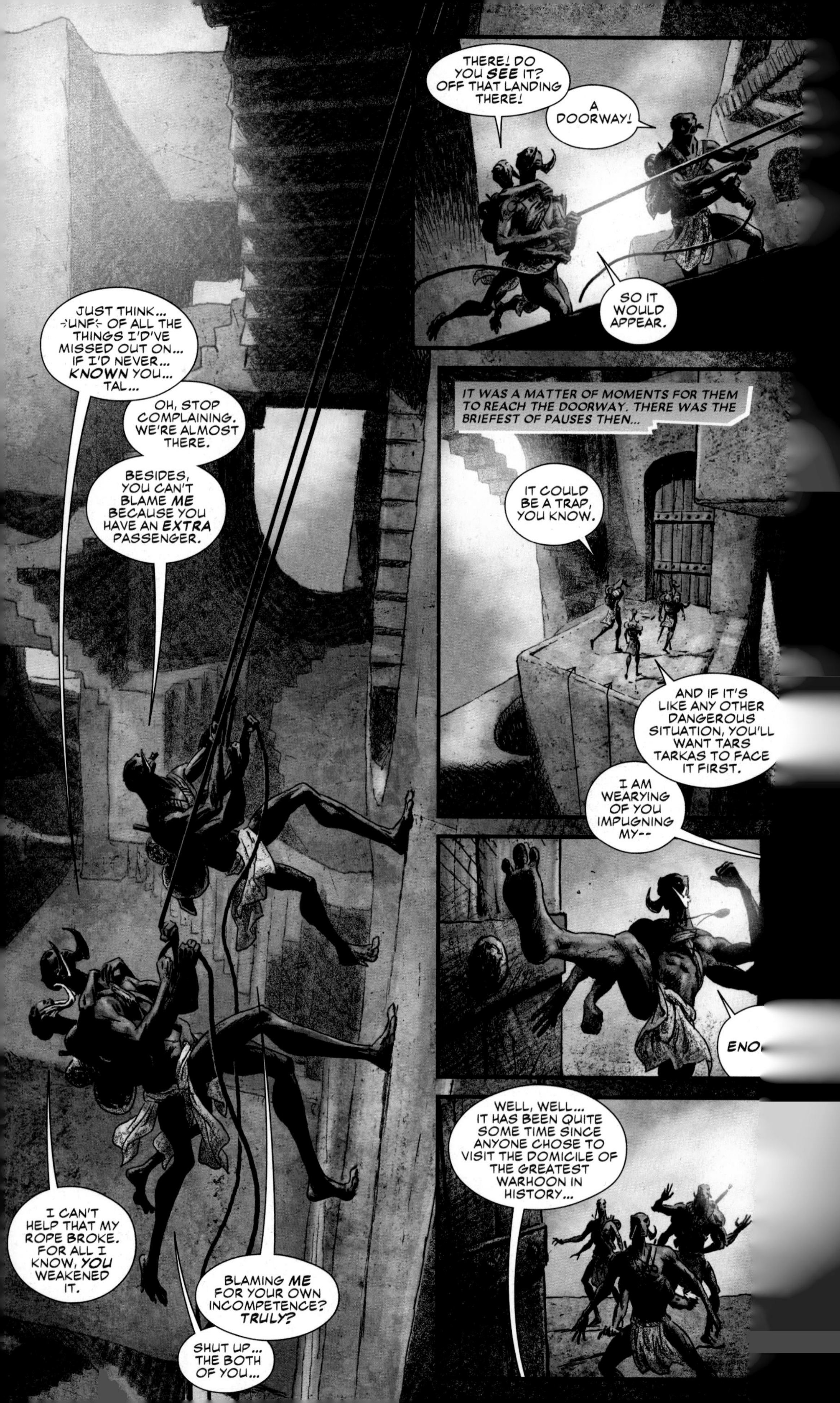
JUST THINK... -UNF- OF ALL THE THINGS I'D'VE MISSED OUT ON... IF I'D NEVER... KNOWN YOU... TAL...
OH, STOP COMPLAINING. WE'RE ALMOST THERE.
BESIDES, YOU CAN'T BLAME ME BECAUSE YOU HAVE AN EXTRA PASSENGER.
I CAN'T HELP THAT MY ROPE BROKE. FOR ALL I KNOW, YOU WEAKENED IT.
BLAMING ME FOR YOUR OWN INCOMPETENCE? TRULY?
SHUT UP... THE BOTH OF YOU...
THERE! DO YOU SEE IT? OFF THAT LANDING THERE!
A DOORWAY!
SO IT WOULD APPEAR.
IT WAS A MATTER OF MOMENTS FOR THEM TO REACH THE DOORWAY. THERE WAS THE BRIEFEST OF PAUSES THEN...
IT COULD BE A TRAP, YOU KNOW.
AND IF IT'S LIKE ANY OTHER DANGEROUS SITUATION, YOU'LL WANT TARS TARKAS TO FACE IT FIRST.
I AM WEARYING OF YOU IMPUGNING MY--
ENO
WELL, WELL... IT HAS BEEN QUITE SOME TIME SINCE ANYONE CHOSE TO VISIT THE DOMICILE OF THE GREATEST WARHOON IN HISTORY...

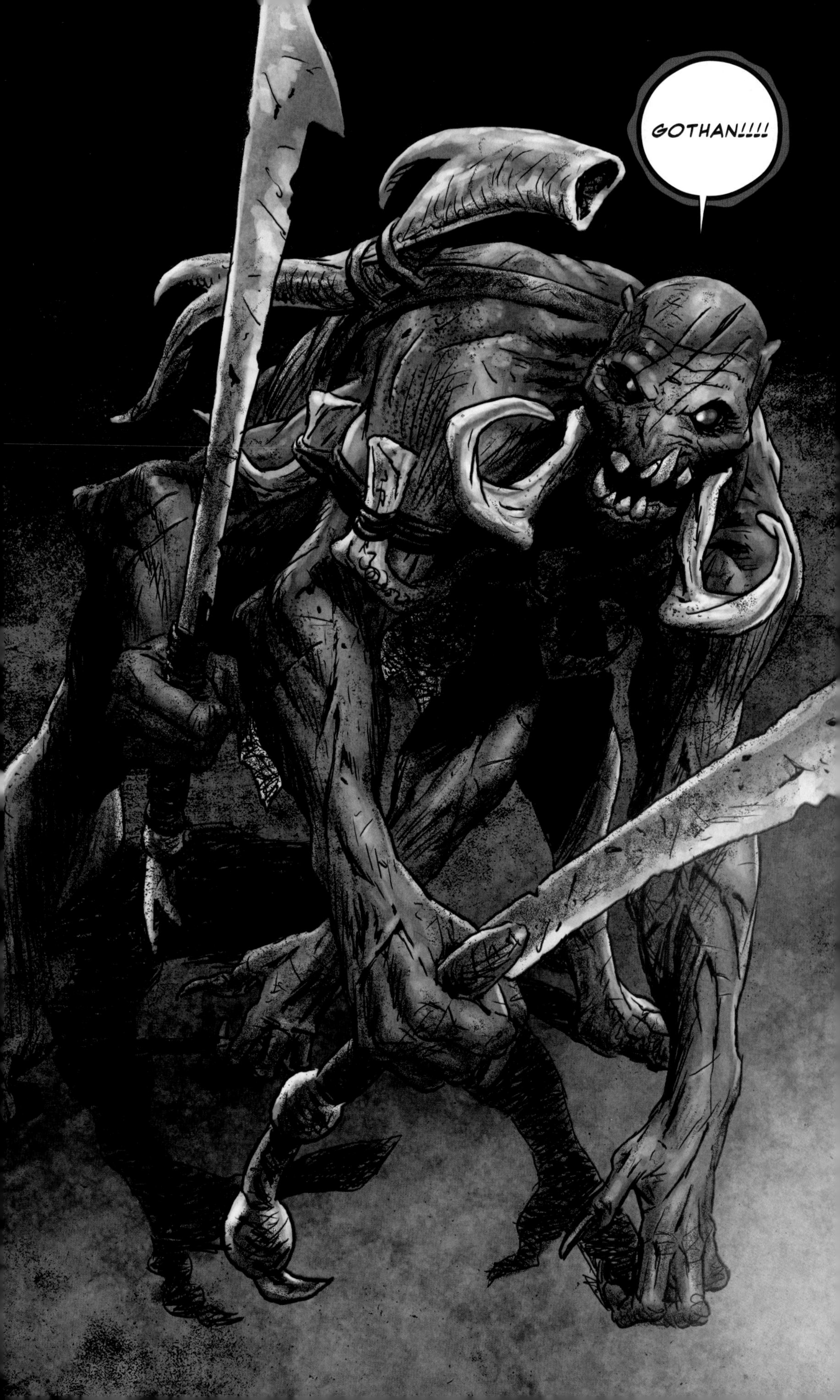
GOTHAN!!!!

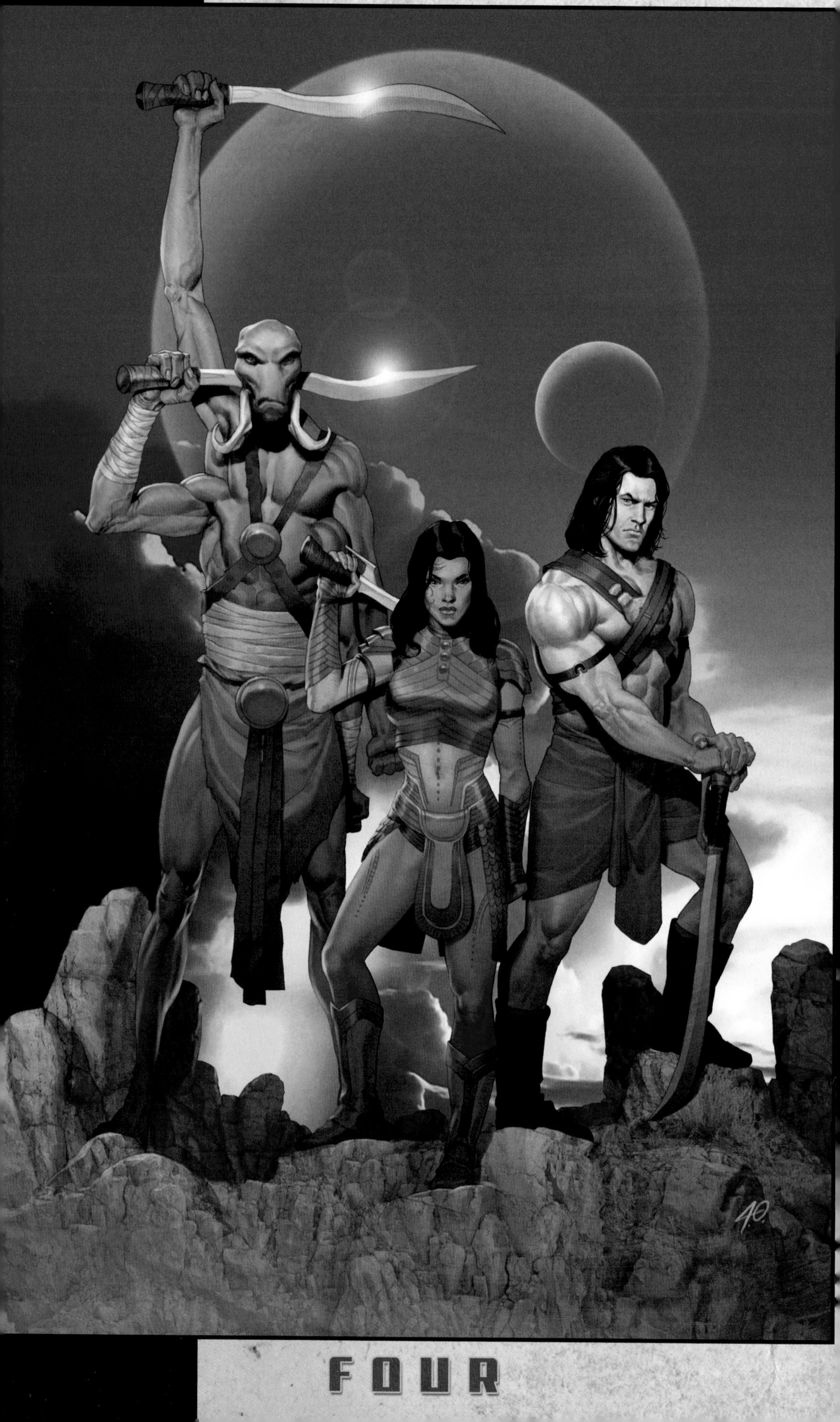

FOUR

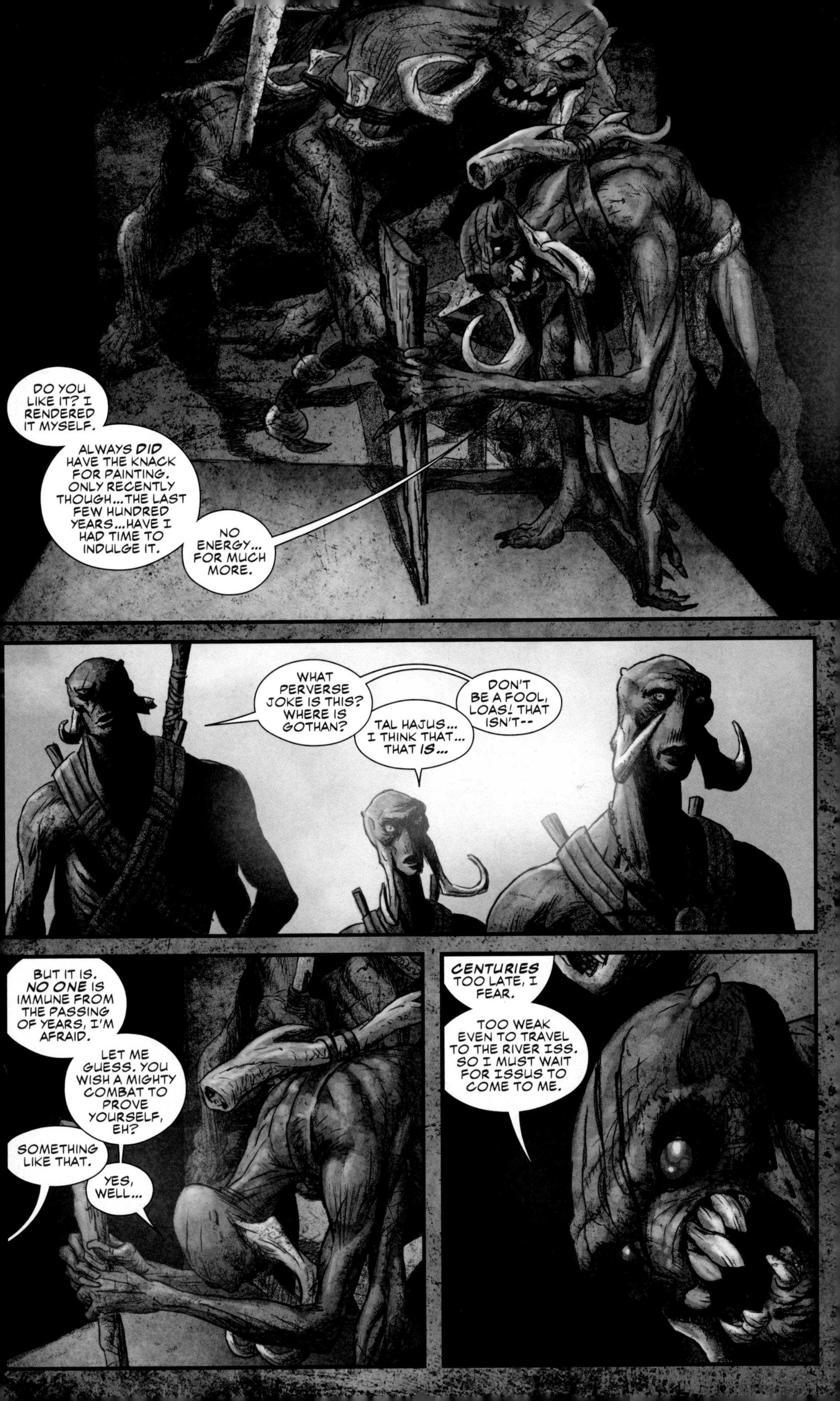
DO YOU LIKE IT? I RENDERED IT MYSELF.
ALWAYS DID HAVE THE KNACK FOR PAINTING. ONLY RECENTLY THOUGH...THE LAST FEW HUNDRED YEARS...HAVE I HAD TIME TO INDULGE IT.
NO ENERGY... FOR MUCH MORE.
WHAT PERVERSE JOKE IS THIS? WHERE IS GOTHAN?
DON'T BE A FOOL, LOAS! THAT ISN'T--
TAL HAJUS... I THINK THAT... THAT IS...
BUT IT IS. NO ONE IS IMMUNE FROM THE PASSING OF YEARS, I'M AFRAID.
LET ME GUESS. YOU WISH A MIGHTY COMBAT TO PROVE YOURSELF, EH?
SOMETHING LIKE THAT.
YES, WELL...
CENTURIES TOO LATE, I FEAR.
TOO WEAK EVEN TO TRAVEL TO THE RIVER ISS. SO I MUST WAIT FOR ISSUS TO COME TO ME.

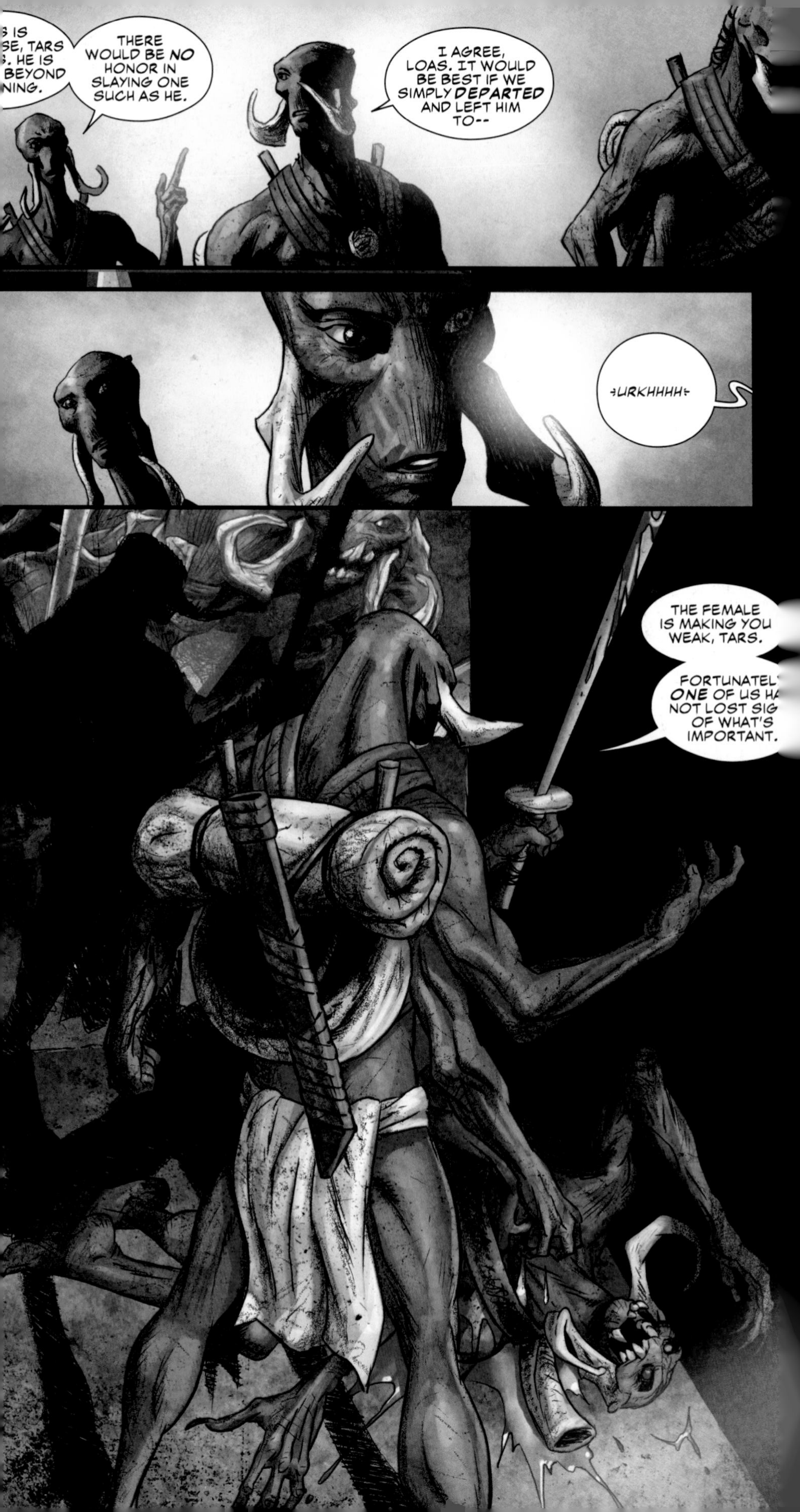

S IS SE, TARS S. HE IS BEYOND NING.
THERE WOULD BE NO HONOR IN SLAYING ONE SUCH AS HE.
I AGREE, LOAS. IT WOULD BE BEST IF WE SIMPLY DEPARTED AND LEFT HIM TO--
URKHHHH
THE FEMALE IS MAKING YOU WEAK, TARS.
FORTUNATEL ONE OF US HA NOT LOST SIG OF WHAT'S IMPORTANT.

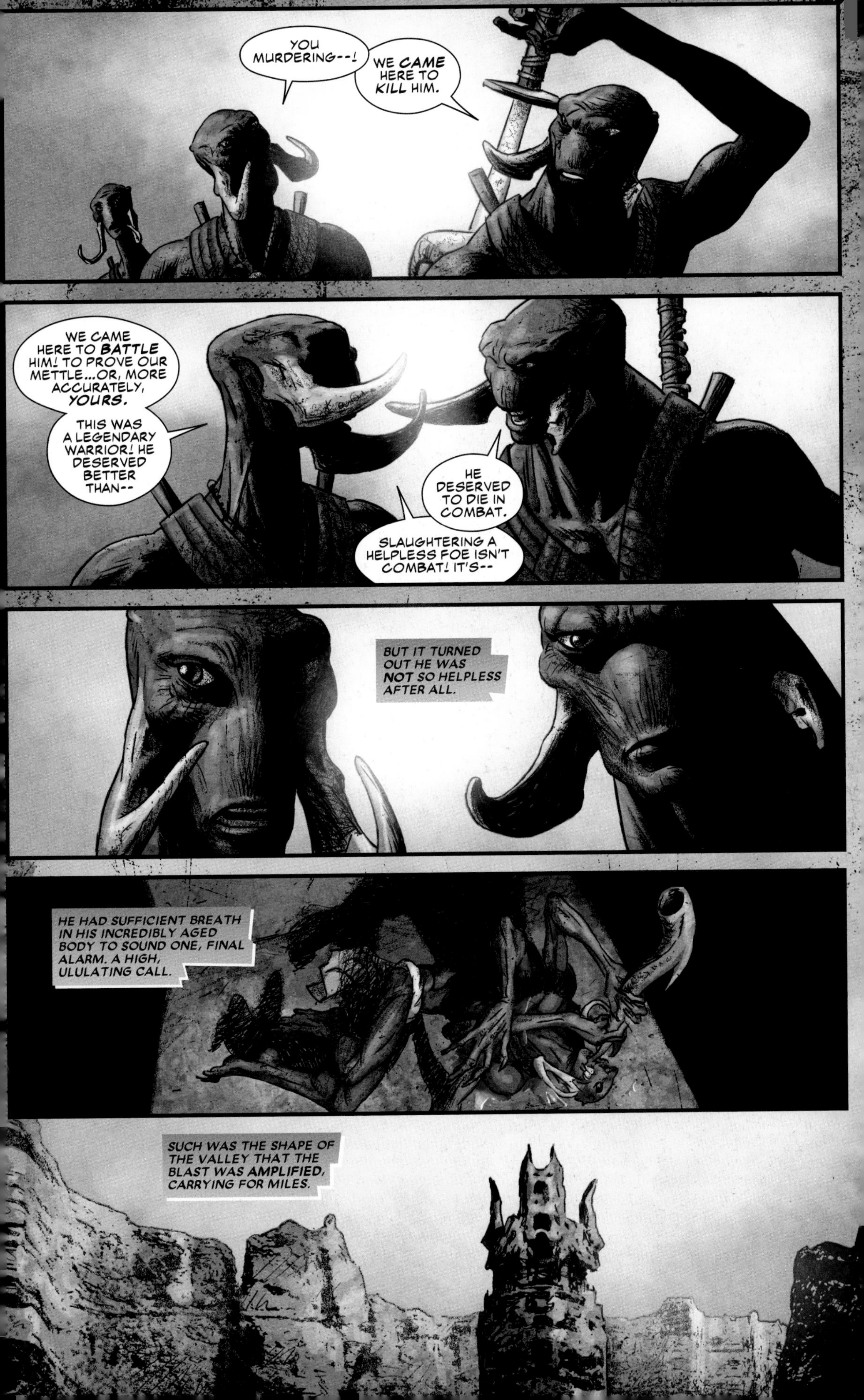

YOU MURDERING--!
WE CAME HERE TO KILL HIM.
WE CAME HERE TO BATTLE HIM! TO PROVE OUR METTLE...OR, MORE ACCURATELY, YOURS.
THIS WAS A LEGENDARY WARRIOR! HE DESERVED BETTER THAN--
HE DESERVED TO DIE IN COMBAT.
SLAUGHTERING A HELPLESS FOE ISN'T COMBAT! IT'S--
BUT IT TURNED OUT HE WAS NOT SO HELPLESS AFTER ALL.
HE HAD SUFFICIENT BREATH IN HIS INCREDIBLY AGED BODY TO SOUND ONE, FINAL ALARM. A HIGH, ULULATING CALL.
SUCH WAS THE SHAPE OF THE VALLEY THAT THE BLAST WAS AMPLIFIED, CARRYING FOR MILES.

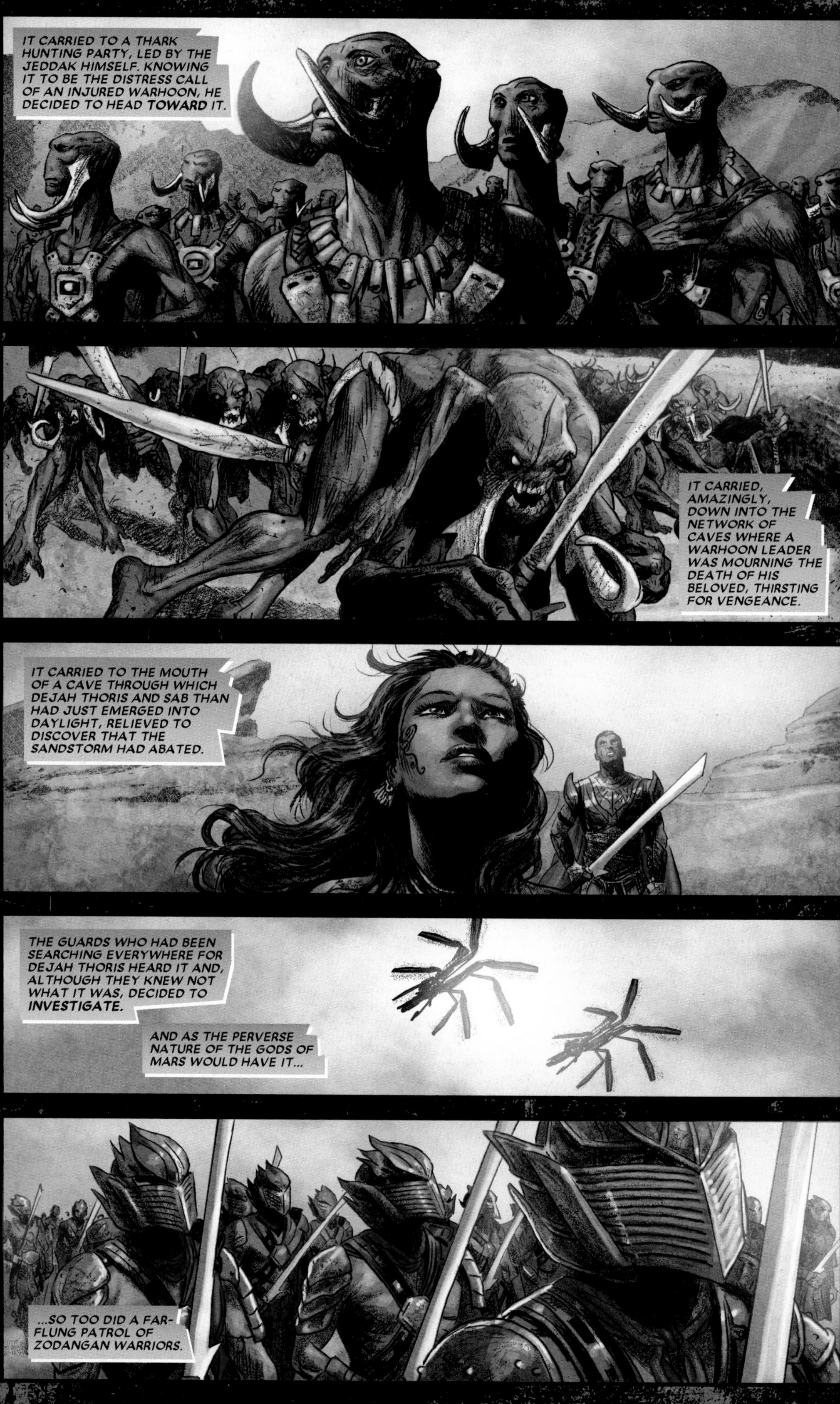

IT CARRIED TO A THARK HUNTING PARTY, LED BY THE JEDDAK HIMSELF. KNOWING IT TO BE THE DISTRESS CALL OF AN INJURED WARHOON, HE DECIDED TO HEAD TOWARD IT.
IT CARRIED, AMAZINGLY, DOWN INTO THE NETWORK OF CAVES WHERE A WARHOON LEADER WAS MOURNING THE DEATH OF HIS BELOVED, THIRSTING FOR VENGEANCE.
IT CARRIED TO THE MOUTH OF A CAVE THROUGH WHICH DEJAH THORIS AND SAB THAN HAD JUST EMERGED INTO DAYLIGHT, RELIEVED TO DISCOVER THAT THE SANDSTORM HAD ABATED.
THE GUARDS WHO HAD BEEN SEARCHING EVERYWHERE FOR DEJAH THORIS HEARD IT AND, ALTHOUGH THEY KNEW NOT WHAT IT WAS, DECIDED TO INVESTIGATE.
AND AS THE PERVERSE NATURE OF THE GODS OF MARS WOULD HAVE IT...
...SO TOO DID A FAR-FLUNG PATROL OF ZODANGAN WARRIORS.

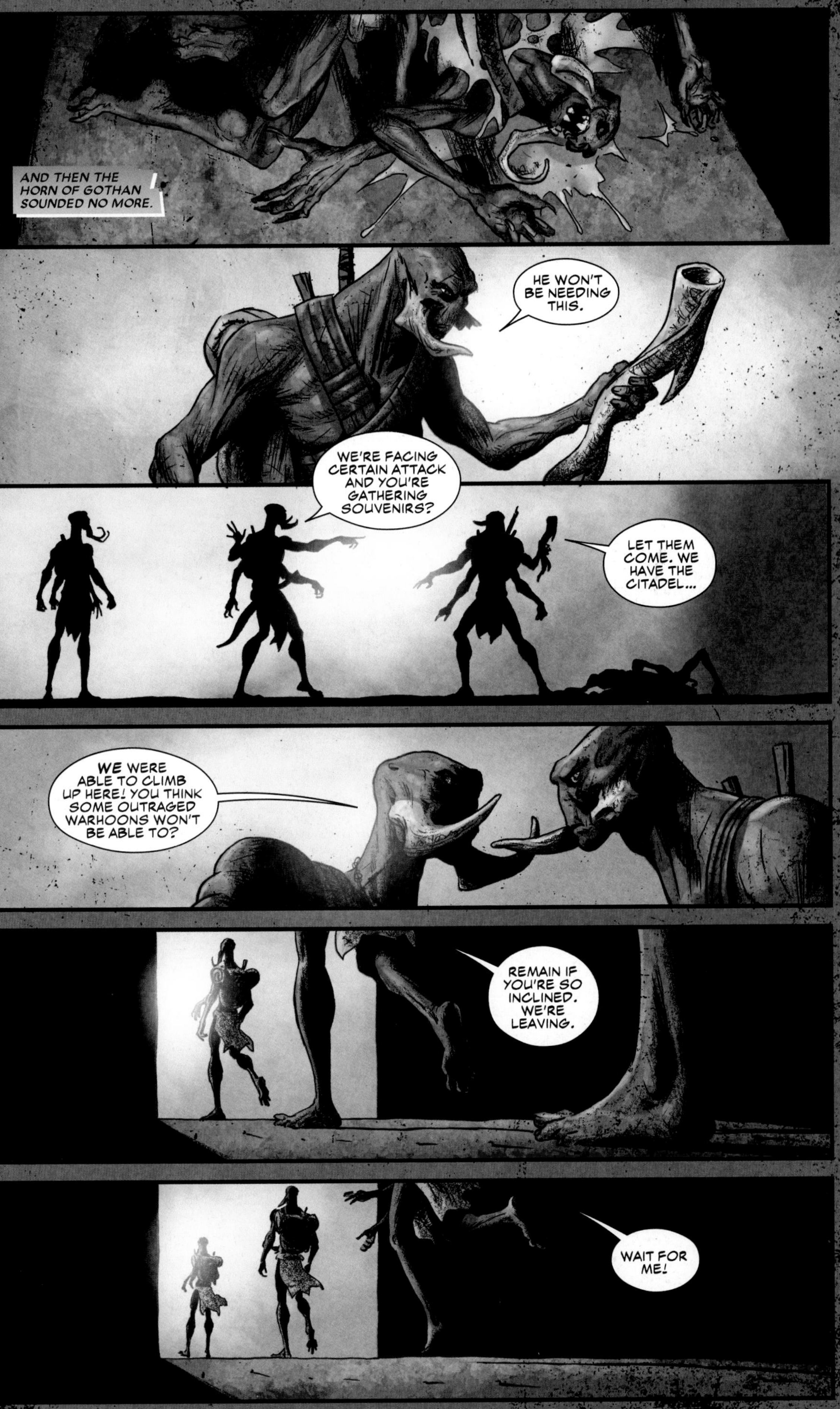
AND THEN THE HORN OF GOTHAN SOUNDED NO MORE.
HE WON'T BE NEEDING THIS.
WE'RE FACING CERTAIN ATTACK AND YOU'RE GATHERING SOUVENIRS?
LET THEM COME. WE HAVE THE CITADEL...
WE WERE ABLE TO CLIMB UP HERE! YOU THINK SOME OUTRAGED WARHOONS WON'T BE ABLE TO?
REMAIN IF YOU'RE SO INCLINED. WE'RE LEAVING.
WAIT FOR ME!

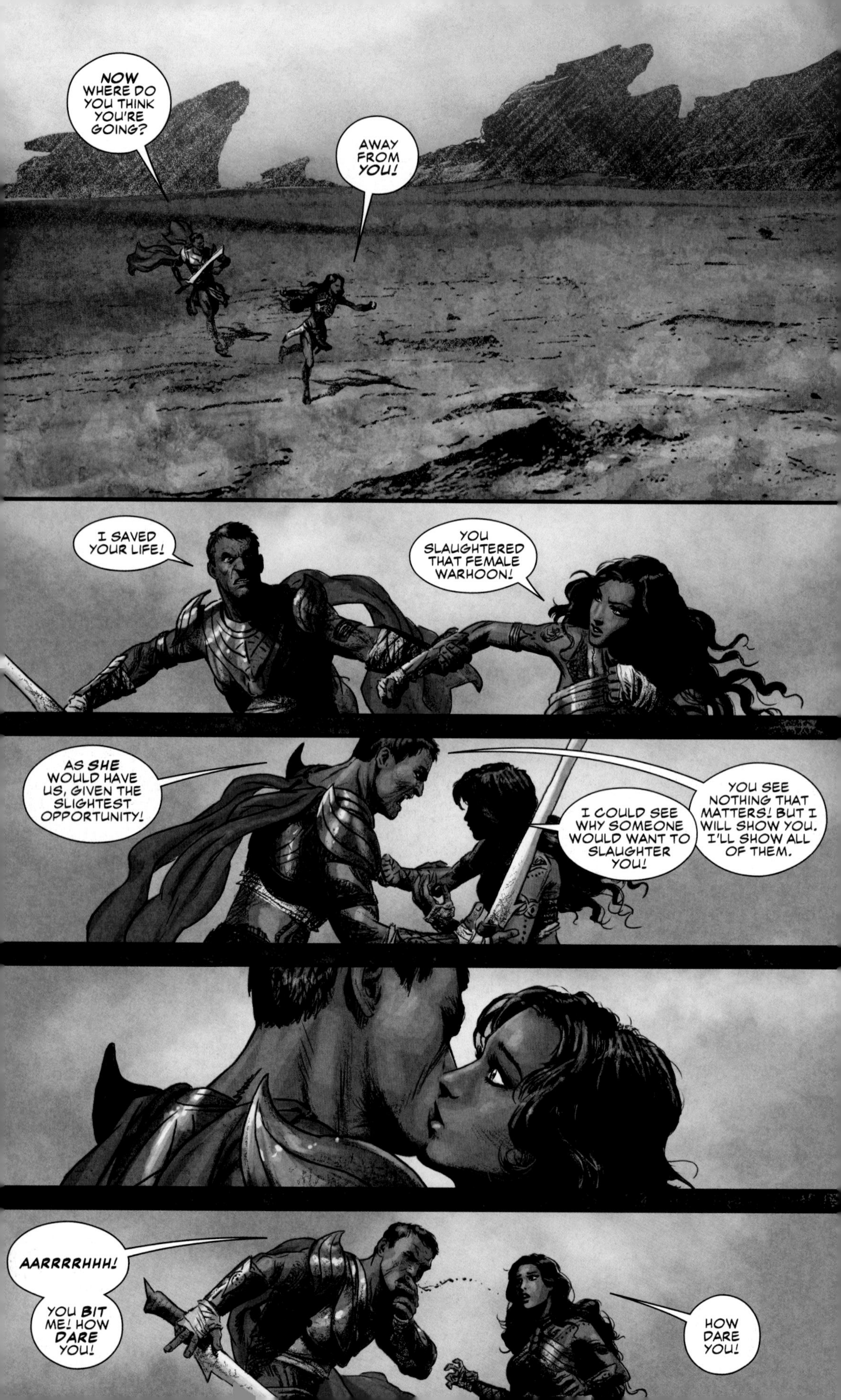
NOW WHERE DO YOU THINK YOU'RE GOING?
AWAY FROM YOU!
I SAVED YOUR LIFE!
YOU SLAUGHTERED THAT FEMALE WARHOON!
AS SHE WOULD HAVE US, GIVEN THE SLIGHTEST OPPORTUNITY!
I COULD SEE WHY SOMEONE WOULD WANT TO SLAUGHTER YOU!
YOU SEE NOTHING THAT MATTERS! BUT I WILL SHOW YOU. I'LL SHOW ALL OF THEM.
AARRRRHHH!
YOU BIT ME! HOW DARE YOU!
HOW DARE YOU!

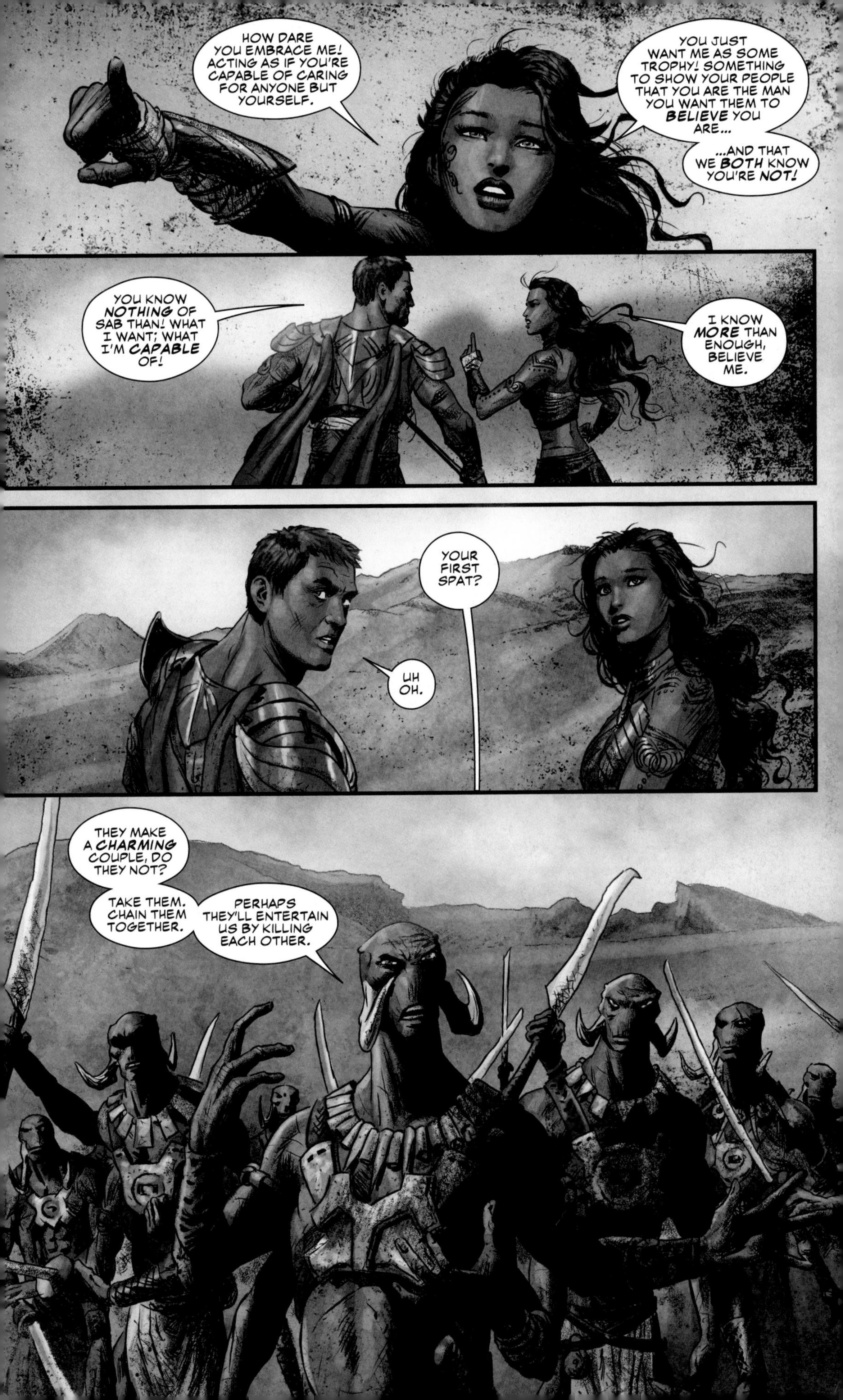
HOW DARE YOU EMBRACE ME! ACTING AS IF YOU'RE CAPABLE OF CARING FOR ANYONE BUT YOURSELF.
YOU JUST WANT ME AS SOME TROPHY! SOMETHING TO SHOW YOUR PEOPLE THAT YOU ARE THE MAN YOU WANT THEM TO BELIEVE YOU ARE...
...AND THAT WE BOTH KNOW YOU'RE NOT!
YOU KNOW NOTHING OF SAB THAN! WHAT I WANT; WHAT I'M CAPABLE OF!
I KNOW MORE THAN ENOUGH, BELIEVE ME.
YOUR FIRST SPAT?
UH OH.
THEY MAKE A CHARMING COUPLE, DO THEY NOT?
TAKE THEM. CHAIN THEM TOGETHER.
PERHAPS THEY'LL ENTERTAIN US BY KILLING EACH OTHER.

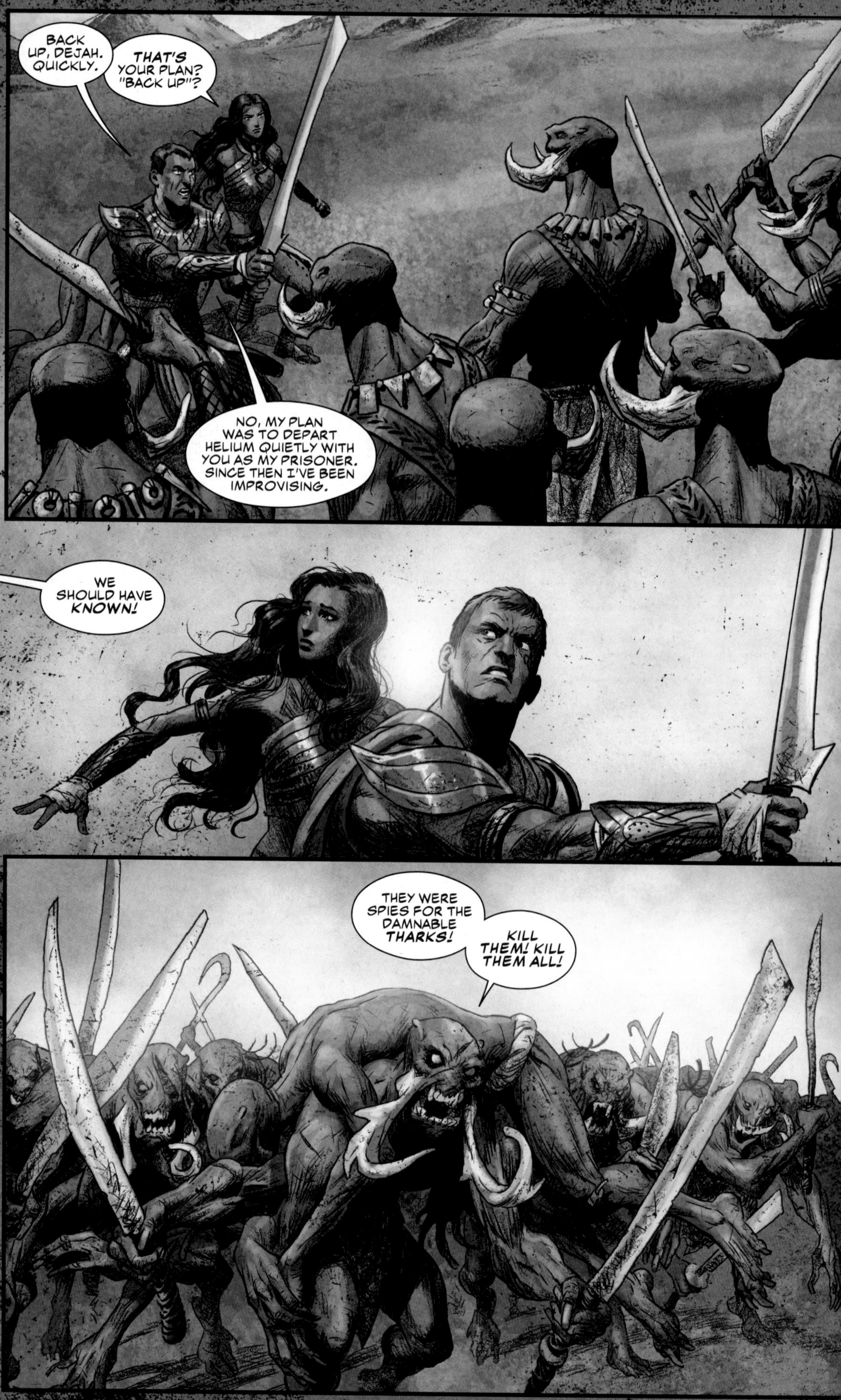
BACK UP, DEJAH. QUICKLY.
THAT'S YOUR PLAN? "BACK UP"?
NO, MY PLAN WAS TO DEPART HELIUM QUIETLY WITH YOU AS MY PRISONER. SINCE THEN I'VE BEEN IMPROVISING.
WE SHOULD HAVE KNOWN!
THEY WERE SPIES FOR THE DAMNABLE THARKS!
KILL THEM! KILL THEM ALL!

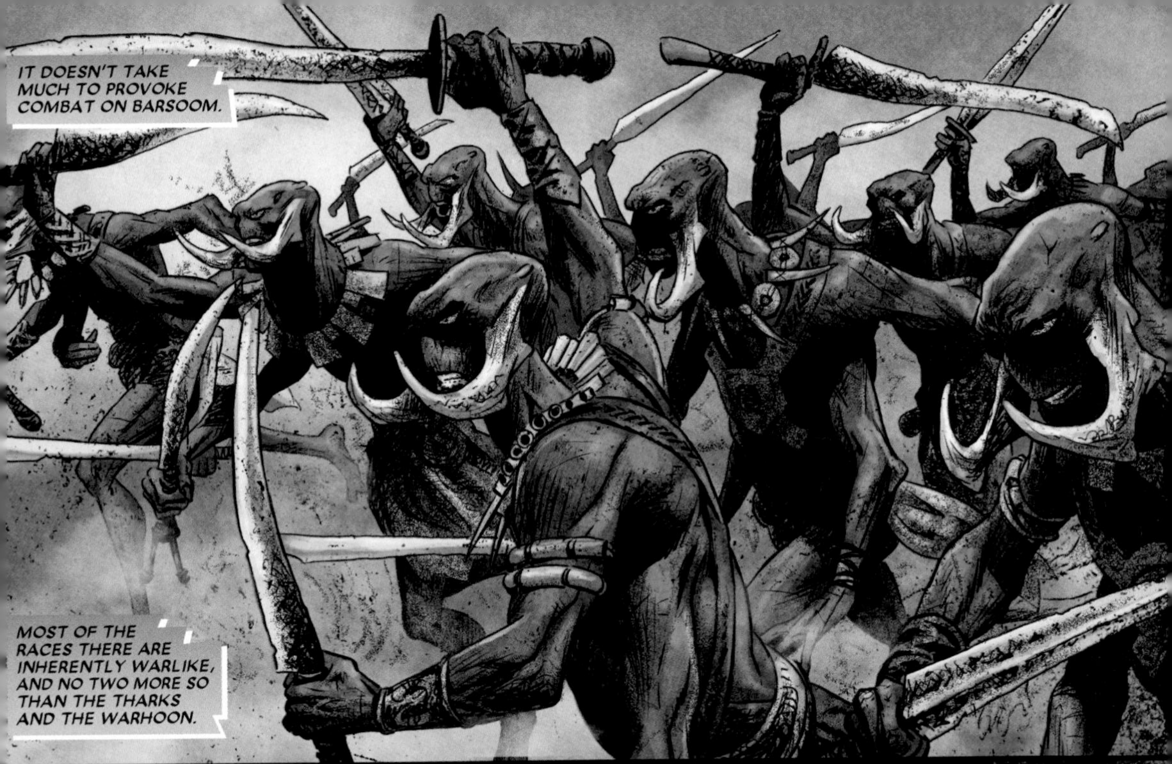
IT DOESN'T TAKE MUCH TO PROVOKE COMBAT ON BARSOOM.
MOST OF THE RACES THERE ARE INHERENTLY WARLIKE, AND NO TWO MORE SO THAN THE THARKS AND THE WARHOON.

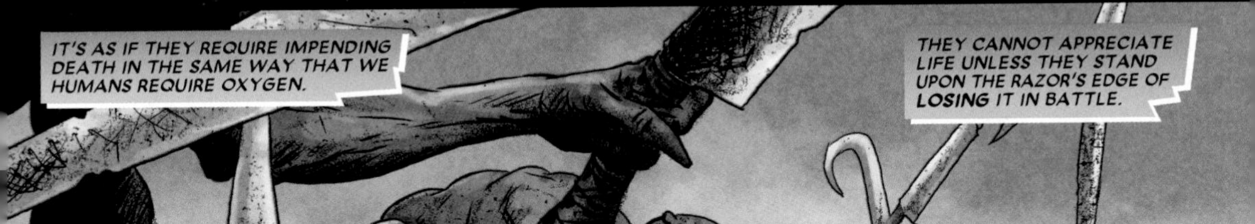
IT'S AS IF THEY REQUIRE IMPENDING DEATH IN THE SAME WAY THAT WE HUMANS REQUIRE OXYGEN.
THEY CANNOT APPRECIATE LIFE UNLESS THEY STAND UPON THE RAZOR'S EDGE OF LOSING IT IN BATTLE.

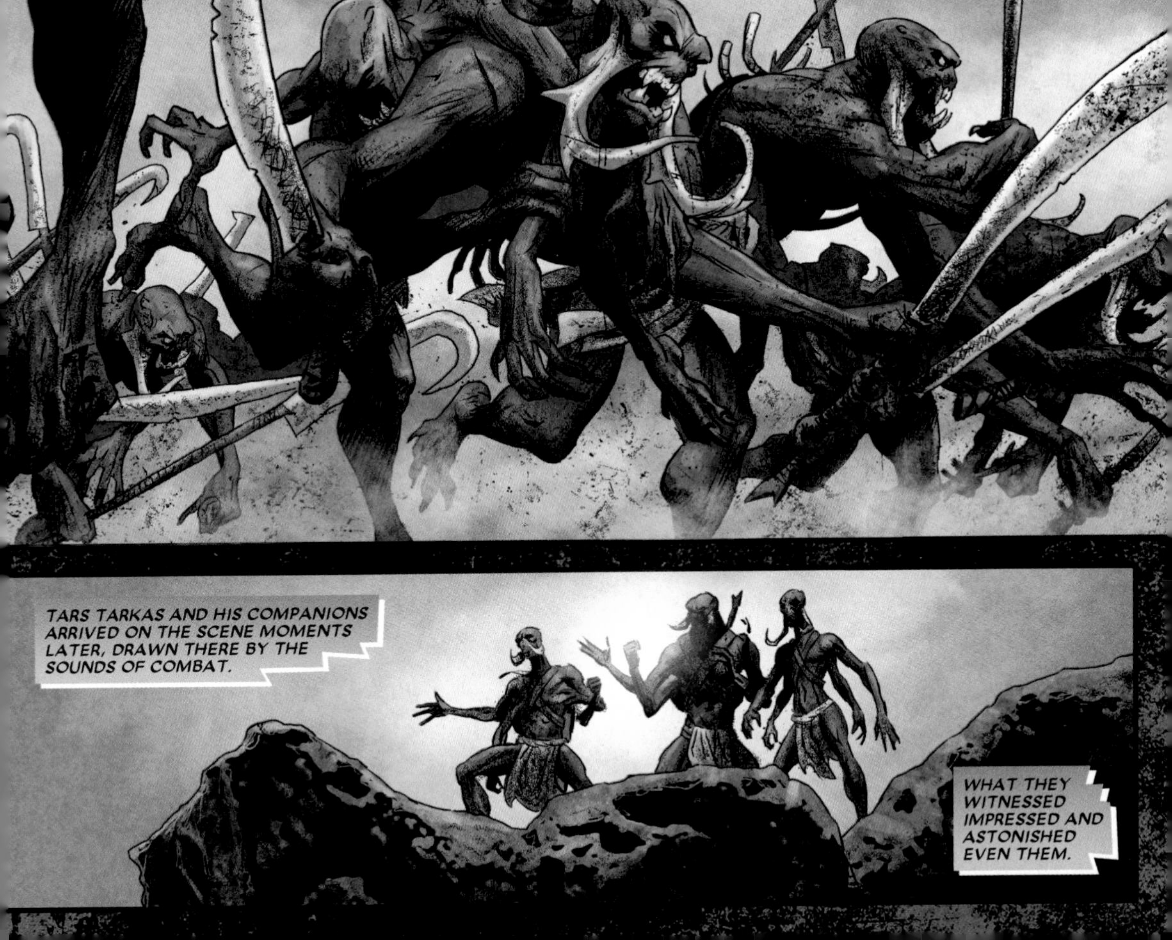
TARS TARKAS AND HIS COMPANIONS ARRIVED ON THE SCENE MOMENTS LATER, DRAWN THERE BY THE SOUNDS OF COMBAT.
WHAT THEY WITNESSED IMPRESSED AND ASTONISHED EVEN THEM.

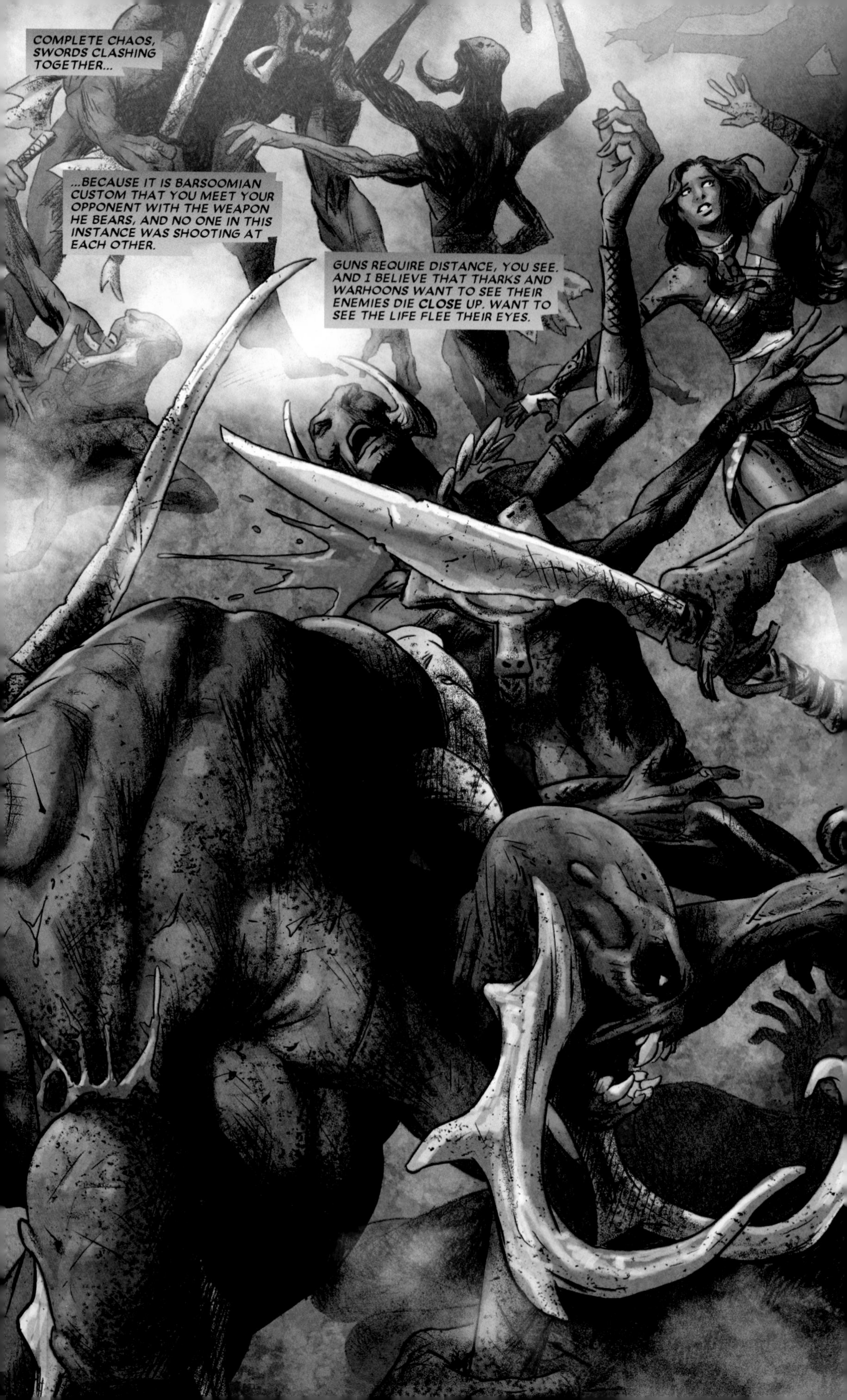
COMPLETE CHAOS, SWORDS CLASHING TOGETHER...
...BECAUSE IT IS BARSOOMIAN CUSTOM THAT YOU MEET YOUR OPPONENT WITH THE WEAPON HE BEARS, AND NO ONE IN THIS INSTANCE WAS SHOOTING AT EACH OTHER.
GUNS REQUIRE DISTANCE, YOU SEE. AND I BELIEVE THAT THARKS AND WARHOONS WANT TO SEE THEIR ENEMIES DIE CLOSE UP. WANT TO SEE THE LIFE FLEE THEIR EYES.

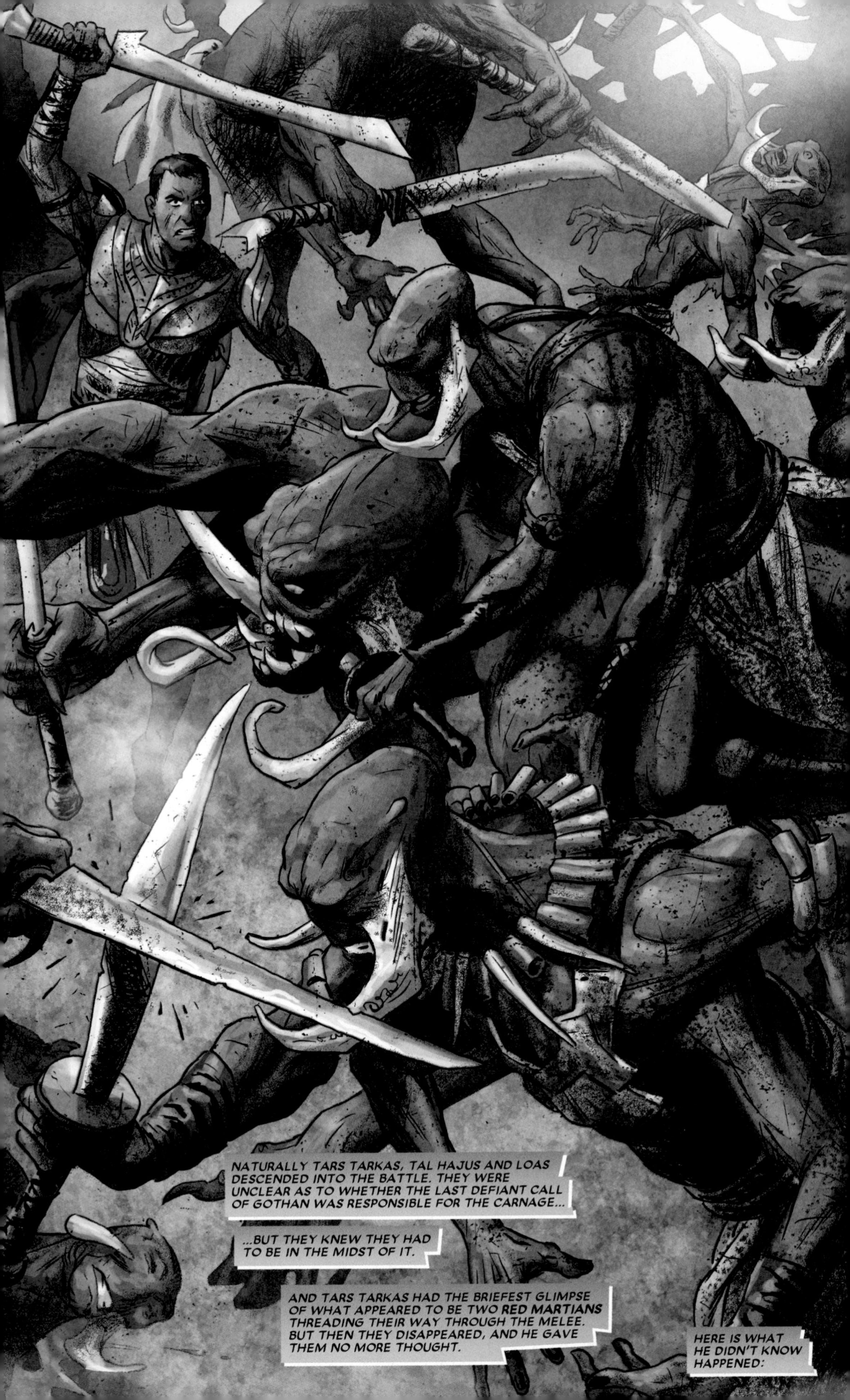
NATURALLY TARS TARKAS, TAL HAJUS AND LOAS DESCENDED INTO THE BATTLE. THEY WERE UNCLEAR AS TO WHETHER THE LAST DEFIANT CALL OF GOTHAN WAS RESPONSIBLE FOR THE CARNAGE...
...BUT THEY KNEW THEY HAD TO BE IN THE MIDST OF IT.
AND TARS TARKAS HAD THE BRIEFEST GLIMPSE OF WHAT APPEARED TO BE TWO RED MARTIANS THREADING THEIR WAY THROUGH THE MELEE. BUT THEN THEY DISAPPEARED, AND HE GAVE THEM NO MORE THOUGHT.
HERE IS WHAT HE DIDN'T KNOW HAPPENED:

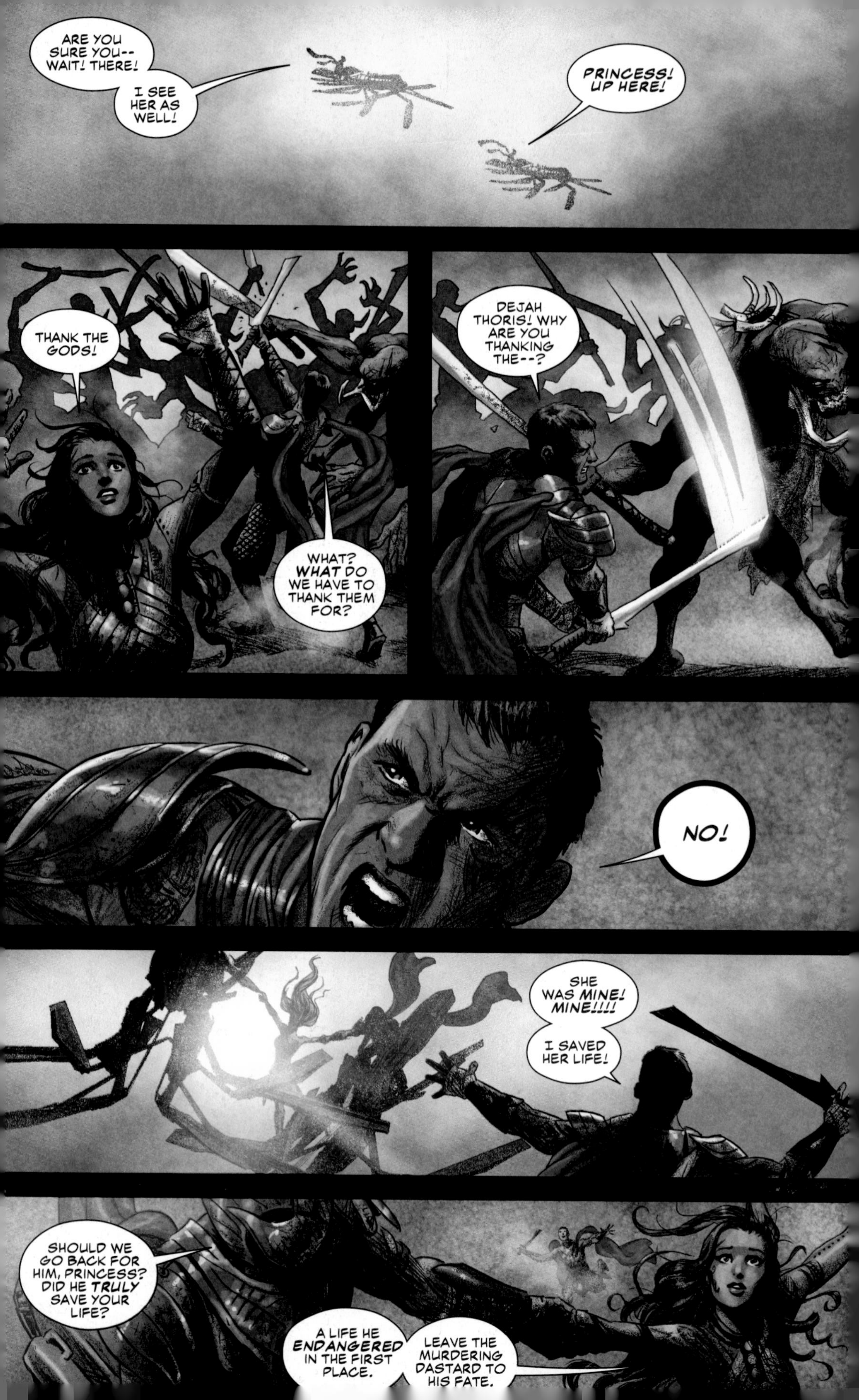
ARE YOU SURE YOU-- WAIT! THERE!
I SEE HER AS WELL!
PRINCESS! UP HERE!
THANK THE GODS!
WHAT? WHAT DO WE HAVE TO THANK THEM FOR?
DEJAH THORIS! WHY ARE YOU THANKING THE--?
NO!
SHE WAS MINE! MINE!!!!
I SAVED HER LIFE!
SHOULD WE GO BACK FOR HIM, PRINCESS? DID HE TRULY SAVE YOUR LIFE?
A LIFE HE ENDANGERED IN THE FIRST PLACE.
LEAVE THE MURDERING DASTARD TO HIS FATE.

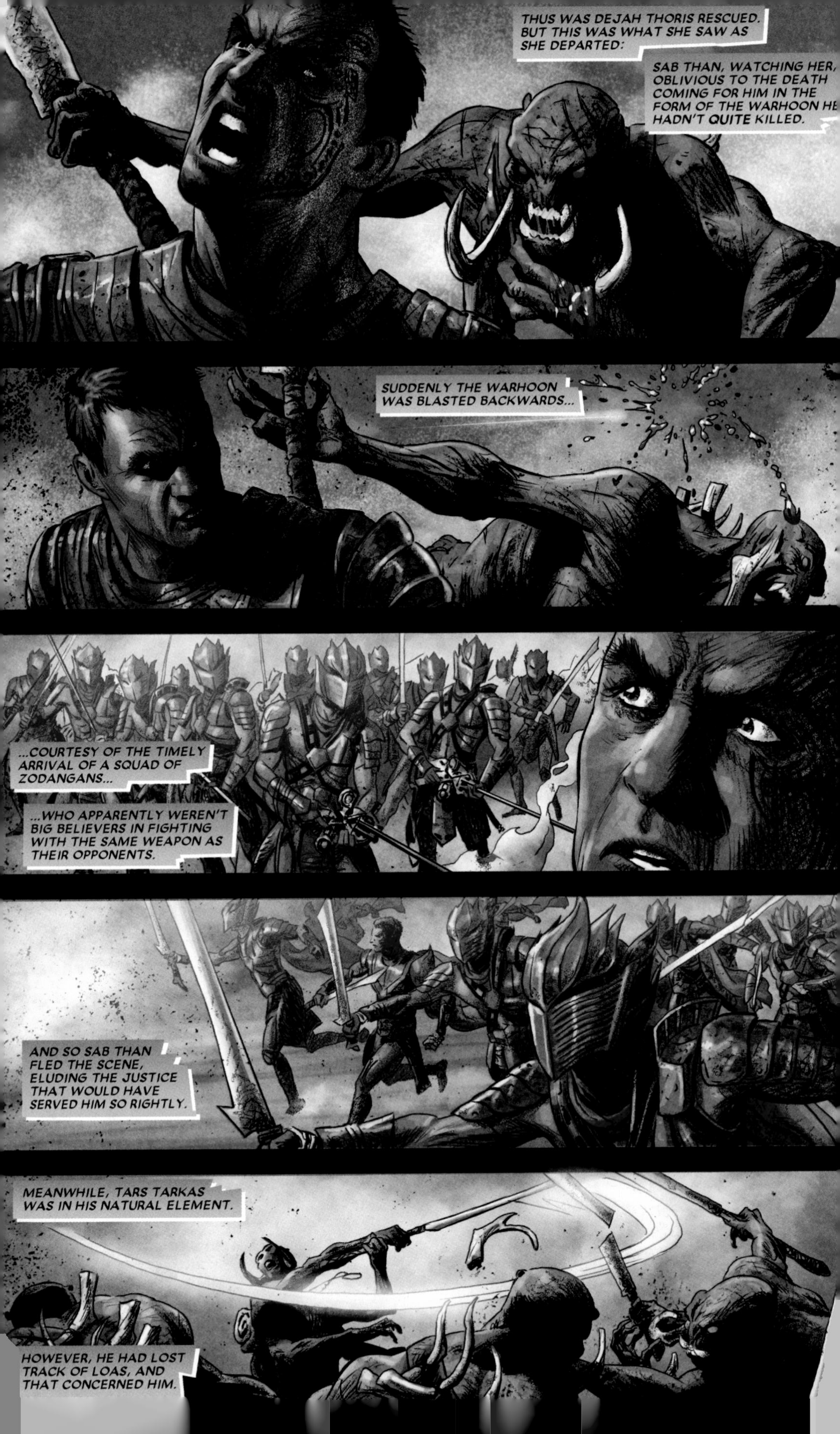
THUS WAS DEJAH THORIS RESCUED. BUT THIS WAS WHAT SHE SAW AS SHE DEPARTED:
SAB THAN, WATCHING HER, OBLIVIOUS TO THE DEATH COMING FOR HIM IN THE FORM OF THE WARHOON HE HADN'T QUITE KILLED.
SUDDENLY THE WARHOON WAS BLASTED BACKWARDS...
...COURTESY OF THE TIMELY ARRIVAL OF A SQUAD OF ZODANGANS...
...WHO APPARENTLY WEREN'T BIG BELIEVERS IN FIGHTING WITH THE SAME WEAPON AS THEIR OPPONENTS.
AND SO SAB THAN FLED THE SCENE, ELUDING THE JUSTICE THAT WOULD HAVE SERVED HIM SO RIGHTLY.
MEANWHILE, TARS TARKAS WAS IN HIS NATURAL ELEMENT.
HOWEVER, HE HAD LOST TRACK OF LOAS, AND THAT CONCERNED HIM.

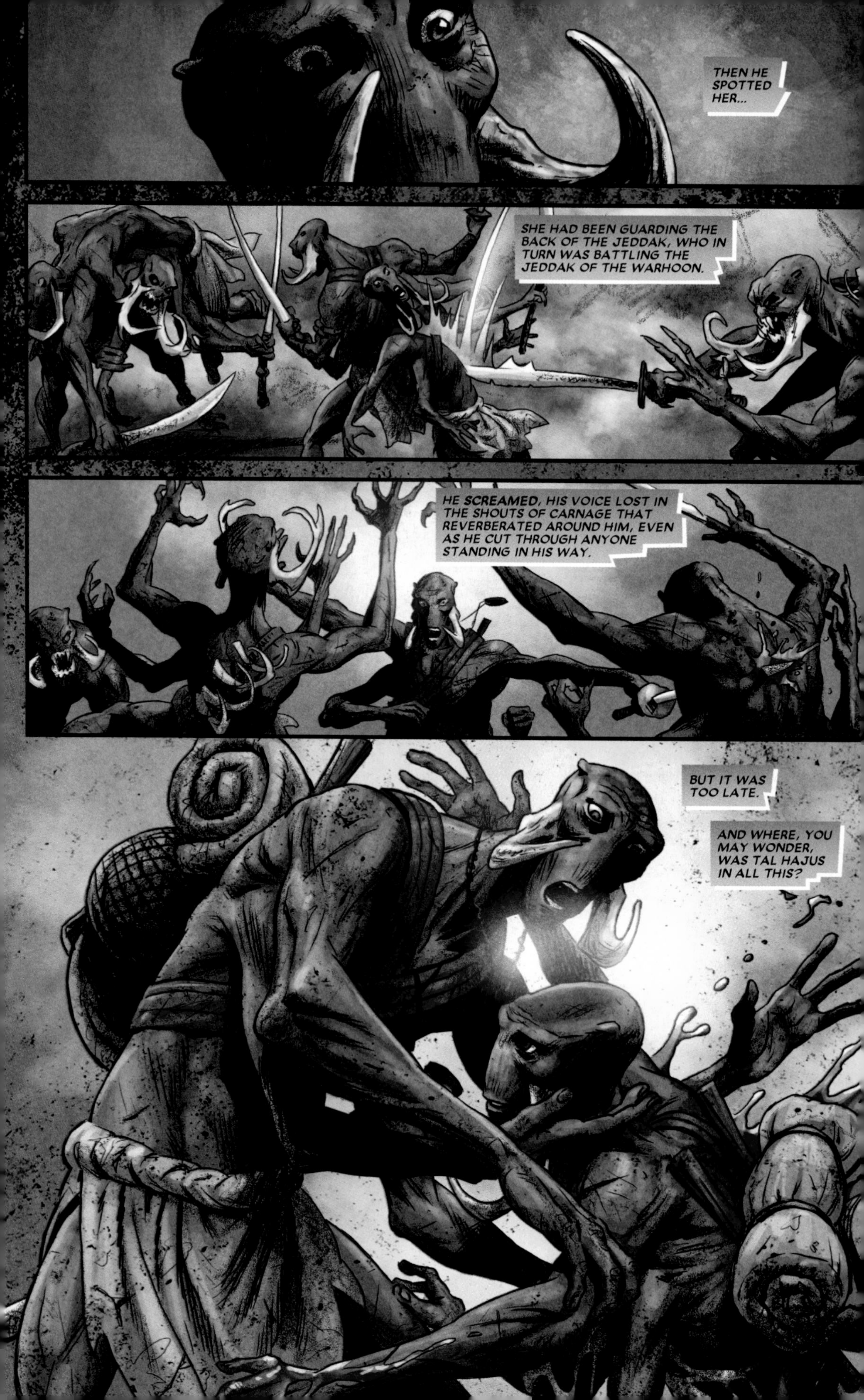
THEN HE SPOTTED HER...
SHE HAD BEEN GUARDING THE BACK OF THE JEDDAK, WHO IN TURN WAS BATTLING THE JEDDAK OF THE WARHOON.
HE SCREAMED, HIS VOICE LOST IN THE SHOUTS OF CARNAGE THAT REVERBERATED AROUND HIM, EVEN AS HE CUT THROUGH ANYONE STANDING IN HIS WAY.
BUT IT WAS TOO LATE.
AND WHERE, YOU MAY WONDER, WAS TAL HAJUS IN ALL THIS?

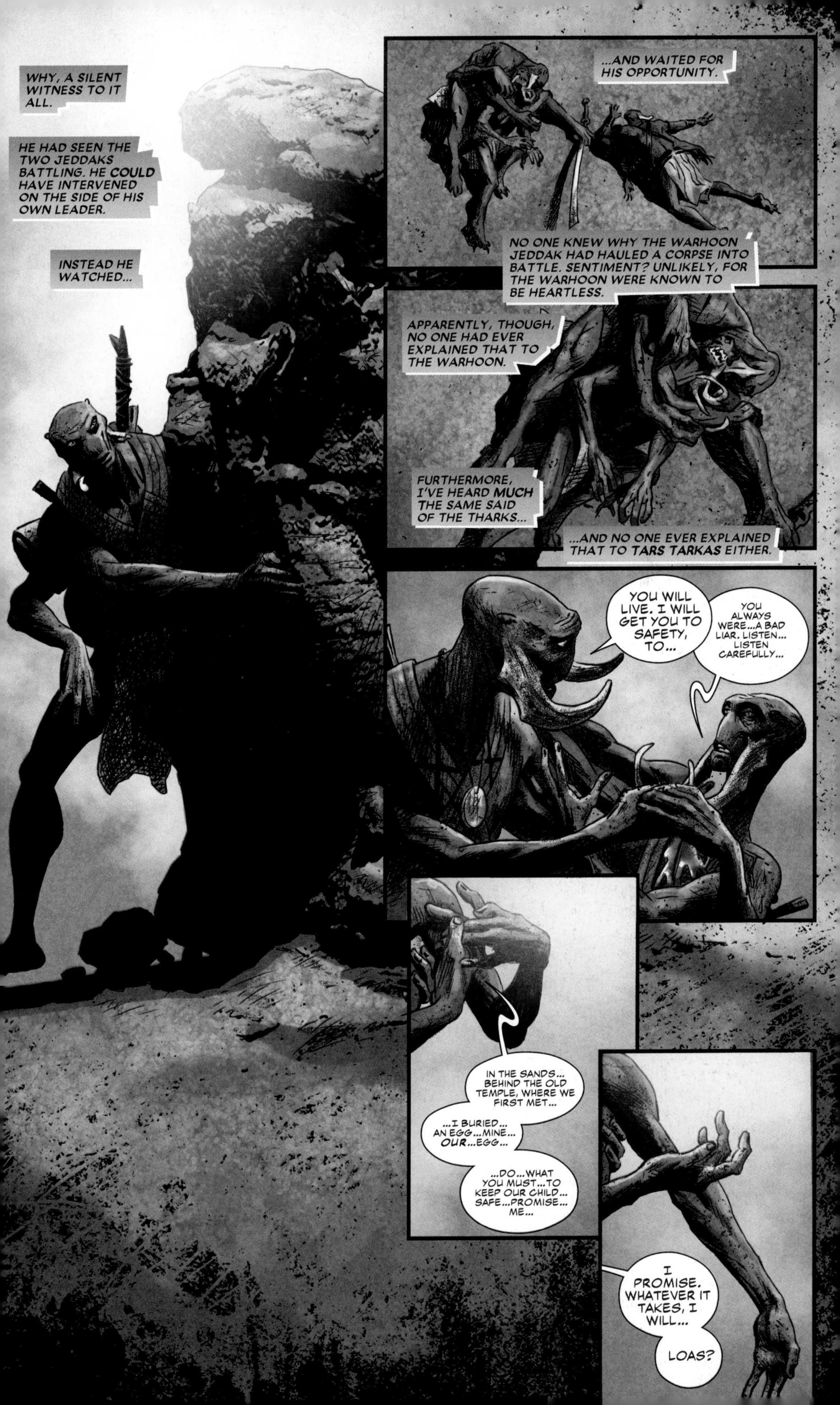
WHY, A SILENT WITNESS TO IT ALL.
HE HAD SEEN THE TWO JEDDAKS BATTLING. HE COULD HAVE INTERVENED ON THE SIDE OF HIS OWN LEADER.
INSTEAD HE WATCHED...
...AND WAITED FOR HIS OPPORTUNITY.
NO ONE KNEW WHY THE WARHOON JEDDAK HAD HAULED A CORPSE INTO BATTLE. SENTIMENT? UNLIKELY, FOR THE WARHOON WERE KNOWN TO BE HEARTLESS.
APPARENTLY, THOUGH, NO ONE HAD EVER EXPLAINED THAT TO THE WARHOON.
FURTHERMORE, I'VE HEARD MUCH THE SAME SAID OF THE THARKS...
...AND NO ONE EVER EXPLAINED THAT TO TARS TARKAS EITHER.
YOU WILL LIVE. I WILL GET YOU TO SAFETY, TO...
YOU ALWAYS WERE...A BAD LIAR. LISTEN... LISTEN CAREFULLY...
IN THE SANDS... BEHIND THE OLD TEMPLE, WHERE WE FIRST MET...
...I BURIED... AN EGG...MINE... OUR...EGG...
...DO...WHAT YOU MUST...TO KEEP OUR CHILD... SAFE...PROMISE... ME...
I PROMISE. WHATEVER IT TAKES, I WILL...
LOAS?

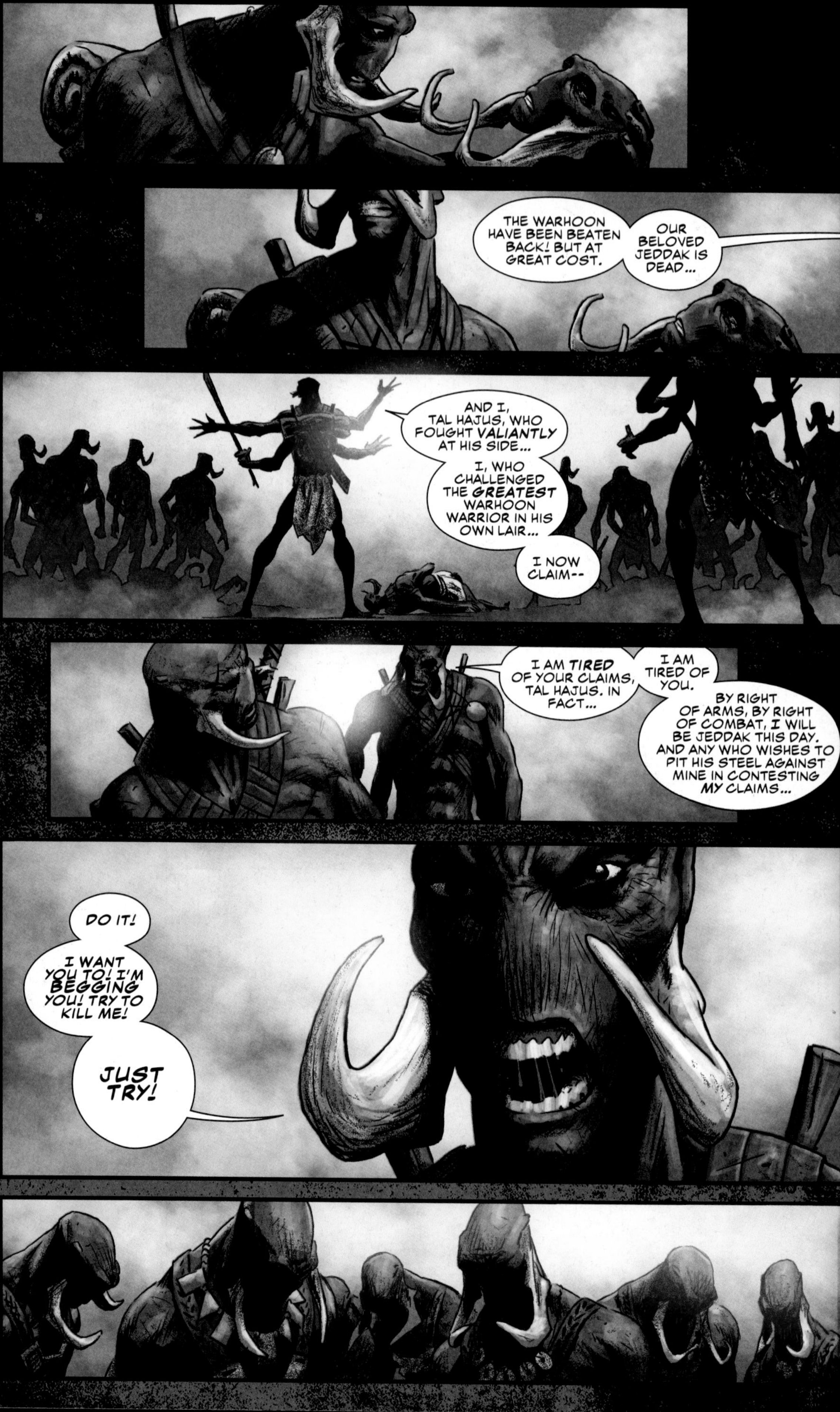
THE WARHOON HAVE BEEN BEATEN BACK! BUT AT GREAT COST.
OUR BELOVED JEDDAK IS DEAD...
AND I, TAL HAJUS, WHO FOUGHT VALIANTLY AT HIS SIDE...
I, WHO CHALLENGED THE GREATEST WARHOON WARRIOR IN HIS OWN LAIR...
I NOW CLAIM--
I AM TIRED OF YOUR CLAIMS, TAL HAJUS. IN FACT...
I AM TIRED OF YOU.
BY RIGHT OF ARMS, BY RIGHT OF COMBAT, I WILL BE JEDDAK THIS DAY. AND ANY WHO WISHES TO PIT HIS STEEL AGAINST MINE IN CONTESTING MY CLAIMS...
DO IT!
I WANT YOU TO! I'M BEGGING YOU! TRY TO KILL ME!
JUST TRY!

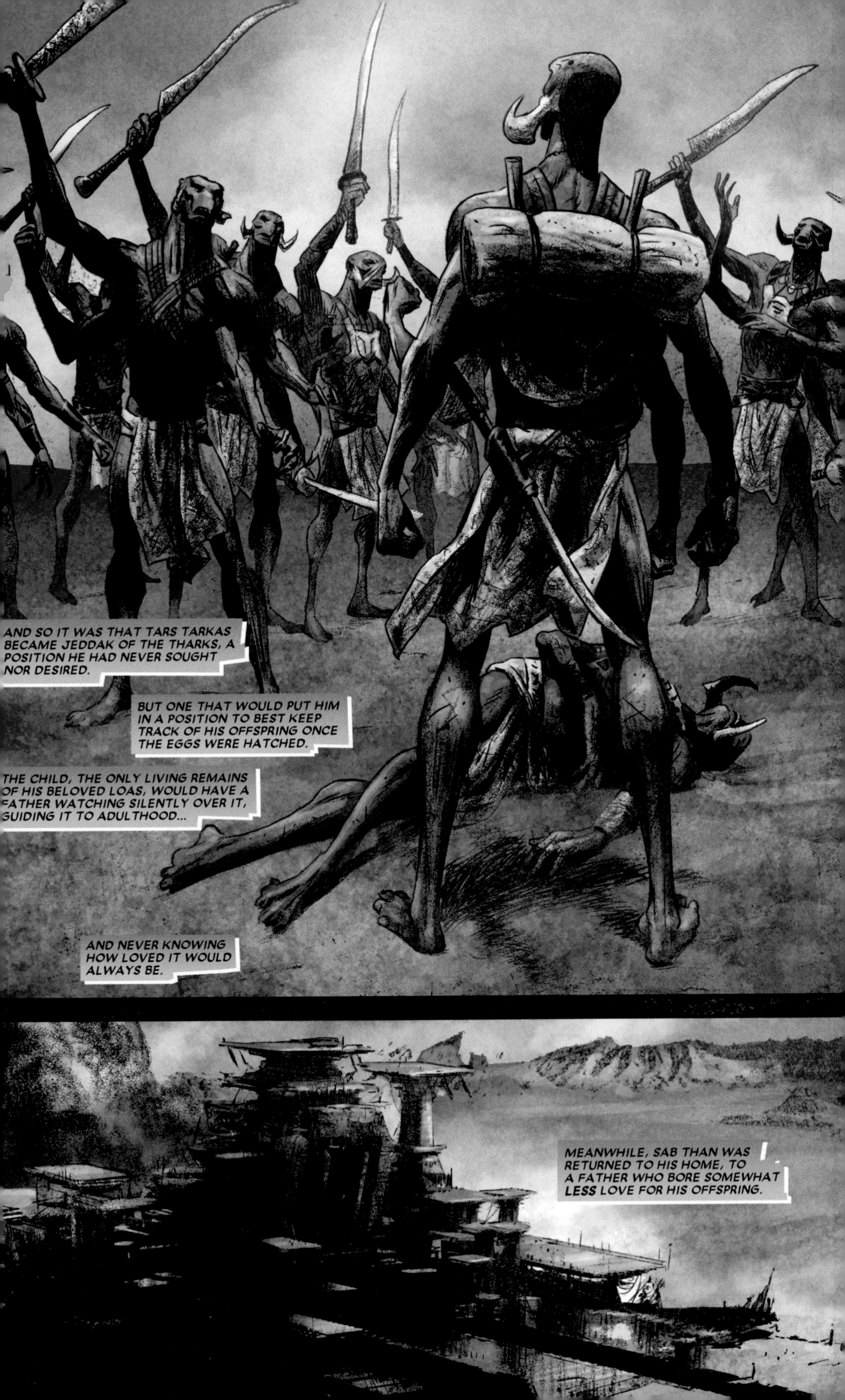
AND SO IT WAS THAT TARS TARKAS BECAME JEDDAK OF THE THARKS, A POSITION HE HAD NEVER SOUGHT NOR DESIRED.
BUT ONE THAT WOULD PUT HIM IN A POSITION TO BEST KEEP TRACK OF HIS OFFSPRING ONCE THE EGGS WERE HATCHED.
THE CHILD, THE ONLY LIVING REMAINS OF HIS BELOVED LOAS, WOULD HAVE A FATHER WATCHING SILENTLY OVER IT, GUIDING IT TO ADULTHOOD...
AND NEVER KNOWING HOW LOVED IT WOULD ALWAYS BE.
MEANWHILE, SAB THAN WAS RETURNED TO HIS HOME, TO A FATHER WHO BORE SOMEWHAT LESS LOVE FOR HIS OFFSPRING.

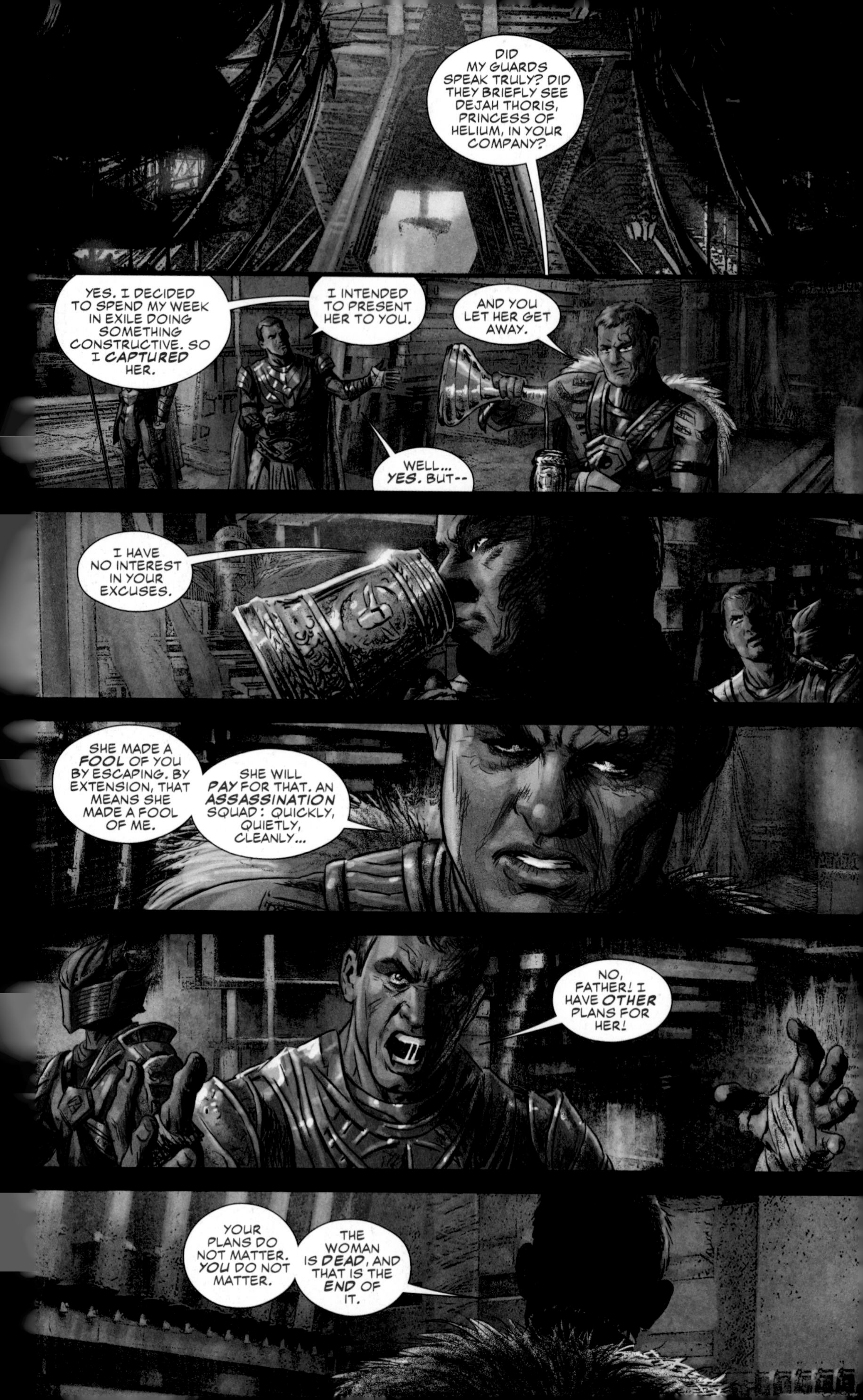

DID MY GUARDS SPEAK TRULY? DID THEY BRIEFLY SEE DEJAH THORIS, PRINCESS OF HELIUM, IN YOUR COMPANY?
YES. I DECIDED TO SPEND MY WEEK IN EXILE DOING SOMETHING CONSTRUCTIVE. SO I CAPTURED HER.
I INTENDED TO PRESENT HER TO YOU.
AND YOU LET HER GET AWAY.
WELL... YES. BUT--
I HAVE NO INTEREST IN YOUR EXCUSES.
SHE MADE A FOOL OF YOU BY ESCAPING. BY EXTENSION, THAT MEANS SHE MADE A FOOL OF ME.
SHE WILL PAY FOR THAT. AN ASSASSINATION SQUAD: QUICKLY, QUIETLY, CLEANLY...
NO, FATHER! I HAVE OTHER PLANS FOR HER!
YOUR PLANS DO NOT MATTER. YOU DO NOT MATTER.
THE WOMAN IS DEAD, AND THAT IS THE END OF IT.

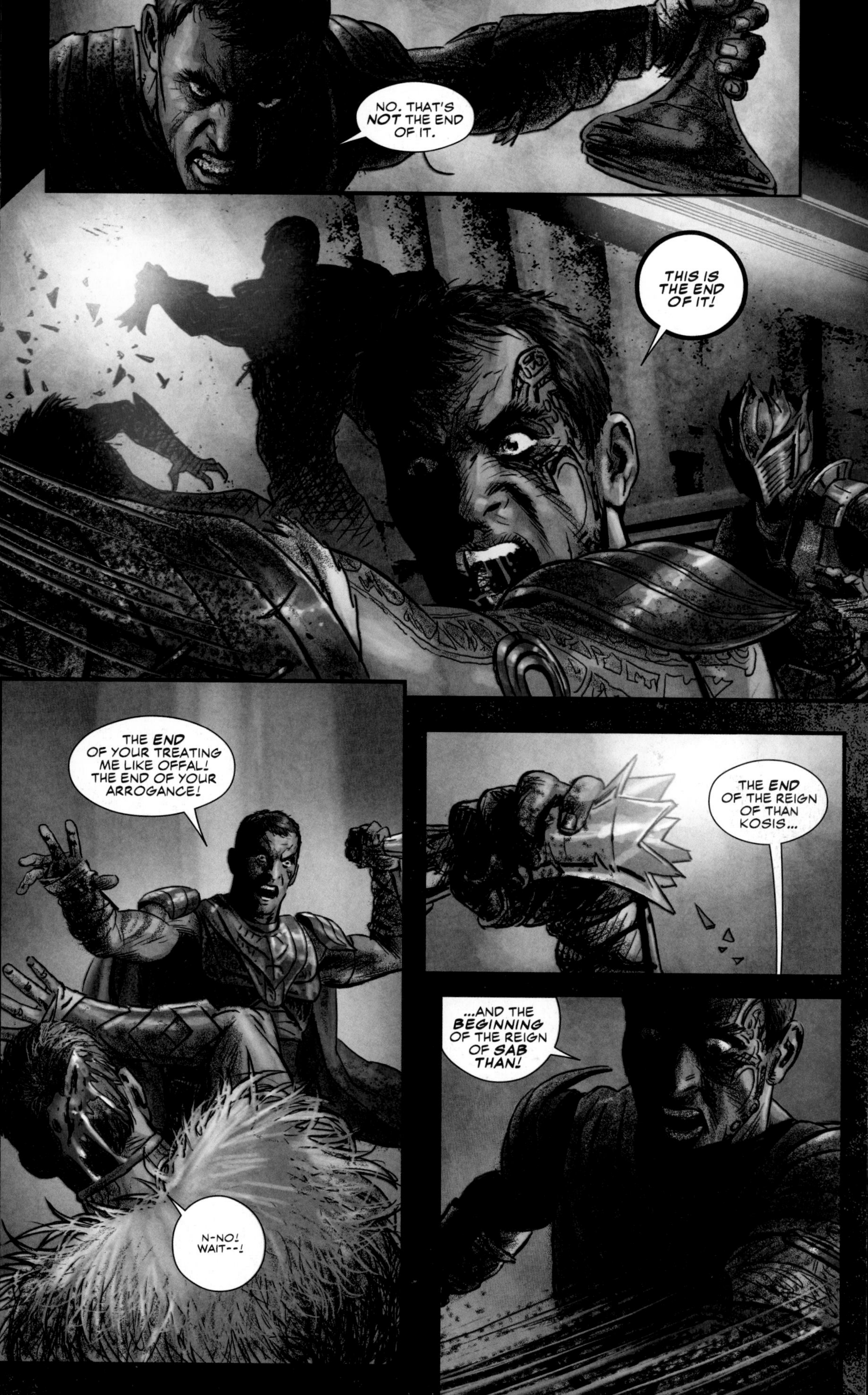
NO. THAT'S NOT THE END OF IT.
THIS IS THE END OF IT!
THE END OF YOUR TREATING ME LIKE OFFAL! THE END OF YOUR ARROGANCE!
N-NO! WAIT--!
THE END OF THE REIGN OF THAN KOSIS...
...AND THE BEGINNING OF THE REIGN OF SAB THAN!

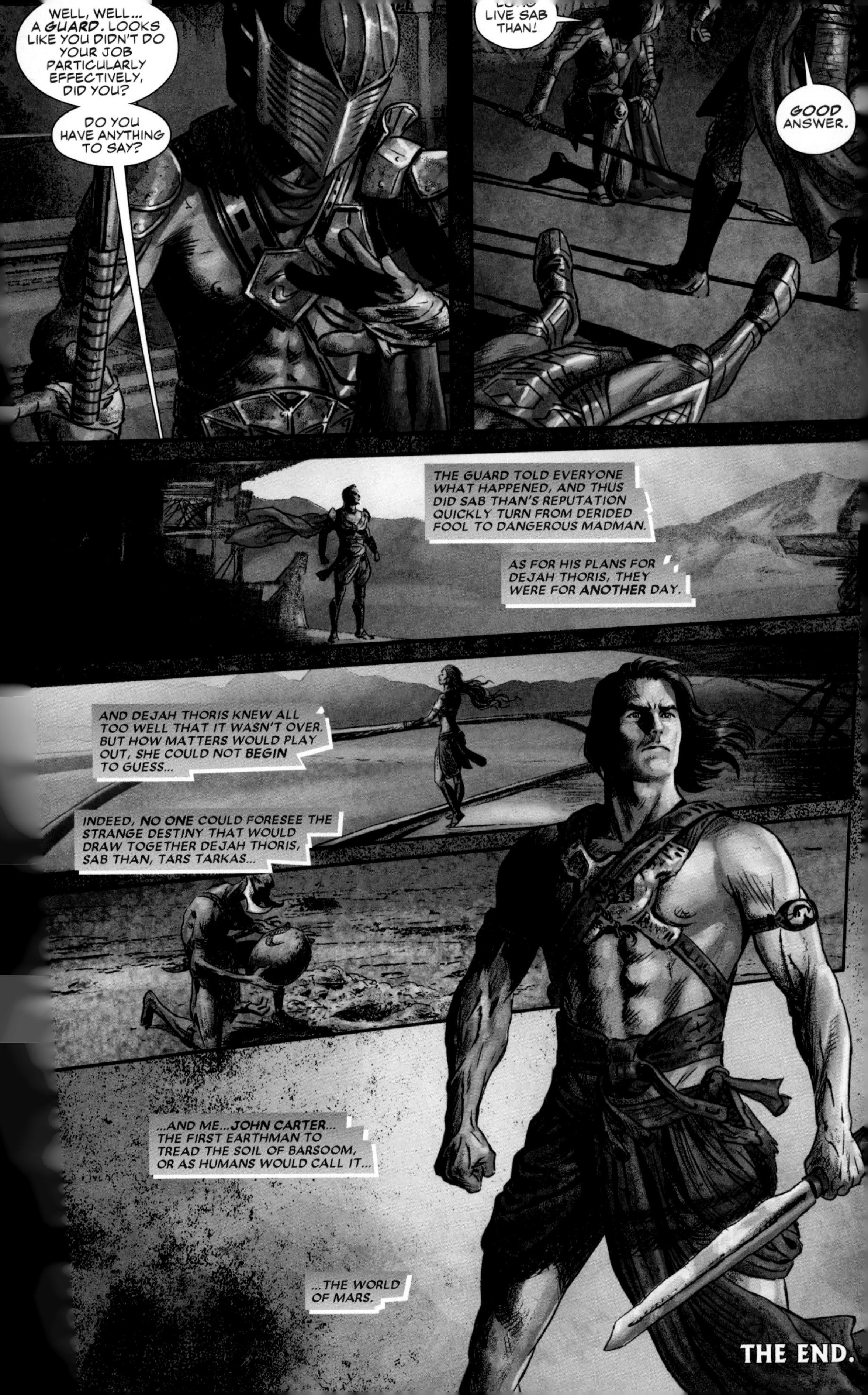
WELL, WELL... A GUARD. LOOKS LIKE YOU DIDN'T DO YOUR JOB PARTICULARLY EFFECTIVELY, DID YOU?
DO YOU HAVE ANYTHING TO SAY?
LIVE SAB THAN!
GOOD ANSWER.
THE GUARD TOLD EVERYONE WHAT HAPPENED, AND THUS DID SAB THAN'S REPUTATION QUICKLY TURN FROM DERIDED FOOL TO DANGEROUS MADMAN.
AS FOR HIS PLANS FOR DEJAH THORIS, THEY WERE FOR ANOTHER DAY.
AND DEJAH THORIS KNEW ALL TOO WELL THAT IT WASN'T OVER. BUT HOW MATTERS WOULD PLAY OUT, SHE COULD NOT BEGIN TO GUESS...
INDEED, NO ONE COULD FORESEE THE STRANGE DESTINY THAT WOULD DRAW TOGETHER DEJAH THORIS, SAB THAN, TARS TARKAS...
...AND ME...JOHN CARTER... THE FIRST EARTHMAN TO TREAD THE SOIL OF BARSOOM, OR AS HUMANS WOULD CALL IT...
...THE WORLD OF MARS.
THE END.

CHARACTER DESIGNS
BY LUKE ROSS

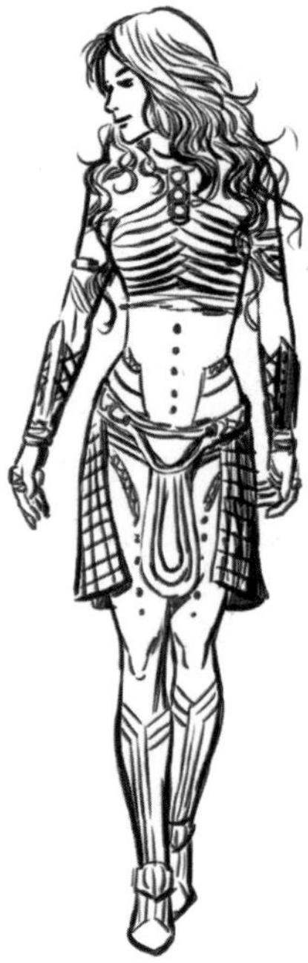

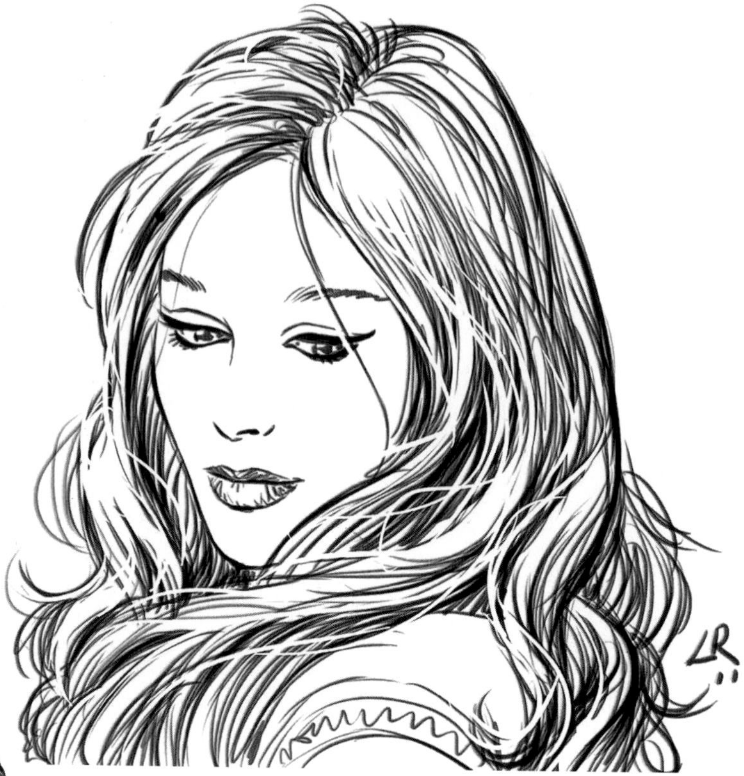

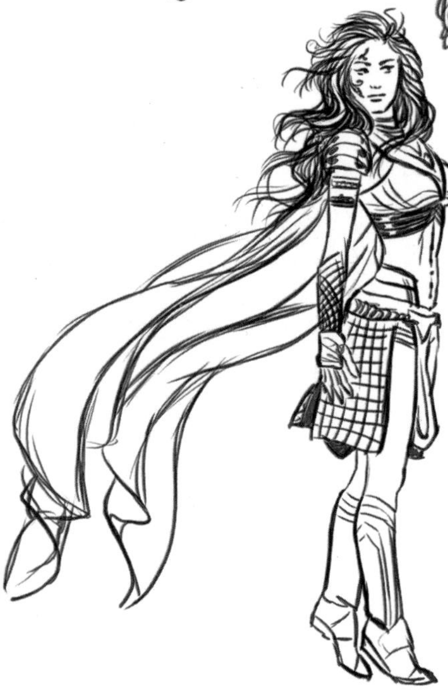

DEJAH THORIS

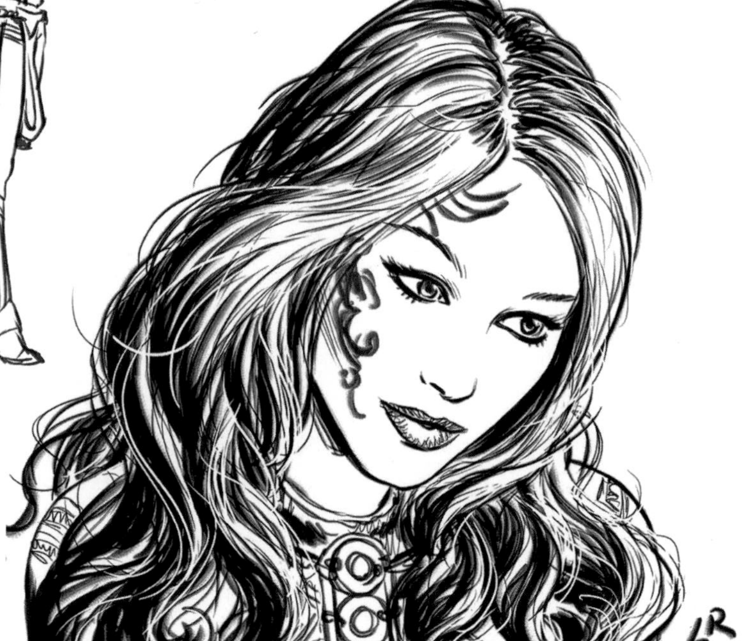

JOHN CARTER

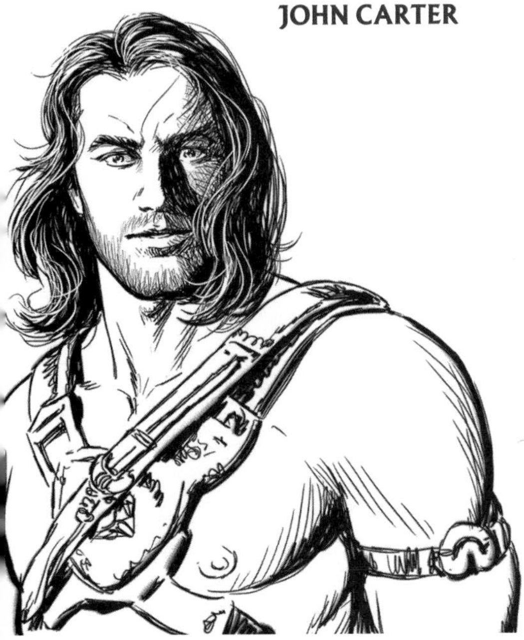

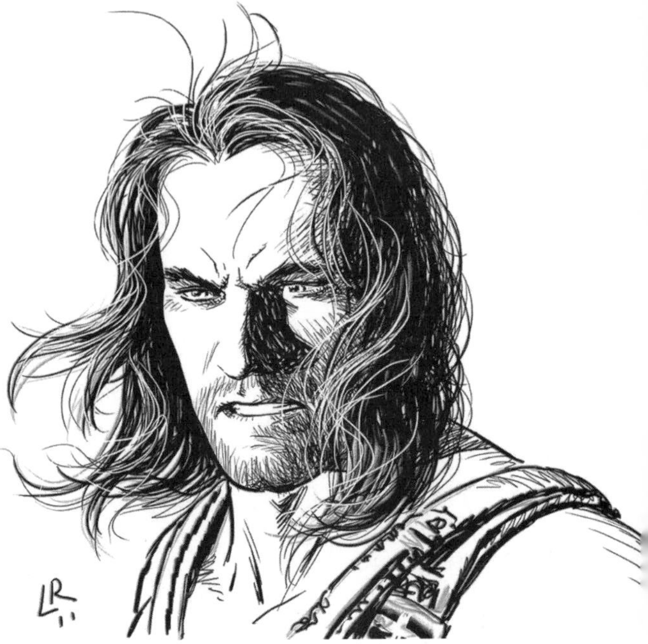

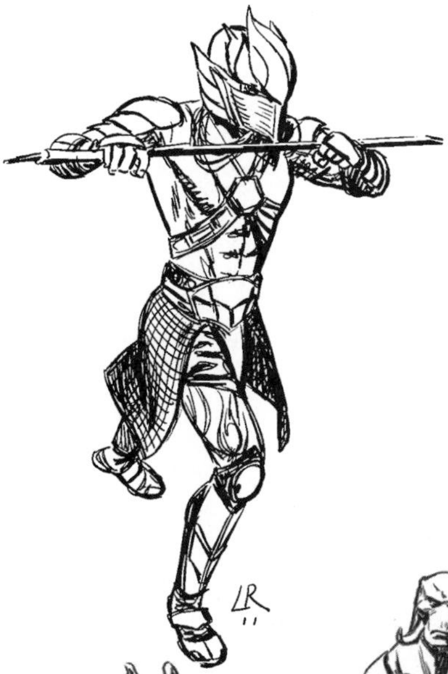

ZODANGAN

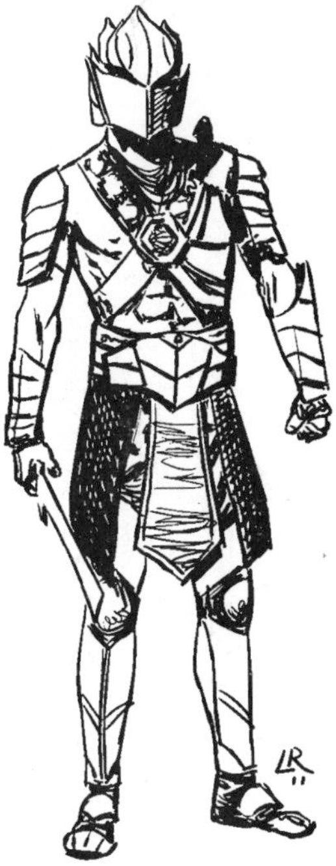

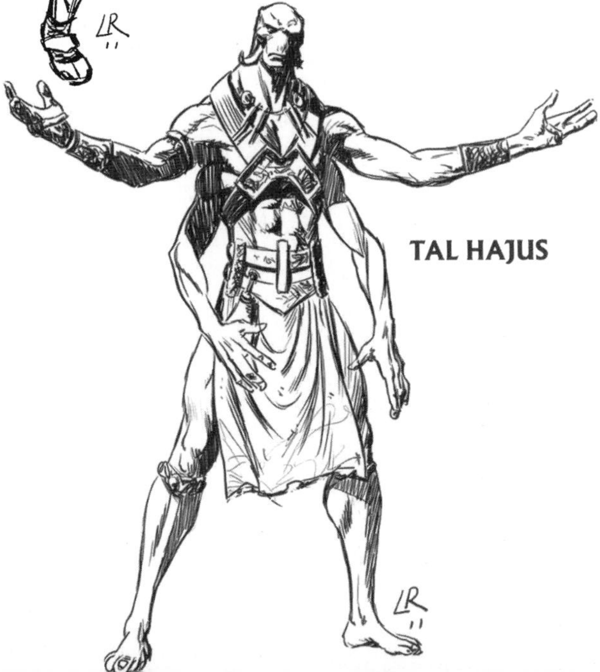

TAL HAJUS

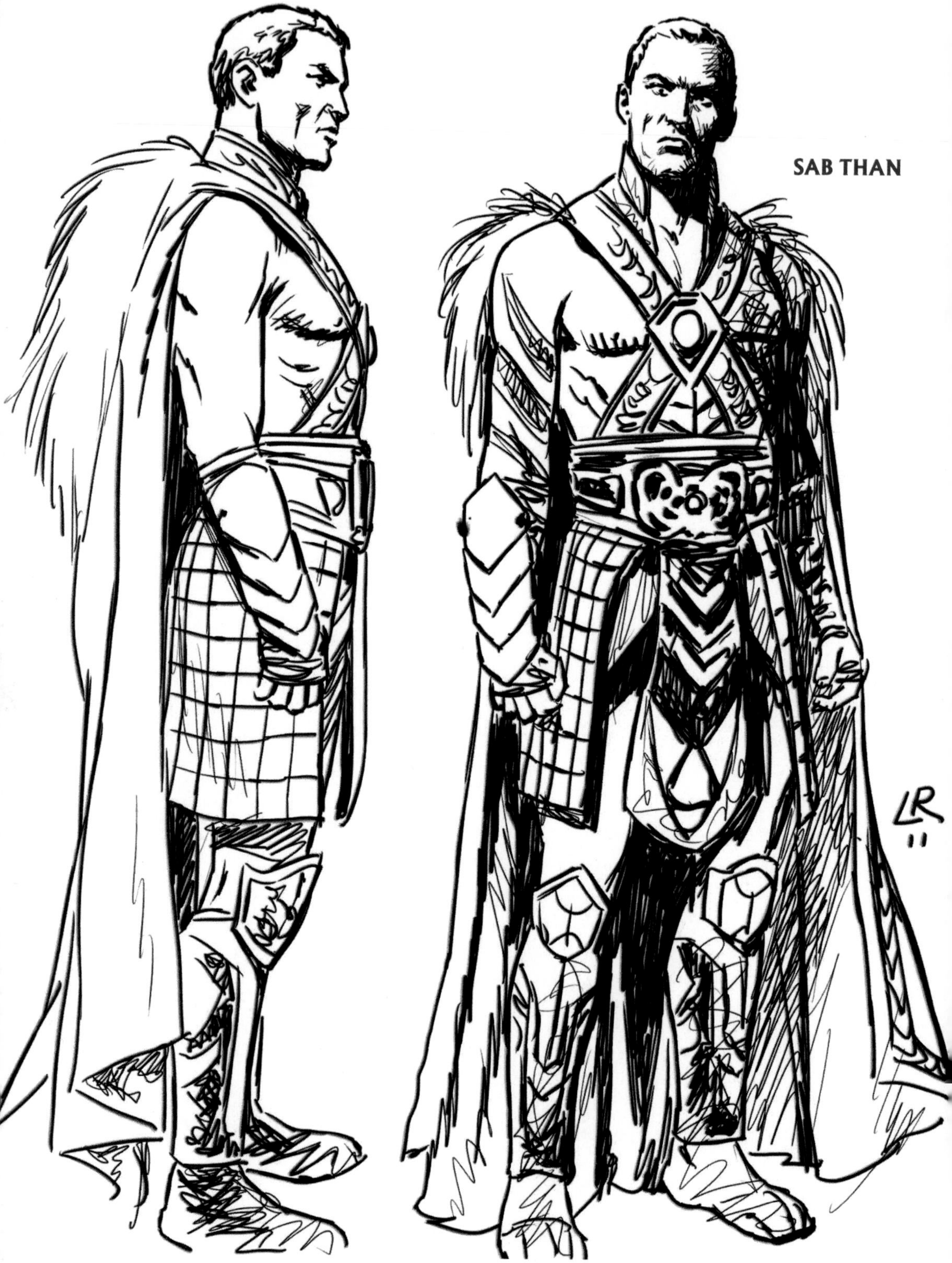
SAB THAN
LR
11

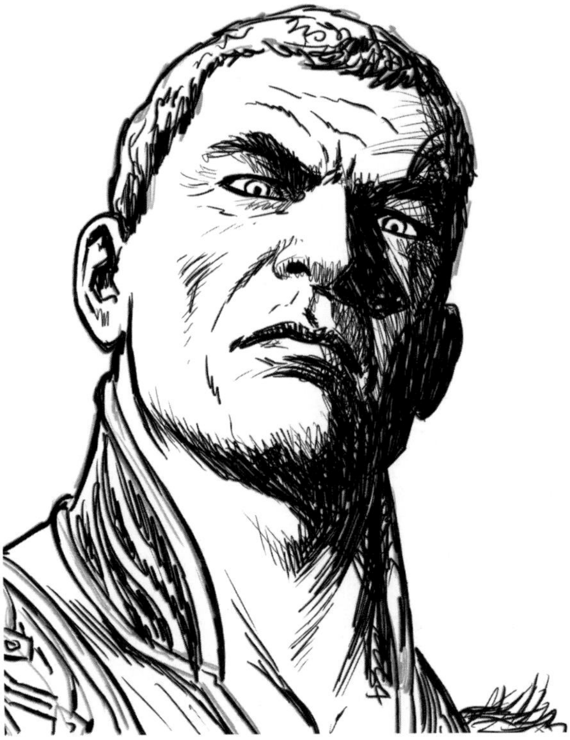

THAN KOSIS

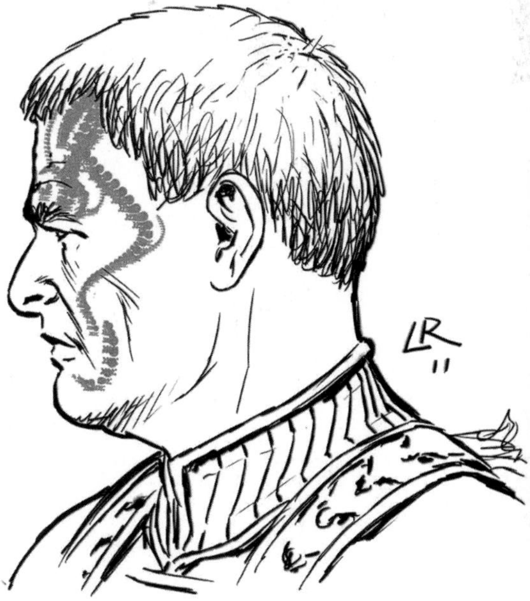

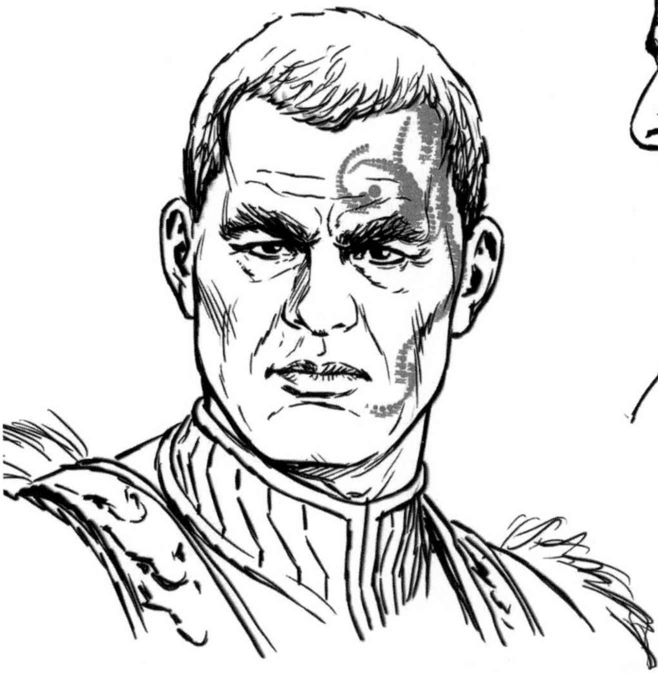

JOHN CARTER: WORLD OF MARS #1

Script by PETER DAVID

Art by LUKE ROSS

PAGE 1

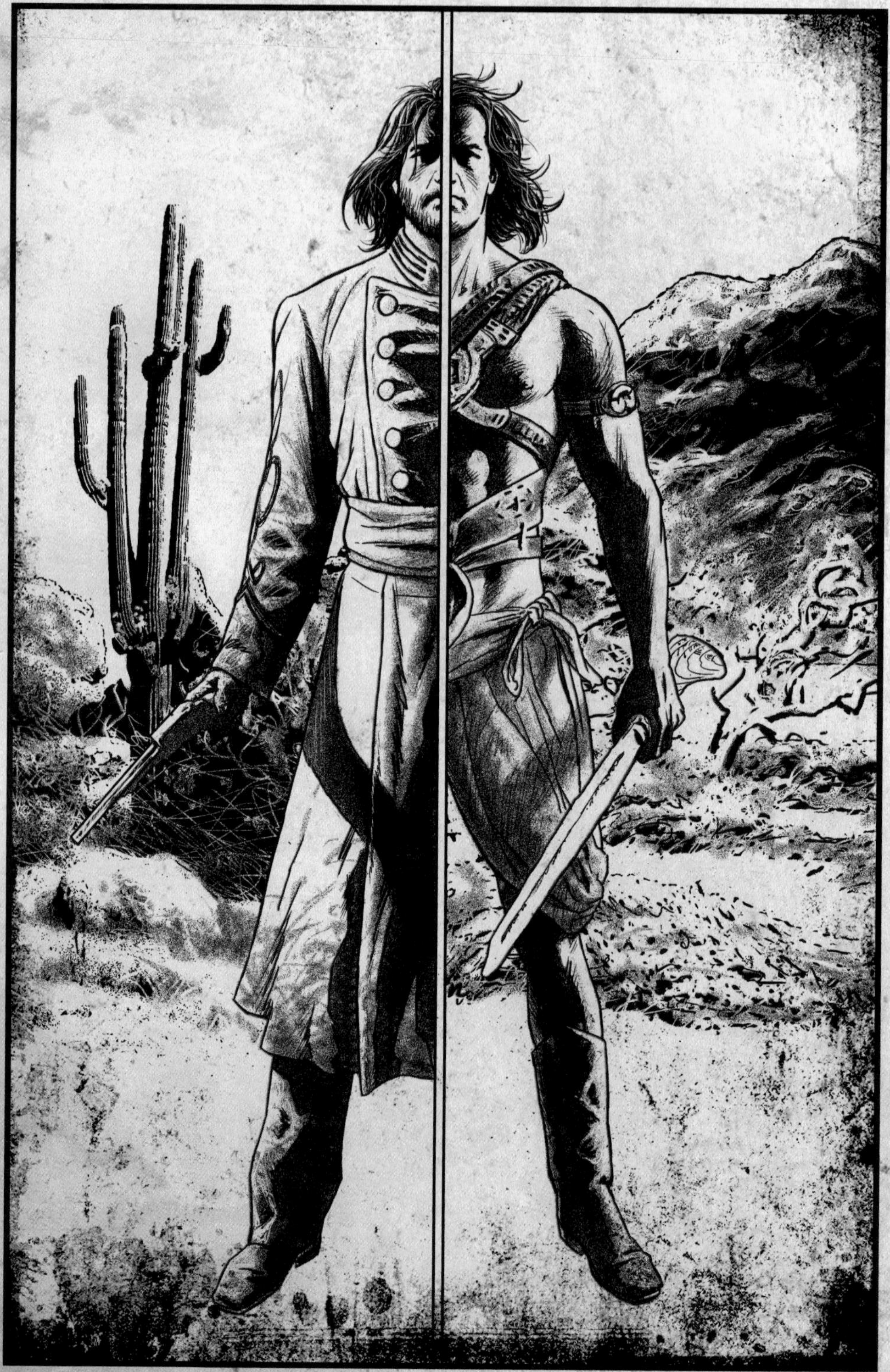

SPLIT FULL PANEL: I'm going for something really old school here. I want us to have a dead on straight shot of John Carter with the panel split vertically down the middle, bisecting Carter. On the left hand side of the page we see Carter in the uniform of a Confederacy soldier, and he's holding a pistol in his hand. The background should be an American desert, and it's night. On the right hand side of the page, he is wearing the loin cloth accoutrements that he's wearing when he is adventuring on Barsoom, and he is holding a sword.

CAPTION 1: My name is John Carter. I am better known as Captain Jack Carter of Virginia.

CAPTION 2: Once I was a normal being, an inhabitant of Earth, although I use the word "normal" in a fairly loose sense.

CAPTION 3: I appear to be about thirty years of age, although I believe I have lived much, much longer than that.

CAPTION 4: Through a rather…unusual…series of events, I found myself walking upon alien soil that no human had ever trod, namely the planet Mars…

CAPTION 5: …or, as its natives call it, Barsoom.

CAPTION 6: Oh yes. Natives, they have, and in abundance. Natives such as…

PAGE 2

A FULL PAGE shot of Dejah Thoris. She is in the "Honeymoon chamber" (see reference from Disney) and is attired in a Hall of Science Blue robe. Carter is leaning against a wall, his arms folded.

CAPTION 1: Dejah Thoris. Princess of the city of Helium.

DEJAH 2: How little you know of our world, John Carter, or the circumstances that shaped it.

DEJAH 3: You act as if nothing of importance could *possibly* have occurred before you arrived here.

JOHN 4: I think that's more how you see me than the way I actually am. But who am I to disagree with a princess?

JOHN 5: Perhaps you would do me the service of educating me as to what I should know?

DEJAH 6: It would be my pleasure.

JOHN 7: And mine as well.

FULL PAGE: A Barsoomian plain. Riding side by side on two mounts are Tars Tarkas and John Carter.

CAPTION 1: And then there's Tars Tarkas, Jeddak of the Tharks.
CAPTION 2: Generally speaking, Red Mmen and Green Mmen of Barsoom get along about as well as red skinned and white skinned men of Earth do.

CAPTION 3: Perhaps we're *not* so alien after all.

JOHN 4: Why are you so unlike others of your race, Tars Tarkas?

TARS 5: *Am* I?

JOHN 6: I would be *dead* were it not for your compassion. An unusual trait for Tharks in general and Jeddaks in particular.

TARS 7: And you would know why, Dotar Sojat?

JOHN 8: If it would interest you to tell it.

TARS 9: And why not? It is a pleasant enough day, and we have a long ride ahead of us.

CAPTION 10: In retrospect, it is amusing that two of the most important individuals in my life had a tale to tell in which they were both participants in each other's narrative...

CAPTION 11: ...but were unaware of it.

CAPTION 12: This is the story that they told me, although it begins neither with Helium nor the Tharks, but instead with events transpiring somewhere else entirely.

PAGE 4

FULL PAGE: Establishing shot of Zodanga, this vast and moving city.

CAPTION 1: With all deference to the last, great Mr. Dickens, it was both the best of times and worst of times and...as you might have surmised, this is a tale of two cities.

CAPTION 2: Although how much better or worse it was doubtless had to do with which major city you happened to dwell within.

CAPTION 3: In this particular case, there were two great cities, old beyond any human imagining can conceive. Helium, I have already mentioned, but let us now focus instead on its centuries old rival, Zodanga.

CAPTION 4: Situated in Barsoom's southwest hemisphere, Zodanga was covered by sentries who paroled just within the walls as our metropolitan police patrol their beats.

CAPTION 5: It resembled a walking refinery: greasy, smelly, smoky, sooty, black and grey, steel and lifeless.

PAGE 5

PANEL A Exterior, the imperial city ~~castle~~ of Zodanga.

CAPTION 1: Barsoomians are insanely long lived by Earth standards; their wars were likewise.

CAPTION 2: A thousand years had Zodanga been locked in hostilities with its seemingly eternal rival, Helium, the Jewel of Barsoom.

CAPTION 3: And there were some…

PANEL B: Interior, the city ~~castle~~. Sab Than is stalking down a corridor, looking well and truly pissed off.

CAPTION 4: …who chafed under their day-to-day existence.

FROM BEHIND HIM 5: Sab Than!

FROM BEHIND HIM 6: *Sab Than!*

PANEL C: Close on Sab Than, having stopped walking, rolling his eyes heavenward.

FROM BEHIND HIM 7: You *will* attend me when I call you!

SAB THAN 8: Oh, will I?
PANEL D: We now reveal his father, Than Kosis, striding toward him. Than Kosis walks with the assistance of a long, ornate staff that he carries in his right hand.

THAN KOSIS 9: *Yes*, you *will!* You may treat others as you wish, but not me.

SAB THAN 10: While you may treat me, your son, in as off-hand a manner as you wish. Belittle me, ignore my opinions…

PANEL E: The two of them face each other.

THAN 11: Yes. One of the privileges of being ruler.

SAB 12: How *convenient* for you.

PANEL F: And Sab Than walks away once more.

THAN 13: Issus *take* that boy. He causes me *nothing* but grief.

PAGE 6

PANEL A: Sab Than stalks into the street.

SAB 1: Issus *take* the man. He causes me *nothing* but grief.

SAB 2: How am I ever to be taken *seriously* if he always ignores my advice over—

PANEL B: And his shoulder impacts with a Zodangan guard, the taller one of two who are walking past.

TALLER GUARD 3: *Unnff!*

SAB 4: One side, fool.

PANEL C: The taller guard glares down at him. The shorter guard is trying to calm the situation.

TALLER GUARD 5: Who are you calling "fool," you oaf?

SHORTER GUARD 6: Softly. That's Sab Th—

TALLER GUARD 7: I *know* who he is.

PANEL D: The taller guard is leaning in toward Sab Than.

TALLER GUARD 8: The man who would be ruler, hiding forever in his father's shadow.

TALLER GUARD 9: Than Kosis' contempt for him is well known.

PANEL E: Sab Than is actually half smiling.

SAB 10: I see. Since my father has no respect for me, you feel you need not, either.

TALLER GUARD 11: More or less.

PAGE 7

PANEL A: And Sab Than slams him in the stomach, doubling the guard over.

SAB 1: *How about now?!*

TALLER GUARD 2: Unfff!

PANEL B: He slams a fist down on the back of the guard's neck, dropping him.

SAB 2: Feeling some more respect *now*?

PANEL C: Close on Sab Than, pounding on the guard who is now below the panel border. He has a look of pure fury in his eyes. If possible, green blood is flying from below. They bleed blue blood.

CAPTION 3: It took three guards to pull him off.

CAPTION 4: His father was…not happy.

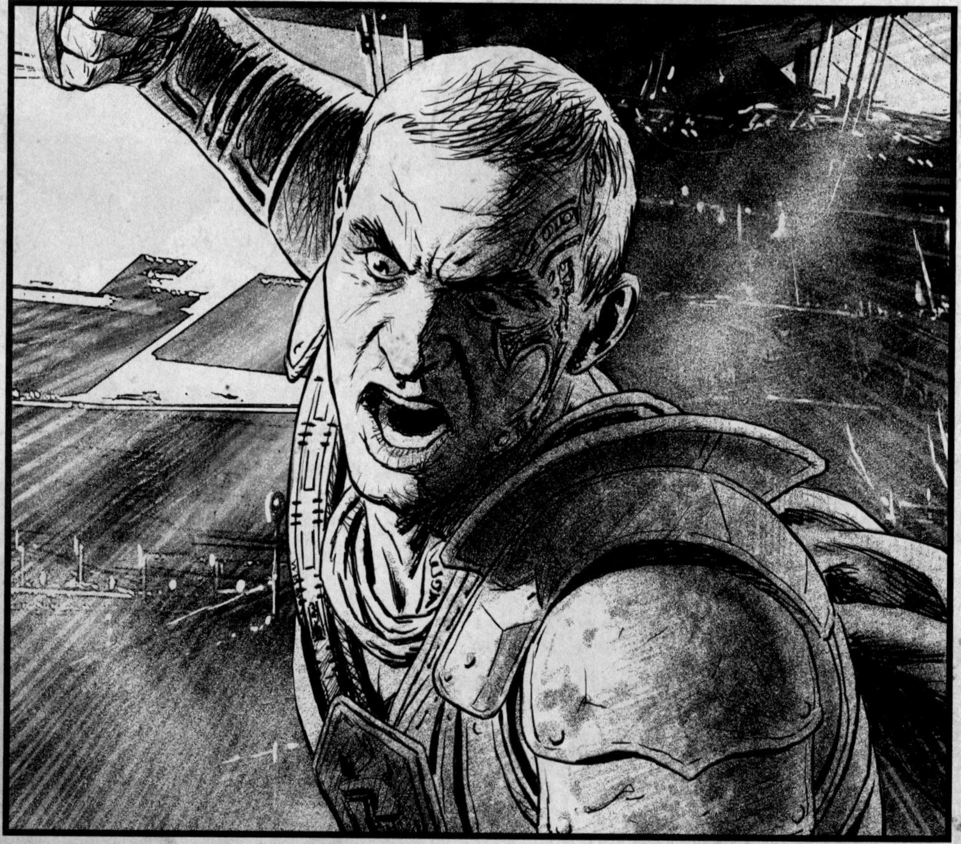

PAGE 8

PANEL A: Interior, the throne room. Than Kosis is bellowing in fury at his son.

THAN 1: Picking a fight with guards? Are you insane!?

SAB 2: He was not giving me the respect that my station requires.

PANEL B: Than Kosis points angrily at Sab Than.

THAN 3: Respect is not something that is *given*! *True* respect is something that's *earned*!

THAN 4: But a brawling, single-minded thug such as you couldn't begin to understand that!

PANEL C: And Sab Than shouts right back at him.

SAB 5: Perhaps what this city needs *is* a brawler! Someone willing to get his hands dirty.

SAB 6: Maybe even end the thousand years war with Helium!

THAN 7: And you think *you* could do that?

PANEL D: Two shot.

SAB 8: *Easily*, if you and your generals would only listen to me!

SAB 9: Rather than countenance a fresh perspective, you shut me out! You treat me as if I'm *not here*!

PANEL E: And Than Kosis calls out, as Sab Than looks suddenly hopeful.

THAN 10: That is an *excellent* idea.

THAN 11: *Guards!*

SAB 12: You…you mean about not ignoring me?

....

PAGE 9

PANEL A: Burly guards are gripping Sab Than firmly by either arm.

THAN 1: No, I mean about you not *being* here.

THAN 2: You are banished from Zodanga for a week.

THAN 3: Get him out of here.

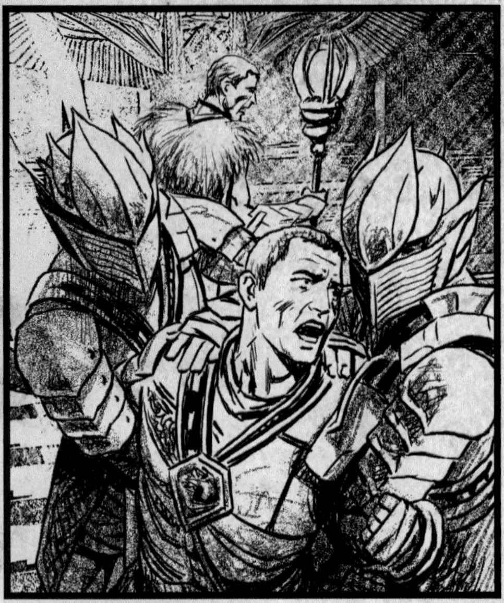

PANEL B: And they're dragging Sab Than out.

SAB 4: *Father!* You cannot *do* this!

THAN 5: And yet here it is, being done.

SAB 6: Where am I supposed to go?

PANEL C: Than Kosis speaks casually over his shoulder words that will come back to haunt him.

THAN 7: Up the River Iss, for all I care.

PANEL D: Sab Than is being dragged out of the throne room.

CAPTION 8: And so it was that Sab Than was, rather *ungently*, shown out of Zodanga.

CAPTION 9: He had no intention of heading up the River Iss, for that was the final journey of those ready to die.

PANEL E Angle on Sab Than, on foot, stalking away from Zodanga, looking well and truly pissed.

CAPTION 10: No, even as he strode away, he developed a plan to show up his father…

CAPTION 11: …a plan involving the incomparable Dejah Thoris. And he headed toward Helium to carry it out.

CAPTION 12: Meanwhile…

PAGE 10

PANEL A: Two swords are clanging together.

CAPTION 1: Two Tharks were engaged in what any outside observer would have considered a life and death struggle.

PANEL B: Pull back to reveal Tars Tarkas and Tal Hajus, battling with swords. Each of them has two swords, but four arms, so feel free to position how they're holding the swords in whatever way you think will make the most dynamic scene. They are battling in the arena, but it is empty of any spectators. This should be the largest panel on the page, obviously. Art note: As Jeddak, Tars

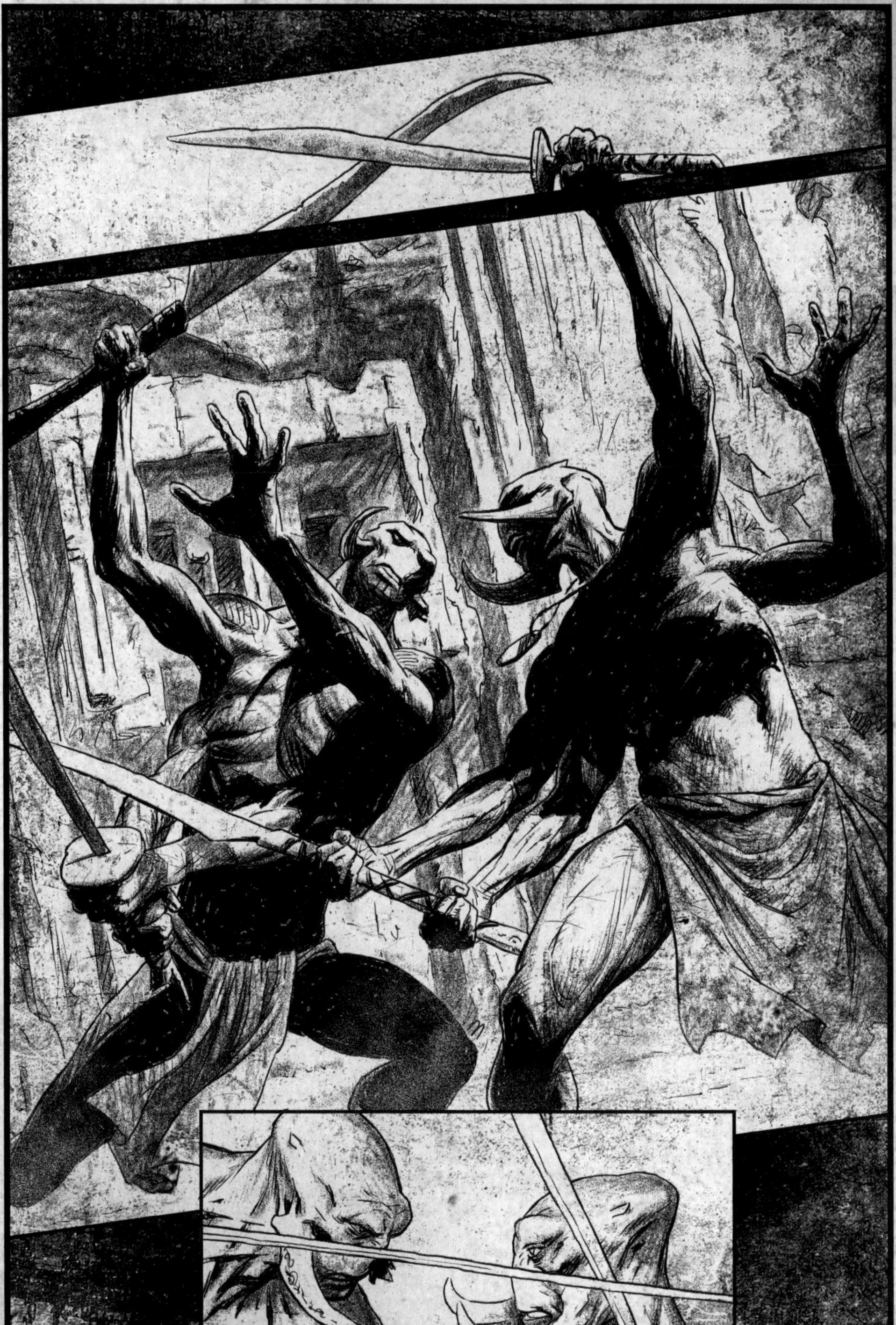

Tarkas will doubtless be wearing various ornaments of office. None of those should be present at this point.

CAPTION 2: But in point of fact, it was simply practice, albeit practice that would likely have left others armless or headless.

PANEL C: Tight on the two of them face to face.

HAJUS 3: You're *weakening*, Tars Tarkas.

TARKAS 4: More like dozing, Tal Hajus. Your technique is *just* that boring.

PAGE 11

PANEL A: Tarkas twists and sends one of Hajus'sswords flying.

TARKAS 1: But if you wish…

HAJUS 2: *No!*

PANEL B: And Tarkas, with one of his free hands, backhands Hajus across the side of his head.

TARKAS 3: I can *force* myself awake.

HAJUS 4: Ooooof!

PANEL C: Hajus is down. Tarkas is standing with one foot on Hajus's remaining sword (which is still in Hajus's hand.) Tarkas has his two swords crisscrossed over Hajus's throat.

TARKAS 5: See? See what happens when you have my *full* attention?

TARKAS 6 *Yield*, Tal. Yi—

PAGE 12

PANEL A: And suddenly Tarkas looks up, noticing something.

TARKAS 1: Eh?

PANEL B: Tarkas's POV. Seated in the stands, far in the distance, is a single observer: Loas, a female Thark.

BALLOON 2: *Loas?*

PANEL C: Push in so we're closer on Loas. She is smiling fetchingly.

BALLOON 3: Well, *this* is an unexpected sur–

PANEL D: With one of his free hands, Hajus punches Tarkas in the back of the knee.

HAJUS 4: *Hah!*

....

PAGE 13

PANEL A: Tarkas is off balance, the struck leg collapsing under him. Hajus is grabbing for one of Tarkas's arms.

TARKAS 1: *Arrrhhh!*

PANEL B: And Hajus, pulling hard, slams Tarkas to the ground.

HAJUS 2: *Got* you!

PANEL C: Now Hajus is atop Tarkas, and he has two hands clamped around Tarkas's throat.
HAJUS 3: Now *your* turn to yield, Tars! I could crush your throat barehanded.

TARKAS 4: Really?

TARKAS 5: Can you crush it before I *gut* you with my *dagger*?

PANEL D: Hajus looks down, between them.

HAJUS 6: Eh?

PANEL E: Sure enough. Tarkas has the point of a dagger touching Hajus's stomach.

HAJUS 7: Hmmm…

PAGE 14

PANEL A: Back to Hajus looking down at Tarkas. They both now have amused expressions on their faces (or as amused as a Thark ever looks.)

HAJUS 1: Call it a *draw*, then?

TARKAS 2: My very thought.

PANEL B: Hajus is now upright and has extended a hand to Tarkas, who is gripping it firmly.

TARKAS 3: Although I *had* you, you know. Dead to rights.

HAJUS 4: Perhaps. But you let yourself get distracted.

PANEL C: He hauls Tarkas to his feet.

HAJUS 5: And I don't even have to look to know by whom.

HAJUS 6: You just *encourage* her, you know, by acknowledging her.

TARKAS 7: I *shouldn't* encourage females?

PANEL D: They stride across the arena.

HAJUS 8: Females are to be used as necessary to sate urges and propagate the race.
HAJUS 9: Anything else is a luxury that a *true* warrior cannot afford.

PANEL E: Loas is now at the edge of the arena grandstands, calling down to the two Tharks.

LOAS 10: I'm so *sorry*, Tars Tarkas. I didn't mean to distract you.

TARKAS 11: You didn't, Loas. I was merely allowing Tal to salvage his pride.

HAJUS 12: Oh, *that's* your tale now, is it?

LOAS 13: So Tars, I was wondering if—

PANEL F: And now Hajus is gripping Tarkas by the arm, pulling the surprised Thark along with him.

HAJUS 14: He has no time to speak with you, female.

TARKAS 15: I *haven't*?

HAJUS 16: No. We've important matters to discuss.

TARKAS 17: We *have*?

HAJUS 18: Yes.

PANEL G: Close on Loas, alone.

LOAS 19: Oh.

PAGE 15

PANEL A: Hajus and Tarkas are now walking away from the arena (i.e., they're outside).

TARKAS 1: What's so important, Tal?

HAJUS 2: My future.

TARKAS 3: Your--?

PANEL B : Closer on the two of them, Hajus scowling fiercely.

HAJUS 4: You're my *oldest* friend, Tars. I've kept *no* secret from you as to my aspirations.

TARKAS 5: To be *Jeddak*, you mean. Yes, I know.

TARKAS 6: Just as I've been candid with *you* about my *lack* of interest in such office.

PANEL C: Close on Hajus, looking annoyed.

HAJUS 7: Yes, well…I'm thinking that now, more

than ever, it's time for a change.

PANEL D: An image of the current Thark Jeddak. He should look somewhat aged, although it's not like you can depict him with white hair. So go for the notion that he's somewhat out of shape. He is at a feast, eating heartily, and there are other Tharks sharing his repast.

CAPTION 8: "Our current Jeddak *may* have been a mighty warrior at one time.

CAPTION 9: "But now he is simply an overweight, out of shape *shadow* of himself.

CAPTION 10: "Yet he manages to retain power because of how generously he treats those who are loyal to him.

CAPTION 11: "It's difficult to crave change when your belly is full and your sword is dull."

PANEL A: Back to Tarkas and Hajus. They are walking up a mountainous incline.

HAJUS 1: If I am to command their attention and respect, I have to do something *dramatic*.

TARKAS 2: Such as?

HAJUS 3: A heroic feat of legendary proportions.

TARKAS 4: Again, such as?

PANEL B: Hajus glances toward him.

HAJUS 5: Know you of…Gothan?

TARKAS 6: *The* Gothan, you mean?

HAJUS 7: Is there another?

PANEL C: A panel featuring a devastating looking Warhoon, massive, frightening, a total bad-ass, wielding a sword dripping with green blood, with dead Tharks and Red Martians piled up around him like cordwood.

CAPTION 8: "The only Gothan *I* know of, Tal, is the Warhoon reputed to be the fiercest, most devastating warrior in the whole of Barsoom.

CAPTION 9: "It's said he remains immortal by feasting on the hearts of his victims.

CAPTION 10: "That no one can defeat him."

PANEL D: Back to Hajus and Tarkas as they continue to walk through the winding pass.

HAJUS 11: I would see for myself.

TARKAS 12: Are you *serious?*

HAJUS 13: Totally.
HAJUS 14: I am going to find and kill Gothan the legend, Tars…

PANEL E: He drapes an arm around a clearly not thrilled Tarkas.

HAJUS 15: …and *you* are going to help me.

PANEL A: And now we cut to a Heliumite patrolman, on a small single-man flyer as he is zipping along the ground (just for the record, Helium also has flyers for single ladies, but if you like it then you should'a put a ring on it) . The patrolman should be wearing various bits of armor or decoration, including a helmet.

CAPTION 1: While this was transpiring, a Heliumite was in routine ground patrol around the perimeter. It was something he had done a thousand times without incident…

PANEL B: And he is unaware that, as he passes a rock formation, Sab Than is leaping off the top of it.

CAPTION 2: …and the problem with that is that it leaves you ill-prepared…

PANEL C: Sab Than lands on the single man flyer behind him, catching him completely off guard.

CAPTION 3: …for the one thousand and *first* time.

PANEL D: Quickly, brutally, Sab Than snaps his neck.

Sfx: SNAP

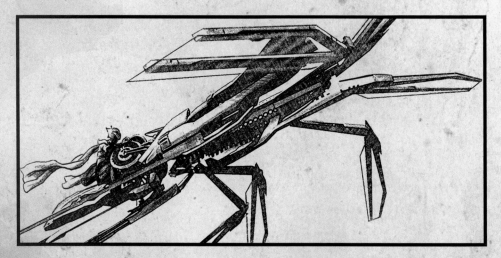

PANEL A: The sled is now on the ground. The body of the guard is lying off to one side. Sab Than is now wearing the guard's accoutrements (including his sword and gun) and is placing the helmet on his head.

SAB THAN 1: I k*new* the Heliumites were soft. You'd never catch a *proper* Zodangan guard that way.

PANEL B: He is now riding the <u>Flyer</u>, heading upwards.

SAB THAN 2: Now then…

PANEL C: Far shot of Helium, hanging there in the air, looking impressive as all get out.

CAPTION 3: "…to get what I came for."

<hr />

PAGE 19

PANEL A: A laboratory on Helium. Dejah Thoris is studying a high-tech looking device that is emitting little pulses of light. Basically think of it as a steam-punk equivalent of a laser.

DEJAH 1: Fascinating. By using radiation to stimulate the light emissions, it's causing a most *potent* oscillation.

DEJAH 2: If it could be amplified, the result could be–

OFF PANEL 3: Princess?

PANEL B: She turns and looks over her shoulder.

DEJAH 4: Yes?

OFF PANEL 5: You're a *hard* lady to find.

DEJAH 6: Not generally. I'm typically here in the laboratory.

DEJAH 7: What can I do for you?

PANEL C: Reverse angle to reveal Sab Than in the guard outfit.

SAB 8: Your noble father wishes to *speak* with you.

SAB 9: He asked me to bring you to him.

DEJAH 10: He sent a *guard* instead of a court messenger?

PANEL D: Closer on Sab Than.

SAB 11: Apparently the cursed Zodangans have some manner of attack planned that involves you.

SAB 12: He dispatched me to see to your safety.

PANEL E: She walks ahead of him.

DEJAH 13: Well then…

DEJAH 14: You to *your* job, then, and me to *mine*.

PANEL F: Close on Dejah Thoris, her face impassive.

OFF PANEL 15: *Your* job, Princess?

DEJAH 16: That's right. My job…

··

PAGE 20

FULL PAGE: And suddenly Dejah Thoris lashes out with her back foot, slamming it into Sab Than's head, snapping it back.

DEJAH 1: …is to see through obvious *imposters* such as *yourself!*

DEJAH 2: I'm familiar with *every* guard who protects Helium against its enemies.

DEJAH 3: I know you not, so there's an obvious conclusion to be drawn. Fortunately…

DEJAH 4: I can also protect *myself!*

CAPTION 5: The wise move, of course, would have been to go *with* him. Out in public, she would then have been able to sound the alarm, call for help, and succor would have come running.

CAPTION 6: But my princess was certain she could handle matters herself, for she is a most prideful creature.

CAPTION 7: Unfortunately, as she would soon learn, pride tends to go before a fall.